PETRIFIED INTELLIGENCE

SUNY series in Hegelian Studies
William Desmond, editor

PETRIFIED INTELLIGENCE

Nature in Hegel's Philosophy

ALISON STONE

STATE UNIVERSITY OF NEW YORK PRESS

Published by
State University of New York Press, Albany

© 2005 State University of New York

All rights reserved

Printed in the United States of America

For information, address State University of New York Press,
90 State Street, Suite 700, Albany, NY 12207

Production by Marilyn P. Semerad
Marketing by Anne M. Valentine

Library of Congress Cataloging-in-Publication Data

Stone, Alison, 1972–
    Petrified intelligence : nature in Hegel's philosophy / Alison Stone.
       p. cm.—(SUNY series in Hegelian studies)
    Includes bibliographical references and index.
    ISBN 0-7914-6293-5 (alk. paper)—0-7914-6294-3 (pbk. : alk. paper)
    1. Hegel, Georg Wilhelm Friedrich, 1770–1831. 2. Philosophy of
nature. I. Title. II. Series.

B2949.N3S76 2004
113'.092—dc22   2004041677

                    10 9 8 7 6 5 4 3 2 1

The feeling of the contradiction between nature and the existing life is the need for its removal; it becomes this need whenever the existing life has lost its authority and all of its worth, when it has become a pure negative.

—Hegel, *Fragment on the Ideal of Social Life*

CONTENTS

ACKNOWLEDGMENTS

A large number of people have helped me, in various ways, with writing this book, and I can only single out a few of them here.

This book was written largely while I held the Thole Research Fellowship in Philosophy at Trinity Hall, University of Cambridge. I am very grateful to the Master and Fellows of Trinity Hall for giving me this opportunity to carry out my research. I have finished the book since joining the Institute for Environment, Philosophy, and Public Policy at Lancaster University, and I am grateful to my colleagues for their support and encouragement of my work.

I am very grateful to Andrew Chitty, who supervised my earlier doctoral thesis on Hegel at the University of Sussex, and helped develop my interest in Hegel. I thank all those who have read and commented on parts of the manuscript, in various incarnations, including John Burbidge, Andrew Chitty, Paul Davies, John Fritzman, Raymond Geuss, Joe McCarney, Jonathan Rée, Andrea Rehberg, Jeremy Spencer, Robert Stern, Céline Surprenant, John Varty, and Thomas Wartenberg. I have benefited from conversations with John Fritzman about the meaning of 'rational necessity' in Hegel. I am grateful to Stephen Houlgate and, especially, Andrew Chitty, Susan James and Robert Stern for advice and encouragement. In particular, I want to thank Simon Gillham, who read through and repeatedly discussed with me the whole manuscript. Special thanks are due to the two anonymous referees for SUNY Press, who read the manuscript very carefully and made many extremely helpful suggestions for improvements. I would like to thank my acquisitions editor at SUNY Press, Jane Bunker, and her former assistant, Olli Baker. I would also like to thank Kurt Stüber for plate 2 from Ernst Haeckel's *Art Forms in Nature,* from Kurt's website www.biolib.de. This image appears on the cover.

Many people have made helpful criticisms and comments on parts of the book that I have presented in talks, on the following occasions especially: "What Is Philosophy of Nature? Hegel's Example," presented at the philosophy seminar, University of Sheffield (2001); "Ethical Implications of Hegel's Philosophy of Nature," presented at the Social and Political Thought graduate/faculty seminar, University of Sussex (2000); "Hegel on the Difference between Philosophy and Science," presented at the Moral Sciences Club, University of Cambridge (2000); "Hegel's Philosophy of Nature," presented at the Human Sciences seminar, Manchester Metropolitan University (1998) and at the philosophy seminar at the University of Kent (1998).

Earlier versions of parts of the book have been published elsewhere. An earlier version of chapter 2 appeared as "Hegel's Philosophy of Nature: Overcoming the Division between Matter and Thought," in *Hegel*, edited by David Kolb, special issue of *Dialogue: Canadian Philosophical Review* 39: 4 (December 2000), pp. 725–43. An earlier version of chapter 6 appeared as "Ethical Implications of Hegel's Philosophy of Nature," in *British Journal for the History of Philosophy* 10: 2 (2002), pp. 255–72. Parts of chapter 5 appeared in "Feminist Criticisms and Reinterpretations of Hegel" in *Bulletin of the Hegel Society of Great Britain* 45/46 (2003), pp. 93–109.

Above all, I want to thank Simon Gillham for his help, encouragement, and patience while I was writing this book.

INTRODUCTION

The Problem of Hegel's Philosophy of Nature

This book is a critical introduction to Hegel's metaphysics and philosophy of nature. My central aim is to show that Hegel's philosophy can make an important contribution to contemporary thinking about the metaphysical and ethical status of nature. In particular, I want to suggest that his decisive contribution is to open up the philosophy of nature as a project and as a conceptual space occupying a distinctive region within the philosophical landscape.[1] Hegel's question concerning the possibility of a specifically philosophical approach to nature is not narrowly historical: above all, I wish to show that it is centrally relevant to environmental concerns. Insofar as environmental degradation stems from technological developments that ultimately derive from modern science, we may suspect that science embodies a problematic approach to the natural world. Through Hegel's work, I shall argue, we can identify a determinate problem with the scientific approach: it rests on inadequate metaphysical assumptions. Since Hegel believes that there can be a form of specifically philosophical inquiry into nature, grounded on different and more adequate metaphysical assumptions, the further implication of his work is that this specially philosophical form of inquiry into nature could provide the basis for a more environmentally sustainable way of life.

The idea that Hegel's philosophy of nature could speak to important social and philosophical problems is not a popular one. Ever since its initial publication in outline form in 1817, Hegel's philosophy of nature has been dismissed, rejected, and ridiculed by most philosophers. As Terry Pinkard notes in his recent biography of Hegel, the philosophy of nature was "ignored for the most part in his own time . . . [and] it fell into complete disrepute immediately after his death and has rarely been looked at since by anybody other than dedicated Hegel scholars."[2] Indeed, even the majority of Hegel scholars have been distinctly unsympathetic toward his philosophy of nature. Alexandre Kojève, for example, castigates Hegel's "absurd philosophy of Nature, his insensate critique of Newton, and his own 'magical' physics which discredited his system."[3] The reason so many readers have given the *Philosophy of Nature* short shrift is that they have perceived it to present a speculative, a priori, theory of the natural world that competes with standard scientific accounts. Most of Hegel's readers agree that this presupposes an absurdly inflated assessment of the powers of pure a priori reasoning, which is in reality capable of generating only a tissue of fantastic imaginings about nature, as Hegel was inevitably left with.[4]

The perhaps surprising starting point for my own interpretation of Hegel is that he does, indeed, use a priori reasoning to construct his basic theory of nature. Although he also incorporates large quantities of material from contemporary science, he does this only when he can interpret scientific claims as corresponding to his basic a priori theory. This method of reinterpreting scientific claims in light of a basic a priori theory is what I shall call "strong a priorism." My contention that Hegel's approach to nature is a priori in this strong sense may seem unpromising in view of the long-standing hostility to speculative philosophizing about nature. However, I will maintain that Hegel's strong a priorism is actually viable insofar as it rests upon his *metaphysics* of nature, a metaphysics which is of interest precisely because it challenges the metaphysics presupposed in science and so, too, the degradation of nature which arguably issues from that scientific metaphysics.

According to my reading, in reinterpreting scientific claims in terms of his basic a priori theory, Hegel is *redescribing* those claims in terms of the particular metaphysical conception of nature that informs his a priori theory. He believes, then, that all scientific theorizing embodies certain metaphysical assumptions about nature—assumptions which he rejects, constructing his alternative theory on the basis of contrasting metaphysical assumptions. For Hegel, the central assumption underlying science is that natural forms are bare things.[5] In contrast, his own metaphysical view is that natural forms are (in a certain qualified sense) rational agents, which act and transform themselves in accordance with rational requirements.[6] Hegel believes that his metaphysics of nature is more adequate than that presupposed within science, a view for which two main arguments can be found in his work: first, that his "rationalist" view of nature (as I will call it)[7] is closer to the basic way in which we experience nature, and, second, that his rationalist view allows us to recognize that all natural forms are intrinsically good, in virtue of the practical effectivity of their inherent rationality. Hegel's work thus establishes the necessity for a philosophical reconceptualization and study of nature distinct from its scientific study (although, importantly, this philosophical mode of study would not be antiscientific or obscurantist, instead redescribing and incorporating scientific claims wherever possible).

My interpretation of Hegel is unusual not least in its claim that he seeks to revalue nature and to find intrinsic value in natural phenomena, anticipating current environmental thought. By contrast, the standard view is that Hegel downgrades nature, deeming it of little interest compared with the human, historical, and sociopolitical phenomena that predominantly exercise him. According to David Kolb, for example, Hegel does not offer new insights about nature as he does about social issues, "because Hegel was more passionate about social and political matters."[8] Even when Hegel does attend to nature, received wisdom holds, he denigrates it: Jeffrey Reid, for instance, alleges that for Hegel "the purely natural is radically devalued."[9] One might appeal here to Hegel's designation of nature as the "rubbish" (*Abfall*) of the idea (EN §248R/1: 209), or to his professed ambition to "do violence" to nature's protean character (§246A/1: 200). Really, though, such remarks do not do justice to the complexity of Hegel's thinking about the natural world, and they should not be taken to exhaust his attitude to nature.[10]

Hegel's reassessment of nature's metaphysical and ethical status significantly influences the positions he takes up in other areas of philosophy. Every part of Hegel's system affects all the others, yet the impact of his philosophy of nature has been largely overlooked. We therefore need to bring out its wider influence, and I shall focus particularly upon its repercussions for Hegel's thought in metaphysics, ethics, and politics. I will argue that Hegel's aspiration to a descriptively adequate conception of nature supports a "metaphysical" reading of his wider philosophical system: that is, a reading according to which that system aims to furnish a realistic description of the structures of the universe.[11] Most metaphysical interpretations of Hegel find his basic description of the universe contained within the categories of his *Logic*. I suggest, instead, that the *Logic* describes a series of ontological structures considered in abstraction from how they are concretely instantiated in nature and mind. Hegel's description of these concretely instantiated structures is primary, the *Logic* being established only derivatively through abstraction from the philosophies of nature and mind.

Hegel's ethical theory is generally held to be premised upon the value of certain specifically human goods or characteristics, such as self-realization or freedom.[12] Complicating this picture, I maintain that an essential strand in Hegel's ethics is his recognition in the *Philosophy of Nature* of intrinsic value in nature, deriving from its practical rationality.[13] At this point, Hegel joins company with recent environmental thinkers, extending the ethical realm beyond the narrowly human sphere. Nonetheless, his recognition of intrinsic value in natural entities barely registers in Hegel's political philosophy as expressed in the *Philosophy of Right* (1821). His understanding of nature only affects his political thought in the sense that he becomes specifically concerned to *deny* moral considerability to natural entities: to show that, despite their intrinsic value, they make no moral claim upon human agents. In this way the *Philosophy of Nature* continues to exert a sustained if indirect influence on the conceptual structure of the *Philosophy of Right*.

The *Philosophy of Nature*'s influence extends, too, to Hegel's *Philosophy of Mind* (1817; revised 1827, 1831).[14] Sections §399–§402 on "sensibility" (*Empfindung*), especially, read differently when juxtaposed with the *Philosophy of Nature*. In section §401, Hegel postulates a structural connection between the senses (which collectively constitute sensibility) and the natural elements. Analyzing his account of sensibility, we find that he believes human subjects to have a basic form of sentient awareness of nature as elemental—an awareness which the *Philosophy of Nature* strives to articulate. This jars, again, with the accepted view that Hegel believes that philosophical thinking requires a purely rational and impersonal standpoint which breaks with sensibility. Robert Wicks, for example, claims that: "Inspired by Plato, Hegel devalues sensation in favour of pure conception . . . Throughout his philosophical writings, Hegel constantly condemns feeling in general as a mode of knowledge."[15] Hegel's attentiveness to the natural elements shows that this received view distorts his thinking concerning sentient experience, which contains a pronounced strain affirming that philosophical theorizing—particularly philosophical theorizing about nature—must remain consonant with sensibility and articulate sensibility instead of separating from it. By tracing the impact of the *Philosophy of Nature* upon Hegel's system, then, we obtain a new reading of his whole project in which, rather than devaluing nature and sentient experience, he seeks to *re*value nature and to *re*value sensibility in opposition to abstracted Enlightenment rationality.[16]

This reading of Hegel deviates not only from the standard conception of his overall philosophical stance, but also from more established approaches to his *Philosophy of Nature*. Since the 1970s, Hegel scholars have sought to combat the traditional, negative, image of the text, primarily by questioning the earlier orthodoxy that it outlines an essentially a priori and speculative theory of nature to combat scientific accounts.[17] According to these more recent commentators, Hegel's project is not to oppose science but to reconstruct and reorganize contemporary scientific hypotheses and theories in light of the more sophisticated logical or ontological categories of his own philosophy. A weakness of these newer readings of the *Philosophy of Nature*, though, is that by construing it as a working-over of scientific materials from Hegel's time, they tend to strip the text of any substantive interest, reducing it to a document for historians of nineteenth-century science.[18] In response, more recent (especially English-speaking) scholars have begun to evolve increasingly philosophical approaches to the text.[19] Building on such work, I propose a thoroughly philosophical reading of the *Philosophy of Nature*: philosophical in that I stress the text's impact on Hegel's wider metaphysical, ethical, and political projects, as well as its relevance to environmental problems and to widespread concerns about the hegemony and excessive authority of modern science.

In foregrounding how Hegel prefigures environmentalism, I risk anachronism—falsely attributing to Hegel an ecological agenda he cannot possibly have had. Certainly, my interpretations regularly go beyond what is explicitly legible in the *Philosophy of Nature* and the rest of the mature system. At the explicit level, Hegel advances no single, unified, consistent position on the value of nature. Similarly, he has no explicit, unified, position on either the extent of his reliance on a priori reasoning or the content of the metaphysical presuppositions which underlie his theory of nature; nor is there any single set of passages in which he explicitly defends these presuppositions as being superior to those of empirical science. In attributing to Hegel a particular cluster of views regarding nature, I am *reconstructing* the views I find implicit within his texts. These implicit views become most clearly visible when the *Philosophy of Nature* and the other systematic works are read conjointly. In reconstructing Hegel's views, I appeal not only to this implicit textual evidence (which is often fragmentary), but also to considerations of philosophical consistency and cogency. This might seem to align my approach with the type of history of philosophy which sets out, problematically, to reconstruct an author's views based on what he or she *should* have said, had he or she had access to the increased level of argumentative rigor available in the present day. To this it can reasonably be objected that a good interpretation can attribute to authors only views which they *could* have held and expressed under the same description, given their historical and intellectual location. On this view, the meaning of a text is fixed by its immediate context, and the interpreter's job is to rediscover this meaning.[20]

The latter view of meaning has, of course, been sharply contested, conspicuously by Hans-Georg Gadamer. According to Gadamerian hermeneutics, the meaning of a text only arises in the relationship between that text and its interpreter(s).[21] Any text contains innumerable potentials for meaning, which become realized only as subsequent interpreters bring that text into dialogue with their own historical and intellectual contexts. This does not mean that latter-day interpreters can simply project onto texts any meaning they choose: good interpretation still involves engaging with, responding to, and endeavoring to understand the text. As Brian Fay puts it: "interpretation is a process of listening to what others through their words . . . have to say to us (in full recognition that what an act [or text] says to us may well differ from what it says to others in different interpretive situations)."[22] According to this hermeneutic approach, then, Hegel's mature system and philosophy of nature do not have one meaning as fixed by his immediate situation, but an indefinite plurality of potential meanings, each of which can emerge in appropriate contexts. Consequently, there can be no single correct interpretation of Hegel's philosophy of nature. Rather, a current context of environmental problems, and growing interest in the possibility of a reenchantment of nature, makes possible the disclosure of certain previously unrealized meanings within the *Philosophy of Nature*. Hegel's concerns over the adequacy of science and the ethical status of nature, which hitherto have remained only potentially present in the *Philosophy of Nature*, can now be realized and activated.

This broadly hermeneutic approach to Hegel bears on my decision to refer regularly to the controversial "additions" (*Zusätze*) to his texts. The editors of his works compiled these additions posthumously from his lecture notes and from students' transcripts of his lectures, adding the results to the main paragraphs of Hegel's mature works. The editors omitted to indicate the separate sources from which the additions were drawn, often jamming together sets of notes from quite different times. The additions to the *Philosophy of Nature* are especially problematic in this regard, since their editor, Jules Michelet, amalgamated notes and transcripts spanning over two decades.[23] Critical editions of the materials on which Michelet drew are now beginning to be published, although, as yet, none have been translated into English.[24] Some scholars have concluded that the additions cannot be used at all in a viable interpretation of the *Philosophy of Nature*.[25] This seems to me excessively restrictive. While the main paragraphs of Hegel's works should certainly be the primary basis on which an interpretation is constructed, there is no reason why the additions should not be used where they augment and do not contradict this interpretation; this will be my procedure here.

At this point, I should also mention my potentially controversial decision to bracket out the vexed issue of Hegel's relationship with Schelling. Hegel's philosophy of nature is often regarded as an "arcane and derivative" reworking of that of Schelling.[26] Undoubtedly, it is Schelling with whom the notion of philosophy of nature is chiefly associated (partly due to his influence on many notable scientists of the time—the so-called *Naturphilosophen*—whom Hegel signally failed to influence). Schelling virtually invented the program of a philosophy of nature with his *Ideas for a Philosophy of Nature* (1797), and he redefined this program in subsequent works, revising it dramatically in the new context of his "identity philosophy" from 1800.[27] One might therefore think that Schelling's work is the more important point of departure for any contemporary reassessment of philosophy of nature. I concentrate on Hegel, though, in the belief that he develops a more systematic and rigorously worked out version of the project initiated, and sketched out in a succession of conflicting ways, by Schelling. It is Hegel, I will suggest, who effectively systematizes the philosophy of nature as a distinctive conceptual space. There remains, of course, an important question as to how Hegel's philosophy of nature relates to the original version of the project advanced by Schelling. But we cannot properly address this genealogical question without first understanding how Hegel conceives of philosophy of nature, my aim here being to provide this preliminary understanding of Hegel's project.

The question of Hegel's relationship to Schelling inevitably also raises the question of his attitude towards romanticism. My reading accentuates certain strands in Hegel which affiliate him with romanticism: in particular, his belief in the need to overcome disenchantment through a more "magical" picture of nature, which would simultaneously reunite the rational and sensible sides of human personality.[28] Hegel scholars are wont to downplay his affinity with romanticism, partly due to a perception of romanticism as theoretically naïve (and, perhaps, politically conservative as well). This negative picture of romanticism is being made increasingly untenable by the growing body of work reassessing romanticism's theoretical sophistication and political complexity, as well as its decisive influence upon European philosophy since Kant.[29] This reassessment makes it possible to reconsider Hegel's relationship with romanticism, and, specifically, to acknowledge how his thought about nature critically develops key romantic motifs: the critique of empirical science, the need to reanimate the natural world, and the need to reconcile sensibility and understanding.[30]

My interpretation of Hegel will be developed in the following stages. I begin in chapter 1 by addressing the extensive controversy over the place of a priori reasoning in Hegel's theory of nature. As I have already remarked, the question of Hegel's a priorism has always lain at the center of controversy over his *Philosophy of Nature*, with critics accusing him of developing a wholly a priori account of nature that can only be chimerical and fantastic. My intervention into this debate is to defend a controversial reading of Hegel as employing the method which I call "strong a priorism." This method involves first working out rationally what forms nature contains (by tracing how they necessitate one another), then incorporating corresponding empirical scientific claims into the resulting account. I argue that strong a priorism is the most philosophically tenable method open to Hegel, because it enables him to avoid falsely absolutizing fallible empirical claims, instead incorporating them into his theory on a merely interpretive and provisional basis. His theory of nature can therefore be reinterpreted as corresponding to relatively recent scientific views (such as relativity theory),[31] and cannot be dismissed as obsolete or of merely historical interest.

The second chapter interprets Hegel's substantive theory of nature as constructed according to the strong a priori method. I suggest that Hegel elaborates a complex and systematic account of the progressive structure of the natural world, an account that has gone almost entirely unnoticed by secondary commentators.[32] According to this theory, nature gradually progresses from an original division between its two constituent elements, thought and matter, to their final unification, crossing a necessary sequence of hierarchically arranged stages in the process. On the basis of my reconstruction of this theory, I argue that Hegel's theory of nature is metaphysical: that is, he attempts to describe the organizing structures that nature really has, structures which consist of forms of thought that become instantiated in matter in increasingly harmoniously ways. Hegel's metaphysical approach insures that his basic theory of nature is quite different from all the scientific accounts which he subsequently incorporates.

In chapter 3, I examine how Hegel's strong a priori method rests on his distinctively "rationalist" metaphysics of nature. If he is to incorporate scientific claims into his theory only provisionally and interpretively, he must offer an initial account of nature which characterizes it in substantially different terms to all empirical science, and so must frame this account in terms of a metaphysics distinct from that presupposed in empirical science. According to this metaphysics that Hegel espouses, all natural forms are *intrinsically rational*: they act and transform themselves according to rational requirements. He contrasts this to the metaphysics that he takes to be presupposed in empirical science, according to which all natural forms are *bare things* that are intrinsically meaningless. Chapter 3 explicates the difference between these metaphysical conceptions of nature, offering a moderate defence of Hegel's belief that all empirical science rests on this shared metaphysics. I then introduce his important claim that science's metaphysical assumptions are inadequate and that his "rationalist" metaphysical assumptions are more adequate, in the sense that they more accurately capture nature's real character.

This raises the question of whether Hegel is arguing for an alternative, ecologically sensitive, kind of science. He is not—or so I will argue. Rather, he believes that scientific claims must always be redescribed and resituated within his broader, more metaphysically adequate, philosophical framework. We therefore need to reconstruct the arguments embedded in Hegel's mature system which defend his claim that his rationalist metaphysics is more adequate than that of empirical science. In chapter 4, I critically examine Hegel's first two arguments for his rationalist metaphysics of nature, concluding that neither is successful. Hegel's first argument is that his metaphysics can better explain the range of natural processes and events. This argument makes sense in the cultural context of *Naturphilosophie* in Hegel's time. Ultimately, though, this argument from explanatory power turns upon a formal point about the logical structure of explanation, and so fails to show that Hegel's metaphysics is superior in respect of substantive truth. His second argument appeals to the systematic derivation of his metaphysics of nature from his general metaphysical standpoint, which has allegedly been proven uniquely true through the critique of rival metaphysical outlooks carried out in the *Phenomenology of Spirit* (1807). This argument invokes the notorious problem concerning the transition from the general metaphysics of Hegel's *Logic* to his philosophy of nature—a problem central to Schelling's and Feuerbach's disputes with Hegel. I conclude that Hegel's system cannot tenably be construed in linear terms, which makes his argument from systematic derivation inapplicable.

In chapter 5, I consider one of Hegel's two more successful and fruitful arguments for his metaphysics of nature: his "phenomenological" argument. According to this, his rationalist metaphysics is especially adequate because, uniquely, it makes it possible to elaborate a theory of the natural world that articulates our basic form of experience of it, which is sensible (that is, preconceptual). Hegel's ideal of *Bildung* (culture or education) implies his general commitment to a principle that adequate theories must articulate sensible experience. Through a reading of §399–§402 of his *Philosophy of Mind*, I argue that Hegel thinks we have a basic sensible awareness of nature as composed of the elements. His theory of nature can then be seen to attempt to articulate this awareness, in that it portrays nature as pervasively elemental. Further, Hegel suggests that his rationalist metaphysics uniquely allows him to develop this theory, by enabling him to conceptualize the dynamism and fluidity of the natural elements. I conclude, though, that Hegel's phenomenological argument remains crucially incomplete, since he does not fully explain why sensibility should be considered veridical in the first place.

In chapter 6, I reconstruct Hegel's "ethical" argument for his rationalist metaphysics of nature, according to which this metaphysics is uniquely adequate because it allows us to recognize that all natural forms are intrinsically good, in virtue of their practical rationality. This argument relies on the broadly Kantian thesis that goodness consists in action from reason. Typically this thesis has been used to devalue natural forms relative to rational human agents, but Hegel's unusual view that all natural forms also act from rationality allows him to extend intrinsic goodness into the whole of nature. This position compares favorably, I shall suggest, with recent assessments of nature's moral status from within environmental philosophy. Nonetheless, Hegel's ethical argument is not fully satisfactory, since his rationalist criterion of goodness ultimately entails that human beings are morally obliged to transform natural entities without restraint (as emerges in his *Philosophy of Right*). Hegel's ethical argument establishes the requirement for a distinctively philosophical conception of nature which can appreciate its intrinsic value, but his rationalist metaphysics fails to satisfy this requirement fully.

Hegel's arguments can be read together as constituting one interconnected defense of his metaphysics, method, and theory of nature. This defence is not wholly successful: even Hegel's phenomenological and ethical arguments do not unequivocally support his rationalist conception of nature. However, those arguments do establish the need for a metaphysical view of nature which allows us to construct a phenomenologically concrete theory that recognizes intrinsic value in nature's constituent forms. In this way, Hegel's arguments have the lasting achievement of opening up the philosophy of nature as a *project*: the project of theorizing natural forms on the basis of a metaphysics which is distinct from that of science, and which is made adequate by its phenomenological richness and ethical implications. Once identified, this project has the potential to be rearticulated outside the parameters of Hegel's thought in ways that could contribute to the contemporary task of revaluing the natural world.

ABBREVIATIONS

References to Hegel are parenthetical and refer to English translations whenever available, although I have sometimes amended these, without special notice, following the German originals. Hegel's works are cited by paragraph number (§) where applicable, in which case the page number to the English translation follows the paragraph citation. Otherwise, works are cited by page number with the English pagination (if available) preceding the German. Remarks are cited "R," additions "A." The following abbreviations are used:

Werke   *G. W. F. Hegel: Werke in zwanzig Bänden*, ed. Eva Moldenhauer and Karl Markus Michel (Frankfurt: Suhrkamp, 1969–1972). Works cited below by volume number.

GC   "The Spirit of Christianity and its Fate." In *Early Theological Writings*, trans. T. M. Knox (Philadelphia: University of Pennsylvania Press, 1975).

         "Der Geist des Christentums und sein Schicksal" (1798–1800). In *Frühe Schriften. Werke 1.*

DS   *The Difference between the Fichtean and Schellingian Systems of Philosophy*, trans. Jere Paul Surber (Arascadero, CA: Ridgeview Press, 1978).

         "Differenz des Fichteschen und Schellingschen Systems der Philosophie (1801)." In *Jenaer Schriften 1801–1807. Werke 2.*

PhG   *Phenomenology of Spirit*, trans. A. V. Miller (Oxford: Oxford University Press, 1977).

         Phänomenologie des Geistes (1807). *Werke 3.*

PP   *The Philosophical Propaedeutic*, trans. A. V. Miller (Oxford: Blackwell, 1986).

            "Texte zur Philosophischen Propädeutik." In *Nürnberger und Heidelberger Schriften 1808–1817. Werke 4.*

WL   *Science of Logic*, trans. A. V. Miller (London: Allen and Unwin, 1969).

            Wissenschaft der Logik (1812–1816). *Werke 5–6.*

EL   *Encyclopaedia Logic*, trans. T. F. Geraets, W. A. Suchting, and H. S. Harris (Indianapolis: Hackett, 1991).

            Enzyklopädie der philosophischen Wissenschaften, volume 1 (1817; revised 1827, 1830). *Werke 8.*

EN   *Philosophy of Nature*, ed. and trans. M. J. Petry. 3 vols. (London: Allen and Unwin, 1970).

            Enzyklopädie der philosophischen Wissenschaften, volume 2 (1817; revised 1827, 1830). *Werke 9.*

EM   *Philosophy of Mind*, trans. A. V. Miller and W. Wallace (Oxford: Clarendon Press, 1971).

            Enzyklopädie der philosophischen Wissenschaften, volume 3 (1817; revised 1827, 1830). *Werke 10.*

LNR   *Lectures on Natural Right and Political Science: The First Philosophy of Right, Heidelberg 1817–1819, with Additions from the Lectures of 1818–1819*, transcribed by Peter Wannenmann, trans. J. Michael Stewart and Peter C. Hodgson (Berkeley: University of California Press, 1996).

            Die Philosophie des Rechts: Die Mitschriften Wannenmann (Heidelberg 1917/18) und Homeyer (Berlin 1818/19), ed. Karl-Heinz Ilting (Stuttgart: Klett-Cotta, 1983).

PR   *Elements of the Philosophy of Right*, ed. Allen Wood, trans. H. B. Nisbet (Cambridge: Cambridge University Press, 1991).

            Grundlinien der Philosophie des Rechts, oder Naturrecht und Staatswissenschaft im Grundrisse (1821). *Werke 7.*

PSS   *Philosophy of Subjective Spirit*, ed. and trans. M. J. Petry. 3 vols. (Dordrecht: Reidel, 1978).

VPGe   *Vorlesungen über die Philosophie des Geistes: Berlin 1827/*
            1828, ed. Franz Hespe and Burkhard Tuschling (Hamburg:
            Meiner, 1994).

VG   *Lectures on the Philosophy of World History. Introduction:*
            Reason in History. trans. H. B. Nisbet (Cambridge: Cam-
            bridge University Press, 1975).

            "Einleitung," *Vorlesungen über die Philosophie der*
            Geschichte. Werke 12.

VPG   *Philosophy of History*, trans. J. Sibree (Buffalo, NY:
            Prometheus Books, 1991).

            Vorlesungen über die Philosophie der Geschichte. Werke 12.

VA   *Aesthetics: Lectures on Fine Art*, trans. T. M. Knox. 2 vols.
            (Oxford: Clarendon Press, 1975).

            Vorlesungen über die Ästhetik. Werke 13–15.

VGP   *Lectures on the History of Philosophy*, trans. E. S. Haldane.
            3 vols. (Lincoln: University of Nebraska Press, 1995).

            Vorlesungen über die Geschichte der Philosophie. Werke
            18–20.

1

A PRIORI KNOWLEDGE IN
HEGEL'S PHILOSOPHY OF NATURE

> Bearing in mind the present *misunderstandings and prejudices* in
> regard to the philosophy of nature, it might seem appropriate to
> begin by setting out the *true* concept of this science. . . . What
> we are engaged on here is not a matter of imagination or
> fantasy; it is a matter of the concept and of reason.
>
> —Hegel, *Philosophy of Nature*

The question of Hegel's a priorism has always lain at the heart of debate
over his *Philosophy of Nature*. Critics have regularly accused him of
propounding a speculative, a priori, theory of nature that can only be
fantastic. The first step toward approaching and evaluating the *Philosophy of Nature* is to ascertain to what extent, and in what sense, Hegel
employs a priori reasoning to theorize nature. Unfortunately, his presentation of his substantive theory of nature is so obscure that one cannot
hope to derive an interpretation of his method on its basis alone. The
interpreter must have recourse to the few explicit remarks on method
that he disperses throughout the text, mostly concentrated in its introduction (EN §245–§252).

In these remarks, Hegel repeatedly claims that his method involves
some sort of reconciliation between a priori and empirical approaches
to nature. Unhappily, these claims are ambiguous and inconsistent,
envisaging three disparate forms of reconciliation. Hegel sometimes
suggests that he proceeded by first accepting a selection of contemporary scientific accounts of natural phenomena on empirical grounds,
subsequently reconstructing these accounts in a priori form. Alternatively, he suggests that he developed his basic theory of nature through

unaided a priori reasoning, thereafter incorporating those scientific results which he could interpret as corroborating his theory. Lastly, he may also be read as suggesting that he constituted his account of nature using those scientific claims that he could interpret as instantiating logical categories.

One aim of this chapter is to show that it is unwise to decide upon any of these interpretations without first acknowledging Hegel's own uncertainty and inconsistency. A reading of the *Philosophy of Nature* which does not arise from confrontation with this inconsistency is unlikely to convince, for it will leave open whether alternative lines of interpretation actually make better sense of the text. To paraphrase Hegel's *Phenomenology*, an interpretation that does not first demonstrate its superiority to others is merely a "bare assurance, just as valid as another" (PhG 71/49). Our initial task is therefore to familiarize ourselves with the ambiguities in Hegel's methodological remarks, setting out all the available interpretations of his approach to nature and eliminating those that are philosophically untenable or exegetically implausible. This is the necessary preliminary to any genuinely plausible interpretation of the *Philosophy of Nature*.

Textual Ambiguities in the *Philosophy of Nature*

Hegel largely confines his discussion of the methodology of his *Philosophy of Nature* to its introduction. Here he emphasizes that his method of theorizing nature is not that of natural science (*Naturwissenschaft*), which he understands to possess three defining characteristics. First, of course, natural science is a form of the study of *nature*—which does not as such distinguish it from the philosophical study of nature. Second, natural science is a *systematic* form of enquiry into nature: it attempts to integrate its discoveries and hypotheses into a comprehensive and unified understanding of the natural world. Again, natural science is no different from philosophy of nature in respect of its systematicity. Third, Hegel sees natural science—traditionally enough—as a specifically *empirical* form of the study of nature; this does divide it from the philosophy of nature.[1]

Hegel's usual term for natural science is simply physics (*Physik*), by which he means not the specialized discipline but natural science in all its branches. He frequently calls physics "empirical physics" (*empirische Physik*). According to him, natural science or "physics" is empirical in that it begins with the observation of nature in "perception and experience" (EN 1: 193). However, science is not exclusively observational, for on the basis of observations scientists identify and describe laws and universal kinds within the multitude of observable natural events and entities. Science is a *"theoretical* and *thinking* consideration of nature . . . [which] aims at comprehending that which is universal in nature . . . forces, laws, genera"* (EN §246/1: 196–97). Thus, for Hegel, natural science is "empirical" not because it is exclusively observational but because its theoretical component—the identification of universal genera and laws within perceptible phenomena—is underpinned by its observational component. Unlike philosophical thinking, scientific thinking about nature always starts from and remains informed by observation.[2]

Hegel is fairly clear that the method of philosophy of nature is not empirical, but his positive characterization of it is more equivocal. In the main paragraph (EN §246) in which he describes his method, he offers two incompatible interpretations of it, one directly following the other. According to his first interpretation, the philosopher of nature theorizes nature by initially learning from empirical science and then rationally reconstructing scientific claims.

> Not only must philosophy be in agreement with experience of nature, but the *origin* and *formation* of the philosophical science has empirical physics as its presupposition and condition. The procedure for originating and preparing a science, however, is not the same as the science itself; in this, the former [that is, experience] can no longer appear as the foundation [*als Grundlage*], which, here, should rather be the necessity of the concept. (EN §246R/1: 197)

To insure a proper agreement with empirical scientific findings, the philosopher must "originate" or "prepare" her theory by learning from scientists about the basic forms (the deeper genera, forces, laws, etc.) that organize the perceptible natural world.[3] The philosopher's further task is to provide an additional, nonempirical, justification for these empirically supported scientific claims, in terms of "the necessity of the concept." A passage from the *Encyclopaedia Logic* (in which Hegel begins the methodological preamble continued in the introduction to the *Philosophy of Nature*) suggests that the philosopher should provide this conceptual justification by working out, through a priori reasoning, why each of the natural forms identified by scientists must exist and have the characteristics it does.

> [P]hilosophy does owe its development to the empirical sciences, but it gives to their content the fully essential shape of

> the *freedom* of thinking (the *a priori*) as well as the *validation* [*Bewährung*] of *necessity* (instead of the warranting [*Beglaubigung*] of the content because it is simply found to be present and because it is a fact of experience). (EL §12R/37)

More specifically, Hegel hints that the philosopher should produce this proof of the necessity of empirically identified natural forms by showing that they compose an "intrinsically necessary whole" (EN §246A/1: 201). By implication, the task is to situate each form as the necessary consequence of the one before it, thereby establishing that all the forms identified by empirical scientists require one another, so that given knowledge of any one form we can acquire knowledge of all the rest, independently of experience. Philosophers find in nature the same structuring patterns as empirical scientists, but by a different, rational, route.

Straight after introducing this idea that philosophy of nature involves rationally reconstructing empirical findings, Hegel advances an alternative interpretation of his method which envisages its a priori and empirical components as inversely related. The philosopher should first theorize nature through pure reasoning and only afterwards compare this theory with empirical scientific claims.

> [I]n the philosophical procedure, not only must the object be given according to its *conceptual determination*, but also the *empirical* appearance that corresponds to [*entspricht*] it must be identified, and it must be shown that it actually corresponds to its concept. However, this is not an appeal to experience [*Erfahrung*] in relation to the necessity of the content. (EN §246R/1: 197)

According to this passage, the philosopher's first task is to deduce the existence and character of the forms comprising the natural world—to "give objects" rationally, according to "conceptual determinations." A statement from Hegel's introduction to his *Philosophy of Mind* indicates that the method through which the philosopher must construct this basic theory of nature is by deriving each natural form as the necessary consequence of its predecessor.

> [I]n the empirical sciences, matter is taken up as it is given by experience, from outside . . . in opposition to this, speculative thinking has to demonstrate each of its objects and their development, in their absolute necessity. This happens in that each particular concept is led forth [*abgeleitet*] out of

the self-originating and self-actualising universal concept, or
the logical idea. (EM §379A/5)

The "logical idea" is the last category of Hegel's *Logic*, immediately
preceding nature. The philosopher has to work out what the logical
idea requires as its necessary consequence, and "lead" this forth as the
first natural form, thereafter deducing succeeding natural forms from it.
(Admittedly, Hegel does not speak explicitly of *Deduktion* in this context, but this is clearly equivalent to his "leading forth" and "conceptual giving").[4]

Having by a priori reasoning constructed a skeletal vision of nature, the philosopher subsequently asks whether any of the forms independently identified by empirical scientists "correspond to" (*entsprechen*)
the forms whose existence she has ascertained rationally. For example,
Hegel states: "To prove that space accords with [*gemäß sei*] our concept, we must compare the representation of space with the determination of our concept" (EN §254A/1: 224). Only if an empirical account
"accords" or "corresponds" with some element in Hegel's preconstituted
a priori theory of nature does that empirical account get incorporated.
By supplementing his a priori framework with empirical material in this
way, Hegel corroborates and amplifies his initially skeletal account.

However, for this skeletal account of nature to be properly
nonempirical, its descriptions of nature's component forms cannot be
couched in terms that derive from and so already presuppose the
compatibility of empirical claims. Accordingly, Hegel portrays the
natural forms that he (on this reading) deduces in unfamiliar language.
He begins, for example, with a form called "the universal being-
outside-itself [*Außersichsein*] of nature," which, he then claims, corresponds to space as characterized by empirical scientists. "The primary
or immediate determination of nature is the abstract *universality of its
being-outside-itself*,—its unmediated indifference, *space*" (EN §254/1:
223). The initially unfamiliar form thereby acquires concrete significance
as space. As this illustrates, Hegel's basic a priori theory of nature
portrays natural phenomena in *sui generis*—specifically nonscientific—
terms. This wholly nonempirical theory then becomes embedded in an
overall picture of nature emerging from the subsequent interpolation
of empirical materials.

Hegel's two proposed interpretations of his method are incompatible, assigning inversely symmetrical roles to a priori and empirical
knowledge.[5] The two methods can be called, respectively, the "weak"
and "strong" a priori methods. Schematically, according to the weak a
priori method, we must (1) learn about nature's constituent forms from

scientists, then (2) work out rationally why these forms are as they are, by tracing how they necessitate one another. Conversely, according to the strong a priori method, we must (1) work out rationally what forms nature contains, by tracing how they necessitate one another (given the initial import of the "logical idea'), then we (2) incorporate corresponding empirical claims into the resulting theory. Since Hegel's two methodological self-interpretations are incompatible, he cannot have assembled his theory of nature through both methods (as he suggests). Which of his self-interpretations is authoritative?

One potential way to decide between these interpretations is to see which receives greater corroboration from the surrounding methodological remarks in the text and in the interconnected introductions to the other volumes of the *Encyclopaedia*. Unfortunately, many of these remarks simply duplicate the inconsistency of EN §246:

> [W]e can first say . . . that the philosophy of nature does not need experience; on the one hand, this is true. . . . However we must not envisage the relationship of philosophy to experience as if it did not need experience.[6]

Often, Hegel's other statements are vague enough to license either of the proposed interpretations of his method. For instance:

> The philosophy of nature takes the material which physics has prepared from experience, at the point to which physics has brought it, and reorganises it, without basing itself on experience as the final proof [*Bewährung*]. Physics must therefore work into the hands of philosophy. (EN §246A/1: 201)

This "taking" and "reorganising" seems at first to refer to the initial acceptance and subsequent reconstruction of empirically generated accounts of nature as envisaged by the weak a priori interpretation. But without difficulty one may also read Hegel as referring to the *final* examination of empirical accounts, and incorporation of those that correspond to philosophical claims, as anticipated on the strong a priori interpretation. Elsewhere Hegel states:

> [S]peculative science does not leave the empirical content of the other sciences aside, but recognises and uses it, and in the same way recognises and employs the universal of these sciences, the laws, the genera, etc., for its own content; but it also introduces other categories into these universals and gives them validity [*geltend macht*]. (EL §9R/33)

This could mean that philosophers should accept empirical accounts but amend them ("introduce other categories") so that the forms identified can be recognized as constituting a necessary chain, thereby receiving additional vindication from reason. Or it could mean that philosophers give validity to empirical accounts by identifying them as corresponding to philosophically derived characterizations of natural forms, an identification that "introduces other categories" into those accounts.

However, one statement from the *Logic* lends firmer support to the weak a priori interpretation:

> It is only an ill-minded prejudice to assume that philosophy stands antithetically opposed to any sensible appreciation of experience . . . These shapes [of consciousness, such as science] are recognised by philosophy, and even justified [*gerechtfertigt*] by it. Rather than opposing them, the thinking mind steeps itself in their basic import; it learns from them and strengthens itself. (EL 5)

Yet other comments in the *Philosophy of Nature* speak equally robustly for the strong a priori interpretation, for instance: "The *first* thing is now the *a priori conceptual determination*; the second is to seek out the way and manner that this conceptual determination exists in our representation" (EN §275A/2: 12). "The immanent philosophical element is here as everywhere the internal necessity of the *conceptual determination*, which must then be shown to be *some* natural existence" (EN §276R/2: 17; see also §247A/1: 206). Examples could be multiplied, but Hegel's elusiveness and inconsistency recur everywhere. This makes it impossible to decide between his competing self-interpretations by referring to his other methodological statements, for without difficulty these can be so construed as to support either interpretation.

Perhaps decisive textual evidence comes from the substantive account of nature occupying the *Philosophy of Nature*? Unhelpfully, Hegel's presentation of this substantive account is heavily condensed, often to the point of unintelligibility. In particular, his arguments linking each natural form to its successor are generally too abbreviated and opaque to support either interpretation unequivocally. Admittedly, it is often thought that the overall makeup of this account refutes Hegel's strong a priori self-interpretation, since he includes résumés of copious quantities of material from the sciences of his time, providing detailed sections on, for instance, geometry, magnetism, electricity, and geology. But this would only tell against the strong a priori interpretation if that method instructed the philosopher wholly to ignore or reject scientific claims. In fact, it instructs her to thoroughly consider, and frequently endorse, scientific claims as supplements to her basic nonempirical theory of nature. The extensive presence of scientific findings in the *Philosophy of Nature* is quite compatible with strong a priorism; moreover, most of these findings feature in the additions to Hegel's main paragraphs, which implies that they merely supplement his main argument, as the strong a priori interpretation suggests.

On the other hand, the organization of Hegel's paragraphs does not immediately suggest that he includes empirical claims or concepts only after previously deducing a specifically philosophical form. Almost all the headings demarcating discussions of individual forms are names drawn from empirical science (for example, "sound," "electricity'), implying that his descriptions of those forms originate in that science. Yet on examining the substance of those discussions, one frequently finds that Hegel introduces these empirical names only after first characterizing the relevant natural form in *sui generis* philosophical terms. For example, he claims that there is a type of body characterized by "inner quivering... within itself,—*sound*. The existence of this oscillating in itself appears ... as sound" (EN §299–§299A/2: 69). Similarly, physical bodies "exhibit their *real* selfhood ... as their light, but a light that is intrinsically *differentiated*,—*electrical* relationship" (§323/2: 165). As a whole, then, the makeup and organization of the *Philosophy of Nature* are too ambiguous to justify conclusively either strong or weak a priori readings of the text.

We hoped for clear signals from Hegel as to the correct understanding of his approach to nature, but surveying the textual evidence has only clarified that neither his general methodological statements nor the general organization of his *Philosophy of Nature* unambiguously support reading the work as either strongly or weakly a priori. This negative conclusion is itself important, because commentators often deny that the strong a priori reading of his account of nature has any textual warrant.[7] This is because they overlook the fact that strong a priorism *does* recommend incorporating empirical material into one's philosophical theory of nature. Given this, neither of Hegel's conflicting self-interpretations can be ruled out on textual grounds. This makes it reasonable to choose between them for philosophical reasons, making the charitable assumption that Hegel must have adopted whichever method is more philosophically cogent. Here the prevailing judgment among commentators is that strong a priorism is less philosophically cogent than weak a priorism. In the next two sections I will argue that this consensus is misguided, and that strong a priorism is actually the more philosophically cogent method.

How Cogent Is Strong A Priorism?

Throughout most of the last two centuries, Hegel's theory of nature was widely perceived to use the method that I have called strong a priorism. Strong a priorism has been almost universally agreed to be philosophically untenable: correspondingly, most readers have rejected Hegel's *Philosophy of Nature* as misguided and chimerical. There are two main reasons why strong a priorism has usually been judged untenable. First, it has often been thought to involve outright ignorance or dismissal of scientific information. For instance, Ernan McMullin claims that Hegel's *Philosophy of Nature*

> was . . . conceived by its originator not as arising from, nor even as complementary to, the empirical science of his day, but rather as a critique of that science, providing an alternative science of Nature much more basic than any experimental-mathematical method could attain.[8]

Having assumed that Hegel's strong a priorism drives him to reject and dismiss scientific claims, McMullin complains that: "Here we see Romantic philosophy at its most normative and imperious." Similarly, Milic Capek accuses Hegel of "plain and arrogant denials of . . . scientific discoveries which were generally accepted by the scientific community of his own time."[9] And for Habermas: "It is with Hegel that a fatal misunderstanding arises: the idea that the claim of philosophical reason is equivalent to the usurpation of the legitimacy of independent sciences."[10] This criticism that strong a priorism dismisses or rejects scientific views rests, as I have explained, on a failure to recognize that strong a priorism distinguishes between a basic, nonempirical, theory of nature and an *overall* vision of nature which results when that theory is—as it should be—fleshed out with empirical findings. Although strong a priorism takes no account of scientific material in constructing the basic theory of nature, this method does recognize the need to incorporate scientific material whenever it corresponds to a priori claims.

Second, critics often accuse strong a priorism of attempting to deduce the existence of the same forms that scientists have identified and theorized empirically.[11] If, for example, Hegel first deduces a form that he calls "universal being-outside-itself" and then assimilates this form to space, then surely he is, indirectly, deducing the very same space that scientists have theorized empirically. As John Findlay comments, strong a priorism appears to involve the attempt to "do the work of science"—to deduce empirical results.[12] It seems highly unlikely that any philosopher can actually deduce empirical results: we must therefore suspect that Hegel's prior acquaintance with empirical findings covertly informs his supposedly pure a priori theory of nature in the first place. Yet, even if we assume that Hegel does somehow succeed in first theorizing nature a priori and afterwards equating his conclusions with those of empirical scientists, the problem remains that he ends up conferring absolute (deductive) justification upon scientific formulations that actually have only fallible, provisional, status. Strong a priorism, according to critics, seems destined to produce an "absolutization of empirical results soon to be superseded by further research."[13]

Does strong a priorism attempt to deduce and absolutize fallible empirical findings? We must explore what Hegel means by saying that empirically described natural forms may "correspond to" (*entsprechen*) forms that he has deduced a priori. A good place to approach this notion of "correspondence" is Hegel's discussion of the "empirical" conception of light at EN §275–§276. Throughout this discussion Hegel designates himself a strong a priori thinker, stating unusually clearly that he is first deducing a certain natural form and then subsequently equating it with empirically described light.[14] He explains:

> The proof [*Beweis*] that this conceptual determination, identity-with-self or the initially abstract self of centrality which has matter in it, this simple ideality that is present, is *light* is, as our introduction said, to be conducted empirically. The immanent philosophical element is here as everywhere the internal necessity of the *conceptual determination*, which must then be shown to be *some* natural existence. (EN §276R/2:17)

The philosopher first deduces a certain form—"identity-with-self," "simple present ideality"—and only afterwards "empirically proves" that it is identical to light as described scientifically. Since scientific and philosophical accounts characterize this form in different terms, the aim is to "prove empirically" that under different descriptions they both refer to the same form.

Hegel constructs his "proof" as follows. First, he fastens on some of the properties that each account attributes to its object and interprets these properties as identical. In this case, Hegel has deduced the existence of a unitary body (empirically, the sun) located at the center of a structured system of bodies, and has reasoned that this body has a homogeneous type of matter that manifests its unitary character. He then equates this with the capacity of empirical light to make everything manifest: "it is by being in light that everything may be . . . grasped by us" (EN §275A/2:13). As this example shows, ascertaining which empirical and philosophical properties are identical involves *interpretation*: only through an act of interpretation can light's illuminating quality be equated with the disclosing character of the kind of matter that Hegel has deduced. *Qua* interpretive, these judgments of identity between empirically and philosophically described properties cannot be codified in rules, and so remain always liable to contestation and revision. Consequently, Hegel's "proofs" of identity between empirical and philosophical properties can only be fallible and provisional, unlike the deductive argumentation that (on this strong a priori interpretation) constitutes his basic theory of nature.[15]

Furthermore, for these interpretations to justify Hegel's inference that the relevant forms—light and "identity-with-self"—are identical as a whole, he has to downplay any properties of light that resist interpretation into philosophical terms. He defends this by suggesting that such properties are comparatively inessential or extrinsic. For instance, he contends that light's finite speed is a merely extrinsic property deriving from its relationship to the atmosphere (EN §276A/2: 20–21). Here, Hegel is beginning to *reformulate* scientific accounts (by redescribing the relations amongst the properties scientists ascribe to forms). These reformulations need not be arbitrary: presumably they will be more or less plausible depending upon how far they stray from the original scientific accounts. But the fact that Hegel's reformulations can be more or less well supported by the content of empirical accounts means that they may always become implausible in the face of scientific change. In this respect, too, Hegel's "proofs" of identity between empirical and philosophical forms constitute a contingent, not a necessary, element of his *Philosophy of Nature*. As scientific knowledge develops, his reformulations of many scientific accounts will become implausible and so his rationale for including them in the *Philosophy of Nature* will disappear. The material that he includes could, in principle, be substituted for quite different material with no effect on his basic theory of nature. Hegel acknowledges this in discussing space:

> In that it is our procedure, after establishing the thought that is necessary according to the concept, to ask how this thought looks in our representation, so the further demand [in this context] is that the thought of pure being-outside-itself correspond to the intuition of space. *Even if we made a mistake here, this would not count against the truth of our thought.* In empirical science one adopts the inverse route; in it the empirical intuition

of space is the first, and only then does one come to the thought
of space. (EN §254A/1:224; my emphasis)[16]

The contingency of Hegel's "proofs" of identity between philosophically
and scientifically described forms is doubly important. First, it means
that, assuming that his theory is strong a priori, it contains no inherent
commitment to endorsing the empirical results accepted in his time. It
may always be possible to construe Hegel's theory as corresponding to
more recent scientific views: thus, his theory cannot be rejected as obsolete relative to later science.[17] Second, the contingency of these "proofs"
confirms that Hegel is not attempting to deduce empirical findings. He
incorporates the latter into his *Philosophy of Nature* on a *non*-deduc-
tive, interpretive, and merely provisional basis.[18] Thus, although strong
a priorism has often been denounced for attempting to deduce scientific
results, when carefully examined it sidesteps this trap of trying to deduce fallible empirical findings and lend them absolute justification.

    We can now appreciate more fully the nature of the strong a priori
method, according to which we must (1) work out rationally what
forms nature contains, by tracing how they necessitate one another,
then (2) incorporate "corresponding" empirical claims into the resulting
theory—that is, those empirical claims which describe (or can be reformulated to describe) forms in such terms that they can be provisionally
interpreted as identical to the forms that have been deduced a priori. By
incorporating empirical claims into his theory on this merely provisional, interpretive, basis, Hegel can theorize nature a priori without
absolutizing contemporary science. Thus, strong a priorism avoids the
fallacies usually laid at its door: it offers a philosophically coherent
approach to the study of nature.

How Cogent is Weak A Priorism?

Critics of strong a priorism have tended to assume that Hegel's proposed weak a priori method is the more cogent approach to nature.
This assumption, I want to suggest, is mistaken, as weak a priorism as
Hegel presents it has a serious problem. Although subsequent scholars
have reformulated weak a priorism to avoid this problem, their reformulations succumb to difficulties in turn—difficulties which necessitate
further revisions of weak a priorism, and, ultimately, its transformation
into a somewhat different method, which I will call "a posteriorism."
This "a posteriori" method *is* cogent, but weak a priorism as such—
with which Hegel initially presents us—does not seem to admit of cogent restatement.

Weak a priorism's problem is very simple: with few exceptions, the scientific accounts that (on this reading) Hegel uses for the basic fabric of his theory of nature have been shown by subsequent science either to be false or to give a merely truncated or distorted characterization of natural forms. By seeking rational necessity in the forms described by contemporary empirical scientists, Hegel really *is* doomed to absolutize fallible results. There are two main ways in which he might respond to this objection. First, he could respond that he mistakenly took soon-to-be-superseded scientific claims to have been conclusively justified through the observational methods of science. Although scientists maintained that those claims had empirical support, in reality they reached these claims through fallacious metaphysical reasoning. Hegel levies this charge against scientists in his *Logic*: "The fundamental illusion in scientific empiricism is always that it uses . . . metaphysical categories . . . and it goes on to draw *conclusions*, guided by categories of this sort" (EL §38R/77–78). Scientists themselves are generally unconscious of using metaphysical categories, and this unself-consciousness makes their reasoning more likely to be invalid while causing them to portray their claims as empirically supported—and so misleading the philosopher into accepting those claims and trying to fit the natural forms described into her rational chain. This possible Hegelian response seems to presuppose that philosophers have limited capacities to spot claims with imperfect empirical support, and will typically be led astray by misguided scientific consensus. Tacitly, then, this possible Hegelian response admits the need for continual reconsideration and revision of philosophers" rational reconstructions as scientific progress exposes past errors. This effectively concedes that the arguments of Hegel's *Philosophy of Nature*—and those of any determinate philosophical rearrangement of science—are likely to be uninterestingly misguided.

Second, Hegel might respond that his rational reconstruction is valid and that this reveals that it is subsequent scientists' refutations of the claims he has reconstructed which are mistaken—that it must be those refutations which lack empirical warrant. This entails the falsity of any significantly new scientific claims produced after 1830. Yet this stipulation that only pre-1830 scientific claims can be true seems arbitrary, and this dissolves the credibility of the reasoning by which (on this reading) Hegel reconstructs those claims. So this second possible response to the problem of scientific change again implies that the actual arguments of the *Philosophy of Nature* are unreliable.

The weak a priori method, then, leaves Hegel in a dilemma: he can either deny fallibility to patently fallible empirical claims or embrace fallibility but admit the unreliability of any particular philosophical

reconstruction of science. However, we should not immediately conclude that the weak a priori interpretation of the *Philosophy of Nature*
should be rejected, for weak a priorism can be reformulated in ways
that make it compatible with recognizing the fallibility of scientific claims.
Michael Petry has advanced one such reformulation, introducing his
1970 English translation of the text.[19] Petry's important idea is that
Hegel is not trying to ascertain which of the forms described by science
are necessary, but is only reorganizing scientific concepts and claims in
a systematic arrangement congruent with the architectonic of his logic.
According to Petry, Hegel

> was fully persuaded that the systematic exposition of the
> various sciences ... had its own validity, and whatever we
> may think of this distinction between contingent content and
> general principle, empirical material and philosophic form, it
> is essential that we should not overlook it.[20]

A properly systematic arrangement of scientific concepts and claims
ranks them in a hierarchy of levels of complexity, corresponding to the
levels of categorial complexity outlined in Hegel's *Logic*. According to
Petry, Hegel believes that philosophers can rightly criticize empirical
scientists when they misrecognize the level of complexity at which their
own discourse operates and therefore generate theories that threaten to
confuse the systematic organization. Brigitte Falkenburg independently
provides a helpful articulation of the kind of approach that Petry attributes to Hegel:

> The systematic order of organizing the concepts of physics
> into a system of natural kinds is prescribed by the systematic
> order of conceptual types of structure as expounded in the
> *Logic*, starting from the most abstract (or structurally poor)
> concepts and ending up at the most complex (or structurally
> complete) concepts.[21]

The method that Petry attributes to Hegel is still weak a priori, insofar
as it rearranges scientific materials into an order governed by the a
priori structure of logical categories. But Petry's reconstruction of weak
a priorism overcomes the defect of Hegel's initial formulation, for according to Petry Hegel does not attempt to ascertain which scientifically
described forms are necessary, but tries, more modestly, to ascertain
how far scientific descriptions of these forms can be arranged into a
structure compatible with a priori logical principles. So reinterpreted,

Hegel turns out to be furthering the development of science in the modest way befitting a philosopher: he directs scientists away from false paths onto which they intermittently stray through lack of grasp of logical principles and completes their work by recasting it within a conceptually well-ordered framework.

Petry's promising reformulation of weak a priorism still has a difficulty. He believes that logical or systematic considerations guide Hegel's *reorganization* of scientific material, but not his *interpretation* of that material (hence Petry's contrast between systematic form and empirical content). Generally, though, when Hegel incorporates empirical results into his *Philosophy of Nature*, he does not take them up just as he finds them, but translates them into his own terms (for example, we have already encountered his seemingly idiosyncratic description of light as "pure manifestation" and "universal self-identity," terms that recur whenever he discusses light). Gerd Buchdahl offers a reading of the *Philosophy of Nature* which recognizes that Hegel does not merely reorganize scientific material with reference to his logic, but thoroughly reinterprets scientific concepts and hypotheses in terms of logical categories. Buchdahl stresses how this project descends from Kant's inquiry into the conditions of possibility of scientific concepts (in his 1786 *Metaphysical Foundations of Natural Science*). But whereas Kant took given scientific results and showed their connection with basic logical categories that give them intelligibility, Hegel completely reinterprets scientific concepts in light of logical categories. For example, he reinterprets the contemporary scientific concepts of "attraction" and "repulsion" through his logical categories of "one" and "many."[22]

Buchdahl's reading of Hegel also has a problem, as he himself highlights. According to Buchdahl's reading, Hegel thinks that Kant links the categories to empirical results so loosely that they confer no additional credibility upon those results. Hegel wants instead to enhance the credibility of empirical findings by thoroughly reinterpreting them through logical categories. But "if the connection between the metaphysical basis and the empirical results [becomes] very close, one runs the risk that changes in scientific theory will overturn the whole enterprise."[23] In other words, according to Buchdahl, Hegel integrates contemporary scientific results so firmly together with logical categories as to entail that no other results could achieve the same level of logical intelligibility—which once again has the effect of raising fallible scientific claims to absolute status. By thoroughly reinterpreting scientific concepts so that they instantiate logical categories, Hegel turns out to be denying that any other scientific concepts can achieve equivalent logical intelligibility.

The problem, then, is that weak a priorism as Hegel initially presents it cannot readily accommodate the fallibility of scientific findings. In Petry's reformulation, weak a priorism avoids this problem, since it seeks only to organize (variable and fallible) scientific results in conformity to logical categories. Yet Petry's reformulation of weak a priorism appears problematic as a reading of Hegel, since Hegel engages in a much more thoroughgoing reinterpretation of scientific claims in light of his *Logic*. Acknowledging this, however, returns us to the initial problem: by closely reinterpreting scientific claims in light of logical categories, weak a priorism once again threatens to deny fallibility and corrigibility to those claims.

In *Real Process: How Logic and Chemistry Combine in Hegel's Philosophy of Nature* (1996), John Burbidge offers a further reinterpretation of Hegel which avoids this problem. According to Burbidge, Hegel identifies scientific concepts as *im*perfectly instantiating logical categories, thereby allowing both present and future scientific claims to attain equal degrees of—imperfect—logical intelligibility. Burbidge's reading of Hegel can therefore be regarded as the most sustained attempt yet to defend the idea that Hegel organizes and reinterprets scientific findings in light of logical categories. It is worth examining Burbidge's impressively careful, detailed, reading of Hegel in some depth: this will help us to see whether weak a priorism can be reformulated in a philosophically cogent form.

Burbidge tends to assume that scientific descriptions and explanations largely capture the reality of the world: he therefore speaks indifferently of Hegel as assessing how far scientific claims exemplify his logic and how far empirical phenomena exemplify that logic.[24] Burbidge holds, essentially, that Hegel finds that empirical phenomena (or their scientific descriptions) only ever instantiate logical categories imperfectly. Burbidge supports this claim with a detailed study of the relation between Hegel's discussions of "chemism" (*Chemismus*) in the *Logic* and of "chemical process" (*chemische Prozeß*) in the *Philosophy of Nature*. The logical category of chemism arises, according to Burbidge, when we start to think of objects as chemical, that is, as separate but inherently oriented towards one another.[25] This obliges us to think of these objects as being capable of realizing their orientation to one another by coming together within a neutral "medium." However, in thinking this we lose our initial idea that separation is essential to chemical objects. This drives us on to reconceive chemical objects again. After a series of such reconceptions, we come to reflect back on the whole succession, reaching the general conclusion that objects are amenable to being classified in systematically interrelated ways. This sparks our move to the entirely

new category of teleology, embracing the idea that objects are so constituted as to be amenable to our thinking about them.[26] All these developments concern only the *logic* of our thinking about chemical processes,
throughout which, as Burbidge emphasizes: "There is no need to refer . . . to
actual chemical bodies . . . Hegel's discussion of chemism involves a systematic development that is logical on its own account."[27]

In the *Philosophy of Nature*, Burbidge continues, Hegel introduces
his discussion of chemical processes by laying out again the logical
category of the chemical object (as separate but oriented to an other).
Unlike in the *Logic*, though, we then move on to explore how this
category is exemplified in empirical phenomena. We find that nature in
its rich diversity exceeds the framework provided by the logical category of the chemical.[28]

> The contingencies of nature disrupt the systematic coherence
> of the logical argument [so that] for all the value of the
> logical analysis in providing ways of characterizing chemical
> phenomena, there is no one-to-one correlation. Experience
> alone can show what phenomena actually occur, and logic
> does its best to sort that confusion of data into a coherent
> framework.[29]

For instance, the initial empirical form of the chemical process ("galva-
nism") involves objects (metals) that are not strictly chemical, as they
do not perfectly exhibit the characteristic of orientation toward one
another. Similarly, all empirical chemical processes prove to unite the
processes of "combination" and "separation," which are logically conceived as separate. Thus, the characteristics of logical chemism are
exhibited (at best) incompletely in empirical material. Burbidge concludes, in general, that "the logic is not instantiated directly; investigation must find what corresponds in nature to the logical pattern, though
in a quite dispersed and incomplete way."[30] After all, as he points out,
if nature instantiated logical chemism perfectly then Hegel would need
no separate discussion of natural chemical processes, which could simply be mentioned as a footnote to the *Logic*.

That logical categories are instantiated only imperfectly in nature
has dramatic implications for how Hegel's account of nature is systematic, as Burbidge shows. Whenever we think logically, we must proceed
by elaborating successive conceptions of something before we grasp
these as a unity, and likewise in thinking about nature we must first
examine all the aspects of empirical chemical processes and then grasp
them in an overall perspective. Grasping all these aspects together leads

us to conclude that bodies and substances are only evanescent moments of an overarching process, which is grasped through the new category of *life* as a self-organizing process that specifies its own members. As in the *Logic*, this is a *conceptual* transition, from one way of thinking about nature to another. However, in the *Logic*, this final "act of reflective synthesis"[31] resulted in the category of *teleology*, not that of life. The *Philosophy of Nature*, then, "does not just follow the logic, but goes its own way."[32] Because philosophical thought about nature has to organize contingent empirical materials, it generates a series of categories which may well *diverge* from logical categories.[33] These "natural" categories are derived from reflection on empirical results and are justified insofar as they allow us to grasp these results as a unity. The natural categories are therefore *a posteriori*: Burbidge explicitly states that "those reflections that initiated the section on chemical process . . . are generated a posteriori from reflection on earlier experience."[34] This contrasts with strictly logical categories, which are always reached a priori. Accordingly, Burbidge concludes that, unlike the *Logic*, the *Philosophy of Nature* is "radically empirical," or practices a "thoroughgoing empirical approach."[35]

Burbidge's analysis of the *Philosophy of Nature* is important because it shows that, once we recognize that empirical phenomena instantiate logical categories only imperfectly, we must acknowledge that the successive categories through which we apprehend those phenomena cannot be simply the a priori categories of the *Logic*: they must compose an *additional* framework of specifically "natural" categories which organize the contingent findings of empirical science, and which must, therefore, be a posteriori. Let me clarify, at a more general level, why this framework of "natural" categories is necessarily a posteriori. After all, one might suppose that Hegel treats each empirical phenomenon as the imperfect instantiation of a preestablished logical category (so that, for example, space imperfectly instantiates the logical category of "being," time imperfectly instantiates the logical category of "nothingness," and so forth). Burbidge shows that such a reading would be inadmissible, because Hegel's *Logic* does not outline a fixed set of categories anyway. Instead, it articulates a *process* undergone by thinking activity, which generates each successive logical category in order to grasp as a whole its successive formulations of the preceding category. Properly philosophical thought about nature can be no less processual than logical thought in general. We cannot think philosophically about nature by approaching it in terms of a fixed set of categories; we must generate the appropriate categories in actively thinking through the complexity of empirical phenomena. The legitimate categories for thinking nature are therefore those that we generate in order to unify a specific range of complex empirical materials—categories that must, therefore, be a posteriori (derived from reflection on the empirical). The a posteriori justification of natural categories makes them fallible, since they must be rethought as empirical knowledge advances (a rethinking in which, Burbidge shows, Hegel continually engaged). Thus, the fact that variable empirical materials exceed logical categories implies, given Hegel's dynamic understanding of categorial thought, that the appropriate categories for thinking nature must be a posteriori.

I have expounded Burbidge's reading of Hegel at length to see whether his work can be considered to recast weak a priorism in a tenable form. As I have explained, previous scholars—notably Petry and Buchdahl—have plausibly argued that a tenable version of the weak a priori method must investigate not which scientifically described forms are rationally necessary, but how far scientific accounts can be reorganized or reinterpreted in light of a priori logical categories. Yet Burbidge's arguments show that this reconstructive method can only accommodate the contingency and diversity of empirical findings by organizing them not through a priori logical categories but through a distinct set of "natural" categories that are a posteriori. In this way, the interpretive effort to reformulate weak a priorism has transformed it into a significantly different method, which can be called "a posteriorism." It cannot therefore be said that Petry, Buchdahl, or Burbidge have rendered weak a priorism, as such, cogent: this method remains problematic. However, Burbidge's work develops an alternative, a posteriori, interpretation of the *Philosophy of Nature* which *is* philosophically viable. Just as strong a priorism involves neither the dismissal nor the fallacious absolutization of scientific claims, likewise the a posteriori method allows Hegel to learn from science while acknowledging the fallibility of its claims. So, at the end of this inquiry, we seem, disappointingly, to be as far as ever from a conclusion as to the best interpretation of the *Philosophy of Nature*.

Metaphysical Disputes in the Interpretation of the *Philosophy of Nature*

The dispute over whether Hegel's theory of nature should be construed as a posteriori or strong a priori is not narrowly relevant to the understanding of the *Philosophy of Nature*, but it raises broader issues in Hegel interpretation. When closely examined, this dispute between the two interpretations can be seen fundamentally to concern Hegel's *metaphysics*. Thus, this dispute bears significantly upon how we should interpret

Hegel's philosophical outlook as a whole, and specifically upon whether, and in what sense, we should construe Hegel as a metaphysical thinker. Essentially, the strong a priori reading of the *Philosophy of Nature* presupposes that Hegel is presenting a metaphysical theory of nature, according to which nature is structured by successive forms that comprise a necessary chain. On the other hand, the a posteriori reading implicitly presupposes that Hegel's theory of nature is nonmetaphysical and that the basic categories composing this theory follow one another merely contingently. Let me expand on this schematic comparison.

According to strong a priorism, the philosopher of nature must first describe—in *sui generis*, nonscientific, terms—a sequence of objectively existing natural forms, each deriving from the preceding one. Next, the philosopher must appraise how far forms described by scientists can be interpreted as identical to these *sui generis* natural forms. According to the strong a priori interpretation, then, the *Philosophy of Nature* is essentially a metaphysical theory, in the sense that it purports to *describe* really existing structures which are presumed to organize the natural world. These structures are initially characterized under specifically nonscientific descriptions, which are subsequently compared against the descriptions that scientists have given of those structures. Moreover, according to Hegel's basic theory, each objectively existing natural structure or form supplants its predecessor with *necessity*. He refers to the "conceptually generated necessity" of nature's "patterns" (*Gebilde*) (EN §250/1: 215), each of these patterns constituting a "stage" (*Stufe*) which "proceeds of necessity out of" its predecessor (*"aus der andern notwendig hervorgeht"*) (§249/1: 212). In other words, each form is the necessary consequence of the one preceding it (in a sense of "necessity" that remains to be explained: see chapter 3).

On the other hand, according to the a posteriori method, the philosopher must trace out a series of categories, each of which provides a perspective for grasping a determinate range of empirical phenomena. In each case the philosopher must assess how these categories are contingently instantiated in the relevant range of empirical phenomena, then reflect on this whole range of phenomena to formulate—a posteriori—the next category in the series. On this a posteriori reading, the basic framework of Hegel's *Philosophy of Nature* is no longer a series of descriptions of objectively existing structures; it is now a set of categories for thinking about empirical phenomena. These categories are "nonmetaphysical": they do not purport to correspond, descriptively, to natural forms or structures that really exist. Rather, these categories specify how we must think about empirical phenomena, articulating the key stages in the process by which we render those phenomena intelligible to ourselves. Burbidge himself confirms that his a posteriori reading implies that the *Philosophy of Nature* is essentially nonmetaphysical. In his earlier book, *On Hegel's Logic*, Burbidge interprets the *Logic* as articulating the basic categories that crystallize "the operations of pure thought."[36] In this Burbidge deliberately discards Hegel's (in)famous claim that his logic is a metaphysics (made, for example, at EL §24/56), arguing instead that "pure thought" unfolds without "any contact with an external reality."[37] The confrontation with external reality marks the transition from *Logic* to *Philosophy of Nature*, at which point thought begins to assess how far its categories apply in the phenomenal domain. The basic framework of the *Philosophy of Nature* thus consists in categories devised, a posteriori, in the encounter with phenomenal reality, just as the *Logic* centers on categories devised, a priori, through thought's entirely self-contained reflections upon its own processes. Furthermore, these "natural" categories constituting Hegel's basic theory of nature compose a contingent series: any revisions in empirical knowledge demand the derivation of new, different, categories.

Through their implicit divergence over Hegel's metaphysics, the two readings of the *Philosophy of Nature* broadly align with opposed positions that have emerged from the extensive debate among Hegel scholars over whether his philosophy should be read "metaphysically" or "nonmetaphysically." Broadly, "metaphysical" readings contend that his philosophical system sets out to describe the structures of the world as it really is.[38] By contrast, "nonmetaphysical" readings hold that Hegel's system explicates a set of categories through which we must confer intelligibility upon our experience.[39] These categories do not purport to correspond to really existing structures within the world, but only to specify how we must represent things, or how they must appear to us given the constraints of our mode of representation (what Henry Allison calls our "epistemic conditions").[40] Some prominent nonmetaphysical interpreters, such as Robert Pippin, give this a Fichtean inflection, whereby the categories that Hegel explicates must constrain our thought in virtue of being necessary conditions for the possibility of self-conscious subjectivity.[41] Broadly, then, the strong a priori construal of the *Philosophy of Nature* aligns with the metaphysical interpretation of Hegel, whereas the a posteriori construal is—as Burbidge suggests—closer to the nonmetaphysical school of interpretation. This gives the interpretive dispute surrounding the *Philosophy of Nature* wider importance and relevance for understanding Hegel's entire philosophical outlook.

The distinction between "metaphysical" and "nonmetaphysical" readings of Hegel could, to some extent, be reframed as a distinction between "realist" and "nonrealist" readings (although this nomenclature does not fully capture the complexity of either position). On metaphysical readings, Hegel is a realist: he believes that the world has, objectively, a determinate structure, which we can know about as it really is. Admittedly, it might sound odd to call Hegel a "realist," when he famously styles himself an "absolute idealist."[42] But, as he clarifies, absolute idealism is the view that things "hav[e] the ground of their being not in themselves but in the universal divine idea" (EL §45A). Here, the "idea" is understood as a comprehensive ontological structure that is not merely "subjective"—not merely a function of human thought—but in some sense exists objectively too. Confusingly, then, the metaphysical position that Hegel calls "absolute idealism" is *not* idealism in the usual sense where "idealism" denotes the view that the world either exists—as for Berkeley—or acquires determinate character—as for Kant—only through the mind's constituting activity. Ironically, "absolute idealism" is a form of realism, on which all reality is structured by the "idea."

Nonmetaphysical readings deny that Hegel is a realist, for on these readings Hegel's system articulates a series of categories rather than attempting to describe any objectively existing structures. One might wonder whether this line of interpretation positions Hegel as someone who holds (with Kant) that reality cannot have in itself the character or structure that we represent it as having (since this character is solely a function of our representing activity), and hence that we cannot know about reality as it is independently of us. Such an interpretation would seem to overlook Hegel's adverse comparison of what he calls Kant's "subjective idealism" with his own "absolute idealism" (EL §45A/88–89). In fact, though, nonmetaphysical interpretations avoid construing Hegel's idealism as merely "subjective" by arguing that, for him, even the concept of reality as it is "in itself," independently of us, is a category that we adopt—a self-contradictory category, in fact, which must be transcended. Thus, the nonmetaphysical Hegel can consistently hold both that our categories do not correspond to any real structures and that these categories are absolutely valid (rather than being merely "subjective" vis-à-vis "reality-in-itself").

The metaphysical reading of Hegel is widely repudiated by contemporary scholars, which might seem to tell, simultaneously, against the strong a priori reading of the *Philosophy of Nature*. Often, though, scholars reject the metaphysical view because they associate it with a particular reading of Hegel promoted by Charles Taylor. For Taylor, Hegel sees the whole universe as the creation and expression of *Geist* or God, a macrocosmic subject which seeks to know itself by creating a natural world that embodies and reflects it. *Geist* also creates finite human subjects who can come to recognize *Geist*'s presence in nature, so that through them *Geist* attains full self-consciousness. The Hegel who issues from Taylor's reading is a "metaphysical" thinker in that he endeavors to describe the universe as it really is: a complex ensemble of relations between *Geist*, nature, and human subjects. Many commentators—especially those predominantly concerned with Hegel's sociopolitical thought—presume that Taylor's reading exhausts the possibilities for metaphysical interpretation of Hegel. For example, Alan Patten assumes that any metaphysical construal of Hegel must, following Taylor, suppose him to "start out from [a] fantastical notion of cosmic spirit," a reading which, Patten concludes, "leaves Hegel's position looking pretty unattractive."[43] Similarly, Allen Wood equates Hegel's metaphysics with the theory of cosmic spirit, then concludes that this metaphysics is an "utterly unconvincing" failure to be jettisoned in favor of Hegel's concrete reflections on social issues.[44]

We should hesitate, however, before equating Hegel's metaphysics with Taylor's construal of it. Taylor makes a crucial interpretive mistake: he generalizes claims that Hegel makes specifically within his philosophy of *mind* to encapsulate the content of his entire metaphysics.[45] More precisely, Taylor extrapolates Hegel's claims about the character of human subjects onto the putative cosmic subject that he calls *Geist*/God. When Hegel himself refers to a metaphysical reality embodied in nature and humanity, though, he typically speaks not of *Geist* but of the "idea," or the "logical idea." By this, he essentially means the sum-total of all the forms of thought described in his *Logic*. He observes that:

> [T]he differences between the particular philosophical sciences are only determinations of the idea itself and it is this alone which presents itself in these diverse elements. In nature, it is not something other than the idea that is recognised, but the idea is in the form of *externalisation* [*Entäußerung*]. (EL §18R/42)

Hegel does not equate the omnipresent "idea" with mind: rather, the idea eventually develops *into* mind, which is "concrete and developed" in contrast to the "comparatively abstract, simple logical idea" (EM §377A/ 1). Thus, although Hegel does appear to believe in a nonmaterial reality of some sort which is instantiated in the natural and human domains, he does not identify this reality directly with a cosmic subject as Taylor alleges. Hegel's system is therefore hospitable to a metaphysical reading quite distinct from that of Taylor.

Hegel makes numerous statements supporting such a metaphysical reading of his philosophy, and confirming, especially, that he believes this nonmaterial reality, called "the idea" (or sometimes "the concept," *der Begriff*), to structure and be embodied in all other beings. He famously states that "the concept is what truly comes first, and things are what they are through the activity of the concept that dwells in them" (EL §163A2/241). Elsewhere he reiterates that all these things only exist insofar as they depend upon the idea: "The proposition that the finite is ideal [*ideell*] constitutes idealism. The idealism of philosophy consists in nothing else than in recognizing that the finite is not a veritable being" (WL 154/1:172). Hegel is saying, then, that his (absolute) "idealism" consists in his view that every existent depends, ontologically, upon the idea, which embraces the totality of forms of thought, forms which exist, as Hegel tells us in his *Logic*, "*objectively*" (*objektiv*).

> [T]houghts can be called *objective* thoughts; and among them the forms which are . . . usually taken to be only forms *of conscious* thinking have to be counted too. Thus *logic* coincides with *metaphysics*, with the science of *things* grasped in *thoughts*, which used to be taken to express the *essentialities* of *things*. . . . To say that there is understanding, or reason, in the world is exactly what is contained in the expression "objective thought." This expression is, however, inconvenient precisely because *thought* is all too commonly used as if it belonged only to spirit, or consciousness, while the objective is used primarily just with reference to what is unspiritual. . . . [Hence] the logical is to be sought in a system of thought-determinations in which the antithesis between subjective and objective (in its usual meaning) disappears. This meaning of thinking and of its determinations is more precisely expressed by the ancients when they say that *nous* governs the world. (EL §24-§24A/56)

The central message of this paragraph is that the forms of thought which make up the "idea," and on which all other existents depend, are not merely "subjective" categories. Rather, they primarily exist as objective structures embodied in both nature and mind.[46] For Hegel, mind necessarily develops to a point at which human beings start to think according to subjective categories which duplicate the content of the objective forms of thought (subjective categories which therefore accurately describe the world's real structure). Thus, objective forms of thought do eventually assume subjective guise. Nonetheless, the forms of thought are not *merely* subjective—not merely functions of the human mind; rather, subjective categories are the highly developed form that hitherto nonsubjective thought eventually assumes. Hegel's idealism thereby dissolves the subject/object "antithesis" by arguing that objective thought must ultimately develop into subjective form.

Considerable textual evidence supports this interpretation of Hegel's metaphysics,[47] which avoids Taylor's problem of postulating a creative cosmic subject. Yet even once Hegel's metaphysics is disentangled from Taylor's construal of it, there are further reasons that some commentators will remain unsympathetic to it. The central problem is that the metaphysical reading risks portraying Hegel as an implausibly pre-critical thinker, blithely unconcerned by Kant's strictures on the impossibility of knowing about how reality might be independent of our modes of representation. For instance, Pippin contends that:

> [T]he standard view of how Hegel passes beyond Kant into speculative philosophy makes very puzzling, to the point of unintelligibility, how Hegel could have been the post-Kantian philosopher he understood himself to be . . . Just attributing moderate philosophic intelligence to Hegel should at least make one hesitate before construing him as a post-Kantian philosopher with a pre-critical metaphysics.[48]

So, on philosophical grounds, many scholars think it wise to construe Hegel nonmetaphysically. Admittedly, this necessitates painstaking reconstruction of those passages in Hegel that appear unambiguously metaphysical, but his texts are multifaceted enough to permit such reconstruction.

However, the objection that construing Hegel metaphysically makes him unacceptably naïve is not conclusive. This is for two reasons. First, unlike pre-critical metaphysicians, Hegel does not attempt to describe a reality that he conceives to exist *independently* of our representations. Although Hegel aims to describe objectively existing structures that organize reality, he does not believe that these structures exist independently of our ways of thinking about and representing them, for thought necessarily develops into subjective forms that replicate and describe its earlier, merely objective, structures. Thus, the really existing structures which Hegel endeavors to describe are necessarily interrelated with—not independent of—our forms of representation.[49] Second, Hegel does not simply make assertions about these objective structures. He strenuously attempts to support his metaphysical descriptions through his exhaustive critique of rival metaphysical views in the *Phenomenology*.

This critical strategy may not entirely succeed, but it represents a considered and challenging alternative to traditional epistemology. Hegel's metaphysical approach is therefore not naïvely pre-Kantian, but arises from careful, prolonged, confrontation with epistemological problems.[50]

These considerations imply that, properly understood, Hegel's possible metaphysical project can be at least as cogent as his possible nonmetaphysical project. But I wish, also, to make a stronger claim: namely, that his metaphysical project of describing the world's conceptual structures is considerably more *fruitful* than the nonmetaphysical project of a category theory. The metaphysical project, I want to suggest, is more fruitful both in its philosophical consequences and in its ethical and political implications. Hegel's metaphysical project is fruitful just because its attempt to describe the conceptual structures organizing reality must include an attempt to describe the objective forms or structures that organize the natural world. Insofar as this description of natural forms belongs within the broader description of reality as pervaded by the "idea," this description of nature can be expected to diverge significantly from any of the descriptions available within empirical science. Hegel's metaphysical project, then, must include the intention of developing a metaphysical theory of the natural world which characterizes it in substantially nonscientific terms. This puts him in a position to advance a strong and interesting critique of modern science. If he can show that his descriptions of natural forms rest on a stronger metaphysical basis than the descriptions offered by empirical science, then he can conclude that scientific claims and theories are inadequate, in respect of their defective metaphysical basis. Insofar as Hegel takes a metaphysical approach to nature, then, he can articulate a distinctive critique of the scientific approach: that it rests on inadequate metaphysical foundations.[51]

A problem of this sort within science—that is, of the sort which Hegel articulates as the problem of science's inadequate metaphysical foundations—can plausibly be seen as the root cause of widespread environmental degradation. In large part, this degradation is directly attributable to modern technological developments, which have a more "unprecedented and immediate impact" on nature than has previously been possible.[52] Yet these technological developments themselves stem from modern empirical science, not only in that they result from the application of science, but also, more deeply, in that they enact practical possibilities already encompassed and anticipated within the theoretical characterizations of nature that science provides.[53] It is therefore reasonable to think that these technological developments are damaging because the scientific characterizations of nature in which they are grounded are, in some way, theoretically deficient in the first place. Hegel's metaphysical approach identifies a basis for such a theoretical deficiency in modern science: namely, that science has inadequate metaphysical foundations which both pervade and distort its accounts of nature. In proposing to outline a theory of nature based on his own, more adequate, metaphysics, Hegel opens up the possibility that his more adequate theory could facilitate more environmentally sensitive technological applications and so a more sustainable way of life as a whole.

My suggestion, then, is that Hegel's metaphysical project is not only philosophically cogent but also promises a fresh approach to nature and a sustained and forceful critique of modern empirical science. Moreover, this critique is forceful partly because it avoids simplistic antiscientism. Hegel's critique does not view scientific claims and theories as straightforwardly false and worthless, but, more cautiously, as flawed by their inadequate metaphysical foundation. This calls on us not to reject those claims but to engage with and reassess them, redescribing them in more metaphysically adequate terms.

The fruitfulness of Hegel's possible metaphysical project gives us philosophical reason to interpret him *as* a metaphysical thinker. After all, when we decide on philosophical grounds between competing interpretations of a text, we need not refer solely to the values of consistency and cogency (although presumably those values set minimum conditions for the acceptability of an interpretation). We may also refer to the theoretical or practical *fecundity* of a position in justifying our decision to interpret a text in its terms. Indeed, it appears that considerations of fecundity often (covertly, if not overtly) guide choices of interpretive frameworks for texts. To take one example, contemporary feminist philosophers often reinterpret texts from the history of philosophy in ways that recover submerged protofeminist themes within those texts, this project of recovery being motivated by its fruitfulness in facilitating the elaboration of positive feminist theories.[54]

The Fecundity of the Strong A Priori Reading

Hegel's *Philosophy of Nature* has been repeatedly condemned for adopting the method that I have called strong a priorism, a method which critics have presumed to entail either blanket dismissal or fallacious absolutization of empirical claims. I have argued that these criticisms are misplaced: correctly understood, strong a priorism incorporates scientific claims on a merely provisional and interpretive basis. On the other hand, weak a priorism—which, as Hegel presents it, aims to reconstruct scientifically described forms into a necessary sequence—

does entail the false absolutization of fallible scientific findings. In its unreconstructed form, the weak a priori reading of the *Philosophy of Nature* should be rejected. As we have seen, though, weak a priorism can be reformulated into the considerably more plausible a posteriori method. Strong a priorism may then be judged problematic relative to a posteriorism, in this case because strong a priorism presupposes the validity of a metaphysical approach to nature, which attempts to describe nature's objectively existing structures. This presents itself as a problem, though, only if the project of describing reality's objective structures is regarded as naïvely pre-Kantian. I have suggested that this objection to the metaphysical project is inconclusive, so that strong a priorism's connection with the metaphysical approach need not diminish its cogency. On the contrary, this connection may actually *enhance* its attractiveness, insofar as Hegel's metaphysical project is unusually fruitful, both theoretically and practically. Given this fecundity, I have suggested, we should read Hegel as a metaphysical thinker: this allows us to explore the possibility that he develops a *sui generis* theory of nature and an attendant critique of science. In this light, strong a priorism becomes philosophically fruitful too, providing the method by which Hegel can develop a theory of nature couched in a language alternative to, and more metaphysically adequate than, that of empirical science. As part of reading Hegel metaphysically, then, we should construe his *Philosophy of Nature* in strong a priori terms. This will enable us to understand his theory as a *sui generis*, specifically philosophical, description of nature, and to explore how he compares this description against scientific accounts and reinterprets those accounts in terms of his own metaphysical framework.

The next chapter therefore proposes a strong a priori reading of Hegel's substantive account of nature in the *Philosophy of Nature*. This reading will provide us with an initial overview of Hegel's *sui generis* theory of nature and how it relates to empirical scientific accounts. This reading will also enable us to see how Hegel's *sui generis* theory of nature reflects his general metaphysical project and, in particular, his central metaphysical thesis that all reality embodies and is structured by forms of thought.

2

THE DEVELOPMENT OF NATURE: OVERCOMING THE DIVISION BETWEEN MATTER AND THOUGHT

> Philosophical thinking knows that nature is idealised not merely by us, that nature's externality is not an absolutely insuperable obstacle for nature itself, for its concept; but that the eternal idea dwelling in nature, or, what is the same thing, the implicit mind working within nature, brings about the idealisation, the sublation of the externality, because this form of mind's existence conflicts with the interiority of its essence. Therefore philosophy has, as it were, simply to watch how nature itself sublates its externality, how it takes back its externality to itself into the centre of the idea, or lets this centre step forth into the external, how it frees the hidden concept from the covering of externality and thereby overcomes external necessity. This transition from necessity to freedom is not a simple transition but a series of stages [*Stufengang*] consisting of many moments, the presentation of which makes up the philosophy of nature.
>
> —Hegel, *Philosophy of Mind*

This chapter aims to develop an interpretation of the *Philosophy of Nature* as composed according to the strong a priori method. Contemporary scholars often deny that the text can plausibly be construed in strong a priori terms.[1] This stipulation appears somewhat arbitrary in the face of the text's ambiguity and impenetrability. Hegel himself acknowledges the opacity of the text, although he blames the difficulty, rather disingenuously, upon nature's "contingency, caprice, and lack of order . . . [its] impotence . . . to hold fast to the realisation of the concept" (EN §250R/1: 215–16). The more immediate reason for the text's difficulty is the severe abbreviation of its key arguments and transitions,[2] a problem compounded by Hegel's fearsome technical vocabulary and his frequently allusive writing style. These features make the text of the *Philosophy of Nature* so ambiguous that, without excessive difficulty, it can be interpreted as pursuing any of a variety of approaches. I have already argued, though, that strong a priorism is the most fruitful approach available to Hegel, as it allows him to elaborate a *sui generis* theory of nature and thereby to articulate a potentially forceful critique of science with positive ecological implications. Following this argument, I shall attempt to reconstruct the *Philosophy of Nature* as a strong a priori text.

My aim, then, is to understand Hegel's account of nature as composed of both his basic a priori theory and his subsequent interpolations of materials from empirical science. His basic theory describes the series of really existing forms that he finds embodied in the phenomena of the natural world. These forms are first described in *sui generis,* distinctively nonscientific, terms, and are only subsequently equated with forms described by empirical scientists. Thus, interpreting the *Philosophy of Nature* as strong a priori involves reconstructing the substantive content of Hegel's basic theory of nature: seeing what forms he identifies in nature and reconstructing his descriptions of those forms and their interrelationships. We need also to explore how these basic descriptions inform Hegel's subsequent appropriation and redescription of empirical scientific materials.

Discerning Hegel's basic theory of natural forms is far from easy, given the obscurity of his presentation. We might appeal to his anticipatory division of the *Philosophy of Nature* into three main sections, called the "Mechanics," the "Physics," and the "Organic Physics." Each of these three main stages describes a range of natural forms, all united by a central characteristic. In the introduction, Hegel defines the mechanical sphere as the province of what he calls "singular individual" beings, material beings that are not structured by any conceptual unity. In this sphere, he says, the idea has "the determination of mutual externality and of infinite *singularisation*. Unity of form . . . is external to this" (EN §252/1: 217). Hegel thinks that the ensuing physical sphere contains peculiarly divided beings: they have conceptual structures, but these structures only imperfectly manifest themselves within their material exteriors. Finally, the organic sphere contains a type of matter that is unified with its conceptual dimension, unambiguously organized by and reflecting conceptual unity. This harmony is reflected in the holistic structure of the living organisms that populate this third sphere; within organisms, "the real differences of form are also brought back to the *ideal* unity, which has found itself and is for itself" (§252/1: 217). Broadly, Hegel depicts nature as progressing or developing from a form of matter that is not conceptually organized, to a form of matter that is only partly and imperfectly conceptually organized, and finally to a form of matter that is fully, manifestly, conceptually organized.[3]

It remains unclear, though, how Hegel's anticipatory survey relates to the body of his text. In attempting to reconstitute his theory of natural development in more detail, then, I shall use a perhaps surprising strategy: an extended comparison between the *Philosophy of Nature* and the theory of consciousness outlined in the *Philosophy of Mind*. According to Hegel, consciousness suffers from an initial opposition that impels it to proceed through various forms, each necessarily succeeding its predecessor. Importantly, the initial opposition within consciousness has the very same structure as the initial opposition that Hegel detects between conceptual and material elements in nature. Consequently, the entire development of consciousness closely parallels that within nature. Given this correspondence between the trajectories of nature and consciousness, we can reliably use Hegel's relatively succinct, uncluttered, theory of consciousness to illuminate his largely submerged theory of natural development. The similarities between consciousness and nature obtain only at the very general level, but, for precisely this reason, the comparison between consciousness and nature provides a good overview of the general organization of the stages within nature.

Reconstructing Hegel's basic theory of natural development via his theory of consciousness achieves two things. It confirms that this basic theory of nature is a priori, like the theory of consciousness which it parallels. Hegel's theory of consciousness is a priori in that it traces a hierarchical series of stages, each emerging as the rationally necessary solution to the contradiction within the stage preceding it (it should be noted, though, that what Hegel means by a contradiction is unclear and contested. I will examine this issue in chapter 3, but for now I shall simply assume that Hegel employs the term "contradiction" in an extended sense which encompasses not only strict contradictions but also oppositions and tensions of varying degrees). Since Hegel's basic theory of nature follows a structure parallel to that of his theory of consciousness, his theory of nature, too, must be a priori in the same sense: that is, it traces how each natural stage arises as the rationally necessary solution to the contradiction in the stage before it. Reading the *Philosophy of Nature* together with the theory of consciousness also illuminates how Hegel's basic theory of nature is *sui generis:* namely, in that his theory characterizes nature in nonscientific terms, as threaded through by two basic metaphysical elements, matter and thought. Hegel believes that the natural world progresses through a necessary course of stages from an initial opposition between these two constituent elements to their eventual unification.[4] Each stage in this series represents a specific constellation of relationships between matter and thought, and each such constellation arises to resolve the contradiction within the previous one. Subsequently, Hegel equates these various stages with regions of nature as described by and theorized in empirical science.

A disadvantage of focusing on Hegel's *Philosophy of Nature* at this general level is that I cannot examine in depth his exposition of any individual natural stages, and my reconstructions of these may seem unsatisfyingly brief and compressed. I hope that this disadvantage is offset by the fact that my interpretation of Hegel's general theory of natural progression provides an overall perspective that makes possible the development of more consistent and reliable interpretations of individual natural stages. After all, Hegel's discussions of these individual stages are very uneven in length, detail, style, and level of philosophical abstraction. We can best gain a reliable and coherent understanding of these stages by standing back from their specifics to view the wider progression in which they are located.

In reconstructing Hegel's general theory of natural progression, I first introduce the general similarities between consciousness and nature, then in each following section I offer a comparative study of a form of consciousness and a corresponding stage in natural development. Through these studies it will emerge that, strictly speaking, natural development passes through *four*, not three, fundamental stages. These stages, we will see, are defined by the emergence of sheer materiality, bodies, "physical" qualities, and life. Finally, I shall return to the broader theme of the fertility and critical potential of Hegel's theory of nature, and begin to explain how his unusual theory reflects the distinctive set of metaphysical assumptions from which he is operating.

Consciousness/Nature

This section prepares for the more detailed comparisons between individual forms of consciousness and stages of natural development by identifying some general affinities between the trajectories of consciousness and nature. To make these affinities visible, I will first explicate Hegel's general theory of consciousness and then sketch out how this parallels his general conception of natural development (as indicated in his introductions to the volumes of the *Encyclopaedia*).

In studying Hegel's theory of consciousness, I shall concentrate primarily on his account from the *Philosophy of Mind* (EM §418–§423).[5] Of course, Hegel gives an earlier, much better known, account of consciousness in chapters 1–3 of the *Phenomenology*—an account that has received considerably more scholarly attention. But, for my purposes, there are good reasons to focus on the *Philosophy of Mind* account. First, Hegel wrote and revised it in conjunction with his *Philosophy of Nature* (both belong within the same *Encyclopaedia*). This increases the likelihood that he deliberately and systematically integrated the two accounts, and that their parallels are noncoincidental. Second, Hegel's account of consciousness in the *Phenomenology* is more complicated than that in his *Philosophy of Mind* in several ways, none of which is helpful from the point of view of trying to ascertain the general and basic parallels between forms of consciousness and stages of nature. The account in the *Phenomenology* incorporates Hegel's study of various historically existing epistemological theories; it intertwines the development of consciousness with the historical development of epistemological theory; and it plays a propaedeutic role in assisting the reader to Hegel's absolute idealist standpoint. These complications are missing from the account in the *Philosophy of Mind*, which simply describes consciousness as a stage in the development of mind. This makes the *Philosophy of Mind* more useful for cross-referencing developments within consciousness against developments within nature.

In the *Philosophy of Mind*, Hegel portrays consciousness as necessarily superseding the previous stage of the subject's existence, in which the subject had assumed the form of the "soul" (*Seele*). The soul is a form of subjectivity that remains embroiled in the individual's corporeality, sensations, and emotions. By the end of its development, the soul has become a form of subjectivity that attempts to express itself within its body, molding and habituating the body so that it expresses rational patterns and principles. Yet the subject's body continues to express it inadequately, because, according to Hegel, "shape [*Gestalt*] in its externality is something immediate and natural, and can therefore be only an indefinite and wholly incomplete *sign* for the mind, unable to represent it as it is for itself, as *universal*" (EM §411R/147). This instills in the soul a need to make explicit the body's resilience, which the soul does by (in some way) separating its body from itself. The soul projects its corporeal reality outside of itself: it "excludes from itself the natural totality of its determinations as an object, a world *external to it*" (§412/151). The soul's body becomes an external world:

> The content is the infinite judgement of the subject through which it posits what it is at first as the negative of itself, throws its determinations of feeling out of itself, and has them as an object, as a world before it. What is in consciousness is in feeling, it being readily admitted that everything must be sensed . . . I sense hardness, I am myself the one who has the hardness, and I then distinguish the two, myself and the hardness, the object. (PSS §415A/3: 285)[6]

So, the problem that Hegel identifies for the soul is that it has been trying to express itself within its inherently unsuitable body, and the soul must make explicit its body's inherent unsuitability by "expelling" its corporeal side.

Hegel does not mean, however, that the soul literally casts its body aside and spreads it out to constitute an exterior world. After all, at this point in the *Encyclopaedia* he has already fully explained the existence and structure of the natural world. Rather, his point is that the mind comes to *think* that physical matter is external to it; it adopts the belief that corporeality constitutes a world opposed and exterior to itself. The mind, then, does not literally dispense with its body. We can confirm this from some of Hegel's further remarks addressing the soul's act of "expelling" its corporeality. In particular, he emphasizes that the subject now starts to oppose the external realm by knowing, or being aware of it, as external: the subject "knows" (*weiß*) this object "as *external to it*" (EM §413/153). He also maintains that the soul, by its act of "expelling" its corporeality, redefines itself as an "I" (or 'subject'), an *Ich*. In coming to think of an external world, the subject implicitly understands itself as contrasted to this external realm of materiality, as a subject or "I." Hegel explains: "I am I, thinking activity, I relate myself thinkingly. I is each of us, i.e. as I each is thinking, and in so far as the I relates itself, it relates thinkingly" (PSS §415A/3: 287). This clarifies that the subject's relation to external reality consists in its forming the *conception* of external reality. Hegel concludes that the subject is "*consciousness*" insofar as it thinks of this external realm: the subject knows this object "as external to it," and "as such it is consciousness [*Bewußtsein*]" (EM §413/153). Hegel designates the subject as "consciousness" because it is or has being (*Sein*) insofar as it is "aware" or "knowing" (*bewußt*). In his theory of "consciousness," then, his aim is to describe the subject's consciousness of external reality, outlining the different stages of consciousness through which the subject passes.

Hegel now identifies a crucial contradiction within consciousness. On the one hand, as we have seen, the subject thinks about the material corporeality which is inherently unsuitable for expressing it, conceiving of that materiality as an antithetical, external, realm. Yet, on the other hand, Hegel claims: "The immediate implication of the other's being posited as independent, is that the other is also posited as ideal [*ideell*], it is ideal for and in the I, which is the subject" (PSS §413A/3: 271). He restates the problem: "Consciousness is both, we have a world outside us, it is firmly for itself, and at the same time, insofar as I am consciousness, I know of this object [*Gegenstand*], it is posited as of an ideal nature, it is therefore not independent but sublated" (§414A/3: 275). Hegel's point is that the subject thinks of materiality as having a character quite antithetical to it; but, just in conceiving of materiality, the subject presupposes that materiality is intelligible to it and so has, at least in part, the same rational intelligibility that characterizes the subject. There is a contradiction between (1) the content of the subject's conception of material reality, as wholly opposed to it in character, and (2) the fact that this conception inherently presupposes that material reality is intelligible and, therefore, not wholly antithetical to the subject in character. Hegel thinks that, ultimately, the subject must remove this contradiction by straightforwardly viewing materiality as intelligibly structured, and, in this respect, as resembling the subject. The *telos* of consciousness is therefore *self*-consciousness, for which "my object is no longer an other, but myself" (§417A/3: 293).

The initial opposition within consciousness has the same essential structure as the opposition which, according to Hegel, initially exists within nature. The basic contradiction in consciousness is between the supposedly complete nonrationality of matter and its implicit intelligibility. Analogously, an initial contradiction obtains in nature between its pure materiality and the fact that this pure materiality is, in some sense, already conceptual. Admittedly, a crucial disparity between consciousness and nature is that consciousness suffers from a contradiction within its *conception* of matter, whereas in nature the contradiction holds within actual, objectively existing, matter. This does not prevent the initial contradictions, and the ensuing developmental courses, of consciousness and nature from being structured in a fundamentally identical way.

Just as the conscious subject begins by conceiving of an entirely nonrational materiality, so nature, according to Hegel, first exists purely as a realm of matter. He claims that: "*externality* constitutes the determination in which the idea exists as nature" (EN §247/1: 205).[7] In saying that nature is initially defined by "externality" (*Äußerlichkeit*), Hegel means that it is wholly material. This becomes explicit in the introduction to the *Philosophy of Mind*, in which he offers a helpful retrospective of his foregoing account of natural progression. He explains that in nature:

> [T]he idea appears in the element of mutual externality
> [*Außereinander*] . . . in nature this subsists near this, this
> follows that,—in brief, everything natural is mutually exter-
> nal, *ad infinitum*; furthermore, matter, this universal basis of
> all the formations that are there in nature . . . holds itself
> external to its own self. (EM §381A/9)

In this passage, Hegel makes explicit that he understands matter, fundamentally, as *partes extra partes*, therefore equating it with externality.[8] However, just as the supposedly pure materiality of which the
conscious subject thinks is already implicitly understood as rationally
intelligible, so the "externality" (or matter) that originally constitutes
nature is in fact already conceptual. Hegel states this while discussing
the notion of externality in the *Encyclopaedia Logic*: "when the determinations *of singularity and of mutual externality* have been earmarked
for the sensuous [*Sinnliche*], we can add that these determinations themselves are again thoughts and universals" (EL §20R/50). Admittedly,
this comment addresses not nature but the subjective *concept* of externality. Nonetheless, since Hegel holds that thought exists both subjec-
tively and objectively, his point may be taken to apply also to externality
as an objective determination of items in nature.[9] With respect to nature, then, his point is that its initial state of externality is contradictory,
because externality is in some sense conceptual *just insofar as* it is
entirely material and antithetical to conceptuality. Hegel believes that
nature's initial contradiction, like that of consciousness, must ultimately
be resolved through the emergence of a form of matter which makes
manifest its conceptual or intelligible character. The *telos* of nature is
the emergence of a thoroughly conceptually structured or permeated
form of matter. The similarity between the underlying requirements
propelling the developments of consciousness and nature means that
each passes through a parallel series of stages. Because of this parallel-
ism, the comparison between consciousness and nature can helpfully
illuminate the general trajectory that the *Philosophy of Nature* pursues:
the more directly and boldly presented trajectory that unfolds within
consciousness runs alongside that in nature.

   Having outlined these general affinities between the initial contradictions and developmental trajectories of consciousness and nature, we
can turn to Hegel's theory of the individual stages within these trajectories. Looking first at his theory of consciousness, he begins by analyzing more precisely the contradiction within consciousness as it initially
exists, at which point it takes the form of "sensuous consciousness,"
sinnliche Bewußtsein. With this notion of "sensuous consciousness,"

Hegel reworks his earlier notion of "sense-certainty," which he famously introduces as the first form of consciousness in the *Phenomenology*. In the *Philosophy of Mind*, he argues that the sensuously conscious subject is simply aware of material items as singular external objects. This recasts the *Phenomenology*'s well-known idea that the subject of sense-certainty conceives of each entity simply as a bare individual "this." As Hegel stresses, "sensuous consciousness" is also aware of these singular entities as external; as such, this form of consciousness arises directly out of the soul's initial act of coming to think of its corporeal content as external.

Sensuous Consciousness/Material Externality

In "sensuous consciousness," the subject thinks of matter as simply *external* to it. The subject also thinks of matter as *being*: as Hegel puts it, "the object is determined . . . as *being* [*als seiender*]" (EM §418/158). Lastly, the subject attributes to the objects of its awareness a third feature: *singularity* (*Einzelheit*). Hegel's explanation for this is confusing: "Although it [the object] is in relation to me, it is however an other to itself, this is also what it is, it is therefore the self-external, the other of itself . . . This makes it immediately singular" (PSS §418A/3: 297). Hegel's point, I think, is that the "object" (that is, matter) is seen as entirely antithetical to the subject and hence as lacking any intelligible structure, so that its corporeal complexity can only be understood as a bundle of entirely disconnected elements, each of which is external to the others and exists as a "singularity." In saying, then, that the subject possesses "sensuous" consciousness, Hegel means that it is conscious of matter as a mass of external, singular, beings.

Hegel clarifies: "What is sensuous is not to be presented as being in the senses [*in den Sinnen*], for its thought-determinations are as of the self-external" (PSS §418A/3: 299). In describing this first form of consciousness as sensuous consciousness, Hegel does not mean that the subject is passively receiving sensory impressions, as we might imagine à la Hume. Sensuous consciousness is a mode of *thinking*: the subject consciously conceptualizes its object in a definite way, as singular, external, beings. And consciousness does not think of its object as possessing a profusion of sensible qualities (colors, sounds, etc.). Consciousness thinks of the object as having *only* the three features of singularity, externality, and being: "for sensuous consciousness as such only the said thought-determination [that is, external, singular, being] remains" (EM §418A/160). Admittedly, Hegel may appear uncertain on this—he claims that: "The rich filling [of the object] is made out of the determinations of feeling; they are the *material* of consciousness . . . what the soul in the anthropological sphere *is* and finds *in itself*" (EM §418R/159). However, Hegel means that the content which the subject is conceptualizing as external, singular, beings dates from its preceding "anthropological" phase (when it existed as the soul). The content, now conceptualized under the categories of singularity, externality, and being, is the *same* content that the subject, as soul, previously contained as corporeal feelings and sensations (see PSS §415A/3: 285). Sensuous consciousness comes particularly close to this corporeal content, because the concepts through which it approaches that content are so impoverished. This is why Hegel calls this form of consciousness "sensuous" consciousness—because its concepts are so minimal, it gives the subject particularly great access to the content in question. This recalls Hegel's dictum in the *Phenomenology* that sense-certainty "appears as the *richest* kind of knowledge" even though it "proves itself to be the most abstract and poorest *truth*" (PhG, 58/82).[10]

The problem with sensuous consciousness is that it does not permit the subject to differentiate *between* singular, external, beings. All items have exactly the same features: external, singular, being. The subject therefore cannot actually pick out one such item in contrast to any others: as soon as the subject identifies an item, that item merges into undifferentiation with all other supposedly distinct items. "The content of sensuous consciousness . . . is supposed to be *the* singular; but just this makes it not *a* singular but all singularity" (EM §419A/161).[11] This deficiency arises from the way that sensuous consciousness has conceptualized matter in the first place. The subject has left itself no room to conceive material items as, for example, qualified by properties: items, for it, are just *simple* singularities, lacking *differentiated* content. The contradiction of sensuous consciousness is that the subject has defined singular material entities in such a narrow way that it cannot differentiate any of these putative entities from one another.

This problem of sensuous consciousness reappears in very similar form at the commencement of the *Philosophy of Nature*. At this point nature is entirely material: "The first or immediate determination of nature is the abstract *universality of its self-externality*" (EN §254/1: 223). Hegel describes this universal self-externality as consisting in a set of entities which differ from one another, possessing *Außereinandersein* (mutual externality) and *Nebeneinander* (juxtaposition). He immediately adds that this universal self-externality is empirically described as space or spatial extension. On closer examination, the material units which initially make up nature possess the same three basic properties as the singular beings of which the subject is sensuously conscious.

First, these units are "external" to thought in that they exist entirely independently of any conceptual dimension: they have "immediate externality" (*Äußerlichkeit*) (EN §254/1: 223). Second, these extended units just *are*: they are "the abstract immediacy of being" at the start of nature (WL 843/2: 573). Third, they are immediately *singular*—they make up the sphere of "singularisation" (*Vereinzelung*) (EN §252/1: 217). These units are "singular" in that they are entirely discrete, not unified or organized through any conceptual dimension.

Hegel proceeds to argue that the units of externality have no individuating characteristics through which they *can* be separate or external to one another: they all share the same qualities of externality, being, and singularity. He concludes that nature at this point is, after all, not *partes extra partes*, but completely *un*differentiated.

> [O]n account of its being self-externality, space is juxtaposition of a wholly ideal sort; as this mutual externality is still completely *abstract*, space is simply *continuous*, and is devoid of any determinate difference... on account of its lack of difference, space is merely the possibility, not the *positedness* of mutual externality... and is therefore simply continuous. (EN §254–§254R/1: 223)

The subject could identify no differences within the objects of its sensuous consciousness, having defined them all as possessing the same three characteristics of singularity, externality, and being. Likewise, it proves impossible for nature in its original form to contain any internal differentiation, since all its parts possess the same three characteristics as well.

Furthermore, in that nature as externality proves completely self-identical, Hegel claims that it is an "abstract *universality*" (EN §254/1: 223). As something universal, though, externality proves to be a form of *thought*. According to Hegel's metaphysics, forms of thought exist objectively within the world, as universal patterns or structures that organize the world and give it rational intelligibility. In its lack of differentiation, externality has proven to be a universal, intelligible, structure of just this sort. Far from simply being entirely material, nature as it originally exists turns out to be entirely conceptual at the same time. However, Hegel does not think that this satisfactorily ends the natural opposition of matter to thought. Rather, the fact that matter proves to be entirely conceptual at the same time means that matter is internally contradictory. Or, as Hegel puts it: "Space [that is, externality] is a contradiction, for the negation [that is, difference] within it disintegrates into indifferent subsistence" (EN §257A/1: 229). Externality is defined by two antithetical characteristics, for it is entirely conceptual just in its sheer materiality. This means that externality, nature's initial state, is self-contradictory and unsatisfactory.

From the unsatisfactory character of externality, Hegel deduces the necessary emergence of a better natural form, which he calls "negativity." He equates this negativity with empirical time, stating that: "The truth of space is time, so that space becomes time" (EN §257A/1: 229). Negativity is divided into a plurality of units—empirical "moments" or "nows" (§258/1: 230). These units attempt to establish individual differentiation by negating all the other units, as it were, asserting their difference from those others. Accordingly, each such unit (or "moment") is a "being which, in that it *is*, is *not*, and in that it is *not*, *is*" (§258/1: 229–30). Yet negative units still fail to differ genuinely from one another. They all share the same defining characteristic of negativity, and so prove identical to one another just like units of externality. "Time is as *continuous* as space is, for it is abstract negativity . . . and in this abstraction there is still no real difference" (§258R/1: 230). Negativity remains subject to the same difficulty that beset externality: it is simultaneously both entirely material (in that it is internally differentiated) and entirely conceptual (in that it is completely self-identical).[12]

This comparison between sensuous consciousness and nature's first, entirely material, stage reveals that Hegel envisages both stages as afflicted by the same basic problem.[13] Consciousness, at this juncture, identifies objects as entirely nonconceptual, but it cannot coherently sustain this identification, nor can nature coherently sustain an exclusively material mode of existence. The subject's conception of pure, structureless, reality proves unsustainable because it does not permit the subject to differentiate between entities; similarly, nature's entirely nonconceptual matter proves self-contradictory and unsustainable because it lacks any internal differentiation. Through this argument Hegel takes his first step toward depicting how nature overcomes its original division of matter from thought, by showing that, even when matter exists without any conceptual structure, it proves fully conceptual at the same time. Since this means that nature's initial material form is internally contradictory, it calls for the development of further natural forms to supersede the contradiction.

Perception/Bodies

The subject cannot sustain its belief in singular, external, entities unless it comes to regard those entities as having specifying properties that differentiate them. Here Hegel makes the transition to the next stage of consciousness: *perception* (*Wahrnehmung*). In this, his account of conscious development in the *Philosophy of Mind* follows his earlier narrative in the *Phenomenology*, in which sense-certainty is necessarily succeeded by perception, which is conscious of individual items only insofar as they have universal properties. Likewise, in the *Philosophy of Mind*, Hegel claims that the perceiving subject forms a conception of differentiated entities only by conceptualizing them as distinguished by different properties. The subject henceforth conceptualizes every entity as a "*thing* [which] has *many* properties" (EM §419/160). In so conceiving of entities (as "things"), the subject retains its original conception of entities as singular and external.[14] But the subject now becomes capable of individuating those entities, by conceiving them as possessing distinguishing properties. The properties that the subject now conceptualizes as attached to things are universal: they are "*relations, determinations of reflection,* and *universalities*" (§419/160). Hegel therefore states that perceiving consists in the "conjunction of singular and universal . . . the *single* things of sensuous apperception . . . and the *universality* . . . the multiple *properties*" (§421/162). Presumably, the subject generates conceptions of these universal properties by reflecting on the given corporeal content which it is conceiving as external. If consciousness takes this content into account, by conceptualizing it as a range of universal properties, then this content can provide the basis for differentiating between singular entities.

Hegel judges perception problematic because it simply "mixes" properties with singular entities: "This conjunction of singular and universal is a mixture, because the singular remains the *basic* being and firmly opposed to the universal, to which, however, it is related" (EM §421/162). In some way, the subject regards the sheer singularity of each entity as more fundamental than its possession of properties, believing that entities can persist in their singularity whether they possess properties or not. This seems odd: after all, the subject postulated these properties precisely to confer on entities the individuation they lacked. What Hegel is getting at is this: the subject assigns properties to entities in response to the problem of their lack of differentiation, but without explicitly *realizing* that without those properties the entities cannot endure. The subject therefore continues to uphold its outmoded belief in entities as bare singularities, even as it also responds to the failure of this belief by affixing individuating properties to those entities. As a result, the subject thinks of these properties—mistakenly—as merely contingent to the things that possess them. Thus, a contradiction obtains between the subject's explicit view that properties are inessential to things and its tacit presupposition that these properties are essential, a contradiction which Hegel, rather vaguely, calls "the many-sided contradiction—between the *single* things . . . and the *universality*" (§421/162).[15]

We find a structurally parallel stage within the *Philosophy of Nature*, composed of the two phases of the "Mechanics" which follow the domain of externality and negativity. These are called "Finite Mechanics" and "Absolute Mechanics." Within "Finite Mechanics," Hegel describes the emergence of a new natural form, the material body—which he sometimes calls simply "matter" (*Materie*) and sometimes the "body" (*Körper*).[16] Material bodies emerge in response to the difficulties facing externality and negativity, which, it will be recalled, were simultaneously wholly material and wholly conceptual. Material bodies, unlike negative moments, succeed in achieving individuation by negating a differentiated *quantity* of the surrounding units of externality. Hegel relates this feature of material bodies to the empirical view that bodies are individuated in terms of their mass: "matter has . . . a *quantitative* difference, and is particularized into different quanta,—*masses*" (EN §263/1: 244).[17] Whereas negative moments simply negated all other units and so remained ultimately identical, material bodies negate varying quantities of those other units and so achieve differentiation. Hegel designates these bodies "material" precisely because they retain individual identity and hence do not directly prove to be equally as conceptual as they are material.

Hegel goes on to analyze material bodies into two aspects. First, they exist as discrete, individual, items, and in this respect each is a "singularity which is *for itself*" (EN §261R/1: 238) and is a body strictly speaking: "*masses*, . . . [as] a whole or unit, are *bodies*" (§263/1: 244). Second, each body's quantity of units (empirically, its mass) constitutes its specifying particularity (§263/1: 244). Clearly, bodies are structurally similar to the things conceived by the conscious subject, while the material parts that pick out each body are structurally similar to the properties that the conscious subject assigns to things. Differentiating units perform the same individuating function for bodies in nature that differentiating properties perform for things in consciousness.

Again, though, Hegel thinks that material bodies are defective in merely combining corporeal singularity with differentiating units—just as perception generated a mere "mixture" of things and properties. As Hegel puts it, each body remains "external" to its mass (EN §252A/1: 219). He elaborates on this point: "In the first sphere the determinations [the quantitative units] are still distinguished from the substance . . . substance as such is still shut up within itself and unmanifest" (§274A/2: 11).

> In mechanics, being-for-self is still not an individual stable unity having the power to subordinate plurality to itself . . . matter does not yet possess the individuality which preserves its determinations, and . . . the determinations of the concept in it are still external to one another. (§252A/1: 219)

Hegel's key claim is that bodies fail to "manifest" themselves in their parts. What he is getting at, I suggest, is that the various units of externality have now come to exist *as* properties of bodies, so that their possession by those bodies is essential to what they are. These units ought, therefore, to have a character such that they "manifest" or express their essential status as properties of bodies. Yet, instead, these units continue to exist as bare material units, with exactly the same character they had prior to the emergence of bodies. These units thereby fail to express that they are essentially properties. This is a problem: because units of matter lack the character appropriate to their status as properties, they do not fully exist *as* properties after all. Material units remain only incompletely, or ambiguously, the properties of bodies. Yet because those bodies attain individuation only by possessing properties, their individuation remains incomplete or ambiguous in turn. Insofar as their specifying units do not *fully* belong to them, bodies cannot be fully individuated either. This problem besetting material bodies parallels the problem of perception. Perceptive consciousness allocates properties to things but does not explicitly conceive of those things as existing only through their possession of properties. For their part, bodies individuate themselves by seizing hold of units, but still do not fully possess these units, since the units themselves do not yet fully exist as properties. Just as consciousness fails to grasp things as entirely dependent upon their properties, so bodies objectively fail to possess their properties fully.

Hegel goes on to argue that material bodies must manifest their imperfect level of individuation by colliding and co-constituting a single body. He equates this process of fusion with empirical "attraction": "The singularised entities . . . are all merely units [*Eins*], many units [*Eins*]; they are one [*eins*]. The unit only repels itself from itself; that is the sublation of the separation of the beings which are for themselves, or attraction" (EN §262A/1: 243). Yet the attractive unity cannot persist without differences to absorb, so bodies differentiate themselves again in a complementary process, equated with empirical "repulsion." Hegel concludes that bodies are necessarily subject to tendencies both to fuse and to divide. He identifies this dual subjection with empirical gravity (*die Schwere*). Translated into philosophical terms, gravity means that material bodies move to unite but without ever actually coinciding, reflecting their inability either to fully individuate themselves or to finally converge.[18]

> [G]ravity is the substance of matter ... Matter possesses gravity in so far as it drives towards a middle point; it is essentially composite, ... it seeks its unity and therefore seeks to sublate itself, it seeks its opposite. If it were to reach this, it would no longer be matter, but would have ceased to exist as such; it strives for ideality [*Idealität*], for in its unity it is ideal. (VG 47–48/55)

This philosophical redescription of gravity allows Hegel also to redescribe the solar system, as he does in the "Absolute Mechanics." Schematically, he redescribes the sun as the central point of identity toward which bodies are drawn and from which they are simultaneously repelled. He now identifies these bodies with the planets as they circle around the sun: held apart from it, yet straining to fuse into it (EN §269R/1: 260–61).

Significantly for the overall trajectory of the *Philosophy of Nature*, bodies gain individuation by taking on specific quantities of parts, thereby becoming material in a more full-blooded way than external units or bits of negativity. Material bodies strive to exist as something purely discrete and singular, not organized into any conceptual unity. Yet even these apparently robustly material entities cannot entirely distinguish themselves from one another, and their partial identity with one another is exhibited in their propensity to fuse. Insofar as they remain partly identical with one another, though, bodies continue, after all, to exist as a conceptual unity: that is, as a form of thought. Hegel stresses that gravitating bodies are expressing their "ideality" (VG 47-48/55) and that "the centre [for which they strive] should not be thought of as material [*materiell*]" (EN §262R/1: 242). By straining to unite, bodies are expressing the fact that they are partly identical and that in this respect they comprise an "abstract universal." Thus bodies remain, unsatisfactorily, partly material and partly conceptual. Hegel's theory of material bodies continues his task of depicting how nature overcomes its primal division, by restaging, in a more complicated context, his earlier argument that purely material entities cannot really *be* exclusively material after all.

Understanding/Physical Qualities

In the *Philosophy of Mind*, Hegel goes on to describe how consciousness makes the transition to its third phase: "understanding" (*Verstand*).

Once again, the *Philosophy of Mind* passes back through the earlier narrative of the *Phenomenology*, in which perception necessarily becomes supplanted by "understanding," the consciousness of underlying essences that manifest themselves in perceptible reality. However, the *Philosophy of Mind* considerably simplifies Hegel's earlier, somewhat convoluted, account of the understanding. In the *Philosophy of Mind*, the understanding simply arises when the subject takes the unavoidable step of reconceiving entities as necessarily possessing their properties. This means, Hegel states, that: "The immediate *truth* of perception is that the object is an *appearance* and the object's reflection-into-itself is . . . an *inner side* which is for itself and a universal [*Allgemeines*]" (EM §422/161–62). Having redefined the object as an entity that inherently possesses properties, the subject is led to see this object as something common to, or shared between, these properties. As such the object is literally a universal, something *all-gemein* (common-to-all). Thus the understanding consciousness finally succeeds in individuating its objects, by defining them as possessing their properties necessarily— but in so doing it also redefines these objects as universals. Furthermore, the subject redefines each object's properties as its appearance (*Erscheinung*), as that within which the universal manifests itself: "The contradiction [of perception] is resolved in the first instance by the fact that the multiple determinations of the sensuous, which are independent both of one another and of the inner unity of each single thing, are reduced to the *appearance* of an *inner side* which is for itself" (§422A/ 163). The subject redefines properties as appearances just because it has redefined the things that bear them as universals, pervading all these properties and being detectable within them.

The problem that Hegel identifies for the understanding is this. On the one hand, the understanding conceptualizes appearance as the product of the inner object—as "mediated" or "posited" (PSS §422A/3: 309). On the other hand, the understanding somehow also regards appearance not as the product of the inner object, but rather as "immediate." The subject thinks of appearance as having exactly the same content as when it was formerly conceived as a bundle of properties. Even though the subject now thinks of appearance as manifesting an essence, it attributes to that appearance a character such that it cannot manifest any essence at all, since this character is exactly the same character that appearance had when it was merely a bunch of properties. Thus, whereas the problem of perception was that consciousness held on to an outmoded conception of objects as sheer singular entities, the problem of understanding is that consciousness holds on to an outmoded conception of appearance as a mere bundle of properties.

Because of this problem, the understanding will ultimately be obliged to rethink appearance so that it manifests its essence.[19]

The *Philosophy of Nature* delineates a natural stage that broadly parallels this conscious stage of understanding. This is the "Physics," which follows the "Mechanics," and which comprises the second main section of the *Philosophy of Nature*. In Hegel's phrase, the subject matter of the "Physics" is the "manifestation of essence" (EN §272A/ 2: 9). Each body becomes an "essence" or "form" which displays itself within its parts. As we saw, the problem facing material bodies was that the units that they seized as properties did not manifest their status as properties of bodies. The obvious solution is for each body to make its parts manifest the fact that they are essentially the property of that body. Bodies do this by conferring new qualities upon their parts: accordingly, the "sphere of physics" deals with "qualified matter" (§271/ 1: 282). Since material units would not exhibit these qualities except for the activity upon them of the bodies possessing them, those units come, in receiving such qualities, to manifest their essential status as properties. Summing up this process, Hegel tells us that "matter tears itself away from gravity, manifests itself, determining itself within itself, and determines spatiality [*das Räumliche*] through the form immanent in it" (§272/2: 9). Material bodies need to become fully individuated (and thereby lose their subordination to empirical gravity) by manifesting themselves in their (spatial) parts, which they do by "determining" (*bestimmen*), or qualifying, those parts. The "Physics," then, documents how bodies remodel their parts in qualitatively specific forms.

The central thematic of the "Physics" strongly recalls Hegel's account of understanding consciousness. The understanding thinks of objects as individuated through their necessary possession of properties, which are therefore reconceived as appearance. Likewise, natural bodies strive to individuate themselves by fully possessing their parts, for which purpose they need to remodel those parts so as to become manifest within them. However, the problem with understanding consciousness is that it retains a conception of appearance such that it cannot, in fact, manifest the essence that is held to pervade it. Correspondingly, we find in the *Philosophy of Nature* that bodies repeatedly fail to remodel their parts effectively or comprehensively enough to attain proper manifestation within those parts. Due to this ongoing difficulty, Hegel explains, the "Physics"

> embraces finite corporeality, and is therefore the most difficult
> to grasp . . . the concept is no longer present in an immediate
> way as it is in the first part, nor does it, as in the third part,

show itself as real. Here the concept is hidden; it shows itself
only as the connecting bond of necessity, while that which
appears [*das Erscheinende*] is conceptless. (EN §273A/2: 10)

Hegel partitions the "Physics" into three phases. In the first phase,
bodies begin to qualify their parts, yet those parts retain an unacceptable level of simple materiality. During the second physical phase, bodies attempt to remove this simply material aspect, but only succeed in
destroying their parts altogether. Finally, bodies succeed in thoroughly
qualifying their parts, infusing qualitative variation into their material
exteriors. Let us briefly consider these three phases of the "Physics."

In the first phase, called the "Physics of Universal Individuality,"
Hegel considers bodies as they start to manifest themselves within their
parts. Continuing to equate such bodies with the empirically described
celestial bodies, he identifies their qualified matter with empirical light
and darkness. That is, Hegel reinterprets empirical light and darkness,
philosophically, as the qualities assumed respectively by the material
parts of the sun (the identity of all bodies) and the moons and comets
(different bodies). The material parts of the planets (which are bodies
that are both different from and identical to each other) are identified
as both light and dark, and as acquiring richer and more complex
qualities which Hegel equates with the empirically described "elements."
The central point of this subsection of the "Physics" is to claim, at the
a priori level, that bodies are already superimposing qualities upon their
formerly merely material parts, and to interpret these qualities, empirically, as identical to light, darkness, and the elements.[20]

Nonetheless, bodies' parts remain material underneath their new
qualities, so they still do not fully manifest the bodies within them:
"matter is determined by the immanent form, and in accordance with
the nature of spatiality. This directly gives rise to a *relationship* between
both, the spatial determinateness as such and the matter which belongs
to it" (EN §290/2: 55). In the ensuing phase of the "Physics," the
"Physics of Particular Individuality," bodies actively struggle to supersede the residual materiality of their parts: thus, at this point bodies
become internally divided or "sundered" (*besonder*). First, bodies attempt to modify their materiality; Hegel equates this modified materiality with "specific gravity" or "density" (*Dichtigkeit*). But this still
remains an imposition *upon* materiality; so Hegel reinterprets it as (empirical) "cohesion," as merely the way in which material parts are held
together (§294/2: 61). Next, bodies more actively attempt to destroy
their pure materiality, becoming "sound," which for Hegel negates matter.
Yet these bodies remain paradoxically dependent on matter, requiring

matter in order to negate it (§299/2: 69). As a result, bodies finally adopt a form in which they straightforwardly annihilate their matter: Hegel equates this form with heat (§303/2: 82). This is self-defeating, however: bodies need to become manifest within their parts, not just eliminate them.

This brings us to the concluding physical phase, the "Physics of Total Individuality." At this point, bodies succeed in making themselves apparent:

> [F]orm is now a *totality* which is immanent within material being which offers it no opposition. Selfhood as infinite self-relating form has as such entered into existence; it maintains itself in the externality which is subject to it, and as the freely determining totality of this materiality [*Materielle*], is free individuality. (EN §307/2: 92)

Bodies cease merely to superimpose qualities upon their matter, instead infusing qualitative variation into the very way in which the units of matter exist, so that these units no longer retain any purely quantitative aspect. From this perspective, Hegel redescribes chemical processes as processes in which bodies change all of their qualities and properties, even their "immediate shape, which has particular determinations within it" (§336A/2: 220–21). Nonetheless, a global defect afflicts all the various forms of self-manifesting body introduced at this stage: these bodies "contain . . . relationship to *another*, and it is only in process that the externality and conditionedness . . . are posited as self-sublating" (§308/2: 94). Bodies of all these types manifest themselves in their parts only in reaction *against* their tendency to fuse with other bodies (a tendency that continually resurfaces because bodies are still not properly individuated). Hegel redescribes many empirical forms as instantiating this general structure: most saliently, magnetism, electricity, and chemistry. In Hegel's redescription, for instance, chemical bodies manifest themselves qualitatively only when stimulated to react against other juxtaposed constituents of a chemical process (§329/2: 188). But bodies need to become capable of appearing irrespective of the occurrence of these conditions. They need, then, to engage in an "infinite *self*-stimulating and *self*-sustaining process" (§336/2: 220). This paves the way for the transition into nature's final stage: the organic.

As a whole, the "Physics" details a series of negotiations between bodies and their physical parts. At first, these parts fail to manifest the bodies possessing them, and the "Physics" documents bodies' repeated efforts to overcome this problem by inducing their parts to adopt an appropriately modified form, in which they retain no narrowly material dimension. Even when bodies finally succeed in becoming fully apparent, their success is marred by having a reactive character—in that the success depends on the occurrence of interactive processes. Despite its convoluted structure, the "Physics" remains broadly analogous to the conscious stage of understanding. The understanding conceives entities as both appearing within their properties and failing to appear insofar as those properties continue to be assigned the same character they had prior to their reconception as appearance. Analogously, the physical stage contains bodies which strive to manifest themselves within their matter by qualifying it, yet which cannot achieve full manifestation as long as qualities are merely superimposed on parts that remain, at root, simply material. The later phases of physical development go beyond the understanding in their efforts to overcome this basic problem, but the problem itself has the same structure in both nature and consciousness.

In terms of Hegel's encompassing project of depicting nature's gradual overcoming of the opposition of matter to thought, what progress do we observe within the "Physics"? Recall that the "Mechanics" introduced forms of matter existing independently of any conceptual dimension (as externality, negativity, and material bodies). These forms of matter, Hegel argued, were internally contradictory, for their component units were not (or not fully) individuated, and so proved as much conceptual as material. In nature's physical stage, new forms of thought have emerged—in the guise of bodies, which organize the plurality of their parts and strive to disclose themselves within those parts. Bodies of this type are *universals*, pervading their many parts as intelligible structures and hence as forms of thought (in Hegel's sense of specifically objective thought). He refers, for example, to "the concept existing as a particular body" (EN §324R/2: 167). In contrast to bodies as unities, their parts—discrete, extended, units—remain material. Hegel sums up: "The two distinct moments of real physical body are form as an abstract whole and determinable matter . . . form is pure physical self-relating identity with itself, and has no determinate being" (§308A/2: 94).

This provides a fresh way to characterize the ongoing tension between bodies' need for manifestation and the materiality of their parts. Throughout nature's physical stage, thought is attempting to manifest itself in matter, to give matter an intelligible structure such that it discloses thought; thought remains unmanifest in matter insofar as it allows matter to retain its original absence of structure. The "Physics," then, depicts a natural stage in which matter becomes *partially* pervaded by thought. Matter's original total independence of thought is overcome, but matter is still not adequately permeated and organized by thought. This incomplete permeation of matter by thought defines the "Physics."

Life

The conflict within understanding—the subject's conception of properties both as appearance and yet as unsuitable to manifest an essence—motivates the subject to move to the final form of consciousness: consciousness of living beings. In devising the conception of living beings, the subject resolves the dilemma that arose at the level of understanding, by dropping its belief that entities are not properly manifested in their exteriors; the subject now simply regards entities as outwardly manifest, reconceiving their exteriors as having a character such that they manifest those entities.[21] According to Hegel, in thus conceiving of entities as outwardly revealed, the subject is conceiving of them as organisms. He makes this claim because he defines the living organism precisely as a universal that continuously remodels its material parts so as to disclose itself within them. In that the material parts of organisms now reveal the universal within them, they exist as its "members" (*Glieder*). Hegel likes to emphasize that members, unlike parts, cannot retain their identity unless they belong to the universality of an organism:

> The single members of the body are what they are only through their unity and in relation to it. So, for instance, a hand that has been hewn from the body is a hand in name only, but not in actual fact, as *Aristotle* has already remarked. (EL §216A/291)

In existing as members, an organism's material parts reflect the fact that they depend for their existence and structure upon the universality of that organism. Thus, by devising the conception of the living organism, the subject manages at last to think of matter as thoroughly conceptually permeated or intelligibly structured.[22]

Living organisms as the subject conceives them have a conspicuously similar structure to really existing organisms as described in the *Philosophy of Nature*. Life occupies the *Philosophy of Nature*'s third division, "Organic Physics," which describes the organism as

> the union of the concept with exteriorized existence, in which the concept maintains itself . . . Life is . . . the resolution of the opposition between the concept and reality . . . This reality no longer is in an immediate and independent way . . . in

the abstract concept of the organism, the existence of particularities is compatible with the unity of the concept, for
these particularities are posited as transitory moments of a
single subject. (EN §337A/3: 10–11)

Within living organisms, matter finally manifests the conceptual dimension organizing it. As a result, the universals that unify organic matter
become what Hegel calls "subjects." He says that life "is an elevation
into the first ideality of nature, so that it has become a *fulfilled* and
essentially *self-centred* and *subjective* unity, as it is self-relating and
negative" (§337/3: 9). He also refers to "the vitalised organism, the
subjectivity which constructs its members within itself" (§342/3: 40).

Hegel believes that life advances through three phases, which he
equates with three empirical natural forms: the earth, plants, and animals. Paradoxically, organisms at first are not properly "alive" at all.
Their matter still presents itself as an independent totality lacking any
conceptual interior; as such, life is "self-alienated" (EN §337A/3: 12),
and Hegel equates this with the earth. At the second organic stage, the
parts of organisms still do not perfectly manifest their dependence on
their center. The empirical analogue of this is plants, the parts of which
can always be separated off to start whole new organisms (as when we
take cuttings, for example). Thus, plants are also a deficient life form
for Hegel because:

[T]he process whereby the vegetable subject articulates and
sustains itself is one in which it comes outside itself and falls
apart into several individuals [that is, individual organisms] . . .
the process of formation and of reproduction of the *singular*
individual . . . is a perennial production of new individuals.
(§343–44/3: 45–47)

The last and most perfect organic form possesses the fully developed
kind of subjectivity that is present throughout the limbs and organs
comprising its body. Hegel equates this with animals. The long chain of
natural progression is finally "perfected through animal life, through its
sensibility, since this reveals to us the omnipresence of the one soul in
all points of its corporeality, and so reveals the sublatedness of the
externality of matter" (EM §389A/32).

This comparison between Hegel's accounts of the subject's consciousness of living beings and of really existing organisms reveals marked
similarities between these two accounts. He argues that the subject
devises the conception of living beings specifically because it adopts the

belief that these beings are fully manifest in their exteriors; likewise, living organisms arise as that natural form whose matter openly displays the conceptual unity permeating it. This similarity arises because both living organisms and the conception of living beings realize the underlying requirements that propel the development of nature and consciousness. The subject has, at last, come to conceive of matter as intelligibly structured; this conception accords with the subject's tacit presupposition that matter is intelligible, ending the progression of consciousness. Nature has also overcome matter's antagonism to thought, since organic matter has become thoroughly conceptually permeated and can in no sense exist independently of this conceptual permeation. The developmental trajectories of both consciousness and nature reach their goals, and cease, with the emergence of organisms.

Hegel's Metaphysical Theory of Nature

Hegel offers an unusual and ambitious reinterpretation of nature as the scene of a gradual progression from an original opposition between its two constituent elements, matter and thought, to their eventual unification. At first, nature contains matter without any conceptual dimension, yet this matter proves, ironically, to be conceptual just *in* its materiality. Units of matter attempt to overcome this problem by individuating themselves, in the process transforming themselves into bodies which unify and organize their material parts, yet which at first still permeate those parts only incompletely. The *Philosophy of Nature* concludes with bodies becoming organisms that thoroughly pervade and reveal themselves within their material parts or members. Matter no longer subsists in independent antagonism to the conceptual; instead, matter has become completely structured and organized by thought.

These general lineaments of Hegel's basic theory of nature have emerged through the comparison between nature and consciousness. Hegel organizes the stages of nature on the same model as the forms of consciousness. This is no coincidence, since he identifies both domains as starting from initial states with corresponding structures and contradictions. These initial contradictions compel both consciousness and nature to progress into necessarily succeeding states, which also have corresponding structures, arising as they do in response to corresponding initial contradictions. Consequently, these states in turn develop substantially identical difficulties; hence, the entire courses of development of consciousness and of nature run in tandem. For this reason, comparing Hegel's *Philosophy of Nature* to his theory of consciousness has allowed us to understand his general theory of natural development.

The comparison with consciousness also brings out how Hegel's basic theory of nature is a priori. The stages through which consciousness passes are all rationally necessary, which means that their progression can be worked out through a priori reasoning. Natural stages follow one another with the same rational necessity—each stage resolves the contradiction in its predecessor—and so natural progression, too, can be described through a priori reasoning. Hegel thus believes that a priori reasoning can generate a basic description of natural forms which duplicates in thought the real progression that those forms objectively undergo. His a priori theory is, simultaneously, a metaphysical description of really existing natural forms.[23]

Hegel's basic theory describes natural forms in sui generis—distinctively nonscientific—terms. However, we can now see that the originality of Hegel's theoretical description of natural forms operates on several levels. Above all, it reflects the broader metaphysical project within which his project of giving a metaphysical description of nature is located. This broader project is to describe the forms of thought—collectively called the "idea"—which structure the world as a whole. Hegel's *Logic* describes these forms in abstraction. That is, the *Logic* focuses on the most general structures manifest in all reality: structures such as being, nothingness, becoming, existence, limitation, and so on. The *Philosophy of Nature* traces how these forms are instantiated in nature. As we can now appreciate, the *Philosophy of Nature* does this by describing thought as existing in a series of forms, each defined by its specific combination with a particular form of matter. In the mechanical stages, forms of thought exist which are combined with matter in that they are immediately identical with (fused together with) matter—first, with pure structureless matter, and, second, with material bodies. In the physical stage, forms of thought exist as universals or bodies that are uneasily tethered to their material parts. In the organic stage, forms of thought exist that manifest themselves, harmoniously, in their material members.

Throughout the *Philosophy of Nature*, then, forms of thought do not feature in an abstract guise as in the *Logic*. Instead, thought is depicted as instantiated in, or combined with, matter in successive ways. This bears out Hegel's general statement that:

[T]he differences between the particular philosophical sciences are only determinations of the idea itself, and . . . it is only the idea which presents itself in these diverse elements. In nature, it is not something other than the idea which is known, but the idea is in the form of externalisation. (EL §18R/42)

In this way, Hegel theorizes nature starting from his broader metaphysics of the idea, and this means that he ends up characterizing nature in different terms from empirical science—as the stage for a gradual harmonization of thought and matter. Within this process of harmonization, Hegel identifies distinct stages, each including a specific range of natural forms. He describes each of these forms in specifically philosophical terms, as reflecting a determinate stage in matter/thought relations.

This leaves Hegel with basic descriptions of natural forms that deviate considerably from those available in science. He subsequently compares the two sets of descriptions, reinterpreting and incorporating scientific descriptions whenever possible. For example, he begins with his sui generis description of the first natural form, externality or matter. He then interprets this as identical to scientifically described space, incorporating scientific findings about space into his account. Admittedly, Hegel's presentation is ambiguous, making it far from obvious that he includes empirical descriptions—like that of space—on this merely interpretive basis. This difficulty intensifies in later sections, where Hegel's sui generis descriptions—in particular, his description of organic life—appear inherently to include an empirical reference (that is, to the organic or biological). Even here, though, we can perceive a distinction (as I have tried to suggest) between the basic *philosophical* description of organic structures that Hegel develops a priori and the relatively *concrete* findings that he appends from the biological sciences. This distinction makes it possible to claim that Hegel moves from the initial philosophical description to a subsequent and merely interpretive incorporation of scientific findings.

The ultimate reason for construing Hegel in this way, I have suggested, is that it is philosophically fruitful to do so. It allows us to see him as constructing a metaphysical theory of nature couched in substantially different terms from those of empirical science. This puts him in a position to develop a trenchant critique of modern science, by arguing that its descriptions of nature are inadequate compared to the alternative descriptions of nature that his metaphysical standpoint makes available.

However, the fact that Hegel's descriptions of nature deviate from scientific descriptions does not automatically show that his descriptions are more adequate: this requires further argument. In the absence of such argument, one may object that Hegel's metaphysical project has only led him to a strange and arcane depiction of nature which is too remote for us to accept it—or even to appreciate what would be involved in accepting it. Hegel is, after all, portraying the natural world as made up of quite unfamiliar forms: he talks, for example, about externality, negativity, and bodies that are both identical and differentiated, rather than such more familiar items as space, time, and gravity. Even though Hegel later incorporates those scientifically described items into his account, his basic descriptions of nature remain unfamiliar. Those basic descriptions coalesce into an overall portrayal of nature as the scene of the gradual unification of matter with objective thought—a portrayal quite different from any standard pictures of nature deriving from empirical science. We need, then, to explore why Hegel's basic descriptions of nature should be taken as more adequate than scientific descriptions. As part of this, we need to see why Hegel's absolute idealist metaphysics, which informs and organizes his approach to nature, should be thought to confer this greater level of adequacy upon his descriptions of natural forms. These are the problems to be pursued in the next chapter.

3

THE RATIONALITY OF NATURE

Nature is mind estranged from itself. In nature, mind only *lets
itself go*, a Bacchic god unrestrained and unaware of itself. In
nature, the unity of the concept hides. . . . Estranged from the
idea, nature is only the corpse of the understanding. Nature is
the idea, but only implicitly. That was why Schelling called it a
petrified intelligence, others even a frozen intelligence. Yet God
does not remain petrified and dead, the stones cry out and raise
themselves to mind.

—Hegel, *Philosophy of Nature*

I have argued that Hegel's *Philosophy of Nature* can most productively
be understood as theorizing nature on a strong a priori basis. By this
I mean that Hegel constructs his theory by working out rationally the
basic sequence of natural forms, subsequently incorporating into his
account those empirical claims and hypotheses which he can provisionally interpret as corresponding to the claims of his own theory. As an
integral part of this strong a priori approach, Hegel must initially describe natural forms in sui generis terms. Only by describing nature in
substantially different terms from empirical science can he avoid presupposing in advance the compatibility of particular scientific claims,
instead including those claims on a merely interpretive and provisional
basis. Hegel's *Philosophy of Nature*, then, begins by describing natural
forms in specifically philosophical terms, as constellations of concept/
matter relations. Even though Hegel subsequently reinterprets empirical
descriptions to correspond to his sui generis descriptions, those descriptions remain themselves esoteric. I have suggested that this originality of
Hegel's basic theory of nature is fruitful, enabling him to advance a
strong, yet nonobscurantist, critique of modern science. But why should
the difference of Hegel's theory from science be thought to confer

epistemic *advantage* on that theory and not make it merely an extended flight of fancy? Hegel's deviation from science can be epistemically advantageous if the *metaphysics* that makes his theory original simultaneously makes it more adequate. How does he develop this possibility?

So far, I have explained how Hegel's theory of natural development is informed by his overarching metaphysical project of describing forms of thought that organize reality. This project leads him to understand nature as a sequence of forms of thought which are instantiated in, or combined with, matter in increasingly harmonious ways. Furthermore, he regards each stage in this sequence as the necessary consequence of the previous stage and, specifically, as its *rationally* necessary consequence, since each stage resolves the contradiction in the one before it. This points to a further respect in which Hegel's theory of nature is distinctive: he regards all natural forms as *intrinsically rational*; that is, they all arise, exist, and behave in line with rational requirements.

This aspect of Hegel's theory can be seen to derive, again, from his overarching metaphysical project. In terms of this project, he believes that all the forms of thought that structure reality are intrinsically rational—in that they each resolve the contradictions in their predecessors. This is precisely why he calls them forms of *thought* (Denk*bestimmungen*) and says that they collectively make up the "*idea*" (or "concept"). For him, these forms are not merely universal ontological patterns or structures, but, more particularly, they are rationally interconnected structures: they intrinsically evince rationality. Accordingly, in the *Science of Logic*, Hegel refers to reality in itself as the "reasonable" (*Vernünftig*) (WL 64/1: 61–62). Given this overarching metaphysics, Hegel must consider the forms of thought *qua* materially instantiated in nature to be intrinsically rational in the same sense.

This central idea that natural forms are intrinsically rational underpins Hegel's entire theory of natural development. As we have seen, he begins by describing nature's initial state, identifying its internal contradiction, then working out what natural form must emerge to provide its resolution. Each form exists with the structure it has—its determinate level of unification with matter—because this structure is rationally required, given preexisting problems in preceding natural forms. Thus, Hegel's fundamental belief in the intrinsic rationality of natural forms underpins his more specialized descriptions of them as embodying definite stages in the progression toward unification of matter with thought.

Now, crucially, Hegel believes that his theory can describe natural forms better than empirical science *because* it attributes intrinsic rationality to those forms. In the mature system, he argues that his fundamental metaphysical conception of natural forms as intrinsically rational (hereafter, simply his "rationalist conception" or "rationalist metaphysics" of nature)[1] is more adequate than a contrasting conception of nature which is presupposed in empirical science, and which makes scientific descriptions less adequate than those of Hegel's *Philosophy of Nature*. This scientific conception of nature can also be described as a metaphysical conception, in that it represents science's attempt to capture nature's real character. The alleged problem, though, is that this conception is inadequate compared with the conception of nature as intrinsically rational that issues from Hegel's absolute idealist metaphysics.

The outlines of this critique of science are present in Hegel's mature system, but they remain fragmentary and incomplete, needing reconstruction into coherent form. This chapter aims to reconstruct certain key opening stages in Hegel's argument. First, I try to explicate his conception of natural forms as intrinsically rational (in that they arise and act according to requirements of rational necessity). Second, I explore how this conception of nature differs from the alternative conception that Hegel takes to be presupposed in empirical science, according to which all natural forms are bare things whose behavior is intrinsically meaningless.[2] Third, I distinguish Hegel's rationalist conception of nature from the traditional teleological conception of it, while also offering a moderate defence of his belief that all scientific inquiry presupposes a metaphysics of bare things (even though science might well be thought to be considerably more internally diverse and sophisticated than this). Fourth, having begun to introduce Hegel's rationalist conception of nature, I then clarify how this conception connects to his strong a priori method of theorizing nature. As I will explain, the rationalist conception justifies and requires strong a priorism, through which Hegel can insure that all his descriptions of individual natural forms reflect the appropriate metaphysics. Through this reconsideration of strong a priorism, I introduce Hegel's crucial claim that his metaphysics is more adequate than that of science. Finally, in the fifth section, I address a possible objection to this claim: that, far from being preferable to the scientific conception, Hegel's rationalist view of nature is delusively anthropomorphic, supposing natural forms to act rationally as if they were like human agents. I argue that Hegel significantly qualifies his assertion of intrinsic rationality in natural forms by maintaining that they act rationally in a specifically nonconscious or, in his phrase, "petrified" fashion.

My aim in this chapter, then, is to begin to explain why the deviation of Hegel's theory of nature from standard scientific accounts should be thought to make that theory illuminating rather than merely fantastic. Hegel's essential argument is that this sui generis theory is illuminating to the extent that it reflects his particularly adequate metaphysical conception of nature. According to this, all natural forms act, nonconsciously, according to rationality. Hegel deems this conception more adequate, above all, than the competing scientific conception of nature as a realm of bare, intrinsically meaningless, things. As this anticipatory summary shows, this chapter will not yet answer the question of *why* Hegel deems his rationalist conception of nature more adequate than its scientific adversary. This question will continue to occupy subsequent chapters; for now, we need an initial understanding of what Hegel's metaphysical conception of nature is and how it differs from the metaphysical conception allegedly presupposed in empirical science.

Hegel's Rationalist Conception of Nature

According to Hegel, his descriptions of natural forms differ from any scientific descriptions because they embody a metaphysical conception of nature different from that presupposed in empirical science: "The philosophy of nature distinguishes itself from physics on account of the kind of metaphysics [*Weise der Metaphysik*] it employs" (EN §246A/1: 202).[3] Fundamental to Hegel's distinctive metaphysical conception of nature is his view that all its forms are intrinsically rational. Unhelpfully, though, he gives no clear and uncluttered statement of this view. We must reconstruct it from his substantive theory of natural development, as expounded in the previous chapter. This reconstruction must be rather painstaking given, again, the obscurity of the *Philosophy of Nature*. Nonetheless, by reexamining Hegel's theory of natural development, we can clarify that he conceives natural forms to contain an inner rationality that impels them continuously to transform themselves.

How is this conception of natural forms as intrinsically rational embodied in Hegel's substantive theory of nature? His adherence to this conception is revealed, above all, by his understanding of the mechanism through which natural forms necessitate one another, as exhibited in their development. Hegel believes each form to follow its predecessor necessarily in that it provides the *rationally necessary* solution to the internal *contradiction* within the structure of that predecessor. For example, he believes that the natural form which he calls negativity (empirically, time) necessarily succeeds externality (empirically, space) because negativity provides the rationally necessary solution to the contradiction (*Widerspruch*) from which externality suffers. This contradiction is that externality is both completely homogeneous (and so conceptual) and internally differentiated (and so material): or, as Hegel puts it, "space in itself is the contradiction of indifferent mutual externality and of undifferentiated continuity" (EN §260/1: 236). To take a different example, he maintains that bodies must thoroughly qualify their material parts (empirically, they must undergo chemical change) because this provides the rationally necessary solution to the "contradiction" that those bodies are partly individuated and partly identical with one another (§326/2: 178).

Hegel's idea that natural forms follow one another with "rational necessity" is far from transparent. To clarify it, I will analyze it into three central claims. First is the claim that each natural form contains an "internal contradiction." Second is the claim that each natural form provides the "rationally necessary" solution to a preexisting contradiction within one of the other forms. Hegel's third claim is that all these forms exist or arise *because* they provide the rationally necessary solutions to preexisting contradictions in other forms. Let us examine each claim in turn.

First, Hegel maintains that each natural form contains or suffers from an internal contradiction (*Widerspruch*): that is, each form has two essential characteristics or features that are antithetical to one another.[4] For example, he sees externality as both homogeneous and internally differentiated—so, in effect, both homogeneous and nonhomogeneous (see, again, EN §257A/1: 229). As the case of externality suggests, Hegel envisages each natural form as defined by characteristics which negate one another, which are literally contradictory. This view poses several difficulties. First, it appears likely that Hegel reached this understanding of natural forms by extrapolating the approach he had successfully applied to shapes of human consciousness in the *Phenomenology*, in which he diagnoses how each shape falls into an internal contradiction calling for a determinate successor. Yet it is not obvious that self-contradictory forms can exist in the *non*human world.[5] If they do, then true descriptions of such forms must themselves be contradictory (since they must attribute to natural forms the antithetical characteristics that they really possess). But philosophers are reluctant to concede that there can be true contradictions, primarily because, as Graham Priest sums up, "a contradiction cannot be true since contradictions entail everything, and not everything is true."[6] To make matters worse, Hegel's earlier analysis in the *Phenomenology* of how each shape of consciousness necessarily gives way to its less contradictory successor appears to rely on the very same belief that contradictory views cannot be true and hence must be superseded by other, less contradictory, views.

Even if Hegel can surmount this difficulty, there remains another problem with his thesis that all natural forms house internal contradictions. Many of the natural forms he describes do not, after all, suffer from literal contradictions as externality (supposedly) does. For instance, there is no contradiction in (what Hegel regards as) the fact that bodies can only manifest themselves in their parts insofar as they react against the threat of fusion with other bodies. At most, there is a *tension* in the way bodies depend upon external conditions to meet internal requirements. As this case illustrates, Hegel often uses the notion of "contradiction" to denote mere tensions or oppositions: as John Findlay famously comments, "By the presence of 'contradictions' in thought and reality, Hegel plainly means the presence of opposed, antithetical *tendencies*."[7] Apparently, then, Hegel employs the term "contradiction" in an extended sense to embrace tensions of varying degrees (an extended usage reflected in his regularly taking "tension" (*Spannung*) to be synonymous with "contradiction").[8]

Fortunately, Hegel's extended understanding of contradiction can enhance, rather than vitiate, the cogency of his overall view of natural progression. This extended understanding gives us scope to rethink the literal contradictions he describes (for example, the contradiction within externality) as merely especially acute tensions. This means that Hegel's theory of nature need not entail the objective reality of contradictions in the logical sense. As long as Hegel can show that each natural form harbors a rationally unacceptable tension of some sort, then he can still hold that each of these tensions requires resolution by some determinately improved natural structure. Natural progression can unfold rationally by way of tensions just as much as logical contradictions. Despite this, for ease of exposition, I will generally stick to Hegel's practice of referring to "contradictions" in nature, with the crucial proviso that this term should be understood, as Hegel understands it, to designate tensions, and not contradictions in the strict logical sense.[9]

Hegel's second main claim is that each natural form provides the "rationally necessary" solution to the internal contradiction infesting some other form. For example, negativity provides the rationally necessary solution to the contradiction of externality because negativity is subdivided into units that negate one another and thereby individuate themselves, losing the homogeneity of externality. This solution is "rational" insofar as it resolves a preexisting contradiction, fulfilling the rational requirement that contradictions be eliminated. Yet it is not obvious that the solution which negativity offers is rationally *necessary*, that is, that it is the only possible solution to the contradiction of externality.[10] Why doesn't externality's contradiction call directly for the more fully individuated items (that is, material bodies) each of which negates not just all other units but a determinate quantity of other units? Hegel wants to say that these more fully individuated items resolve, specifically, the later contradiction within negativity, not the earlier contradiction within externality. This reveals that he uses the idea of a "necessary" solution in, again, a somewhat technical sense. For him, a structure provides the "necessary" solution to a preexisting contradiction when this structure resolves that contradiction in a way that introduces the *smallest possible difference* between itself and the structure whose contradiction it amends. In this, Hegel again models the kind of necessity with which natural forms follow one another upon the kind of necessity he has already found in the transitions between shapes of consciousness in the *Phenomenology*. Michael Forster explains this as follows:

> [T]he "necessity" of a transition from a shape of consciousness A to a shape of consciousness B just consists in the complex fact that . . . shape B preserves shape A's constitutive conceptions/concepts but in a way which modifies them so as to eliminate the self-contradiction, and moreover does so while departing less from the meanings of A's constitutive conceptions/concepts than any other . . . shape which performs that function.[11]

Forster's explanation leaves open what it means for a shape to "depart less" from its predecessor than any other. Presumably, a shape—or natural form—departs least when it introduces the minimal level of difference from its predecessor that is compatible with resolving its contradiction, whereas all other forms introduce a greater level of differentiation. But what does it mean to say that a given difference is as small as is compatible with resolving the predecessor's contradiction? We can extrapolate Hegel's answer to this, again, from his substantive account of natural development. Negative units (or moments) differentiate themselves from units of externality to the smallest possible extent insofar as they introduce only *one* new characteristic in addition to those already present in external units: namely, negativity. For Hegel, this negativity is not itself analyzable into a plurality of characteristics—it is quite undifferentiated, as evidenced by the way that units act negatively toward all other units. In contrast, material bodies differ from negative units by adding *another* new characteristic: they always direct their negativity toward some determinate quantity of surrounding units. Thus, Hegel envisages each natural form differentiating itself minimally from its predecessor by adding only one new characteristic to those that the predecessor possessed. Nature's rationally necessary development is therefore simultaneously a progression in levels of complexity, as natural

forms accumulate ever more characteristics, each incorporating or building upon those previously present. In terms of his notion of necessity,
then, Hegel believes that any natural form provides the rationally necessary solution to another form's contradiction just when it resolves that
contradiction while introducing only one characteristic to distinguish
itself from the preceding form. This rather technical notion of "necessity" captures the rationale behind the developmental pattern Hegel
detects within nature, whereby it advances to its most perfect form not
in a "simple transition" but through "a series of stages consisting of
many moments" (EM §381A/13).[12]

The third element in Hegel's idea that natural forms supplant one
another with "rational necessity" is his claim that all natural forms
exist or arise *because* they provide the rationally necessary solutions to
one another's internal contradictions. The claim is that the rational
necessity of a given structure explains its existence or emergence. Confusingly, Hegel sketches two distinct interpretations of how the existence of natural forms conforms to the requirements of rational necessity.
The first can be called the "logical" interpretation. It emerges in a
comment in the *Philosophy of Mind*, where Hegel implies that he derives the series of natural forms by a regressive argument:

> The differences into which the concept of nature unfolds
> itself are more or less mutually independent existences; true,
> through their original unity they stand in connection with
> one another, so that none can be grasped [*begriffen*] without
> the others, but this connection is to a greater or lesser degree
> external to them. (EM §381A/9)

Hegel is suggesting that he begins with the knowledge that externality
exists (given the requirements of the logical idea), then establishes that
externality is internally contradictory and therefore can only subsist
because some other form also exists which resolves its contradiction, a
successor form which, in turn, only exists because it is accompanied by
or embraced within something else which resolves *its* contradiction.
This institutes a pattern to be found throughout nature, with each form
depending logically upon the one that resolves its contradiction. On this
view, the existence of nature conforms to rational requirements in the
sense that nature embodies a comprehensive structure of logical relationships; thus, on this picture, logical requirements exert a prior constraint upon the possible modes of nature's existence.

According to Hegel's alternative conception of how natural forms
conform to rational requirements, each form responds to its internal

contradiction by actually *turning into* the successor form that it requires. The details of Hegel's portrayals of many natural developments support this conception. Consider once more, for example, the development from externality to negativity. Externality has to "posit" its "possibility" of internal differentiation, which strongly suggests that it actively realizes itself by metamorphosing into a set of more fully differentiated entities (empirical points). Having then assimilated these entities to (empirical) lines, Hegel continues: "the line therefore *passes over into* the plane" (EN §256/1: 226; my emphasis), then he adds that, again, planes must "actualize" or "posit" their essential lack of differentiation by making the transition to negativity (characteristically, Hegel does not at this point maintain a clear distinction between the a priori and empirical components of his account).[13] His overall conclusion to this section most plainly endorses the conception of natural rationality with which he is working here:

> The truth of space is time, so that space *becomes* time; our transition to time is not subjective, *space itself makes* the transition. In representation space and time are far outside one another; space is there, and then we *also* have time. Philosophy calls this "also" into question. (§257A/1: 229; emphases altered)[14]

This second conception of natural necessity may be called the "transformative" conception. According to it, all natural forms are intrinsically rational, uniformly transforming themselves so as to overcome their internal contradictions. On this view, nature does not (as Hegel implied before) merely embody rationality as a logical constraint; rather, each of nature's component forms contains some *inner* locus of rationality, which responds to the force of rational requirements by propelling that form to metamorphose in the way that corrects its self-contradiction.[15]

Hegel's transformative conception of the rational necessity in nature faces a difficulty: if each form actively becomes its successor, this suggests that the successor must follow it not only logically but also temporally. This produces an obvious paradox in the case of negativity—which Hegel equates with empirical time—since any explanation of how negativity emerges must presuppose time even before its supposed derivation.[16] In any case, Hegel denies that transitions within nature occur temporally:

> Nature is to be regarded as a *system of stages*, one proceeding necessarily from the other and being the direct [*nächste*]

truth of that from which it results. This is not to be thought
of as a *natural* engendering of one out of the other however,
but an engendering in the inner idea which constitutes the
ground [*Grund*] of nature. *Metamorphosis* applies only to
the concept as such, for only its alteration is development
[*Entwicklung*]. (EN §249/1: 212)

This seems to suggest that each form "becomes" its successor not literally but conceptually, in that it entails or presupposes the latter—a
regressive reading of natural rationality.

Elsewhere, though, Hegel hints at a third possibility: that natural
forms do metamorphose actively into one another, but that this metamorphosis occurs *nontemporally*. He states that the antithesis to the
temporal is the eternal, and that the "inner idea" (of EN §249)—the
totality of natural structures—exists eternally (§258A/1: 232). But he
also stresses that what is eternal is not absolutely "outside of time" but
is uninterruptedly present, never coming into being or ceasing to be
(§247A/1: 207). His revealing example is the supposed "creation" of
the natural world by the logical idea, which is and always has been
going on, incessantly. These comments imply that each natural form
necessitates its successor by metamorphosing into it continuously, while,
reciprocally, being neverendingly regenerated from its own predecessor
(just as, allegedly, the logical idea continuously metamorphoses into the
first natural form, externality, while simultaneously being continually
regenerated itself from the preceding stage of logical development). This
third conception of how natural forms obey rational requirements has
the important advantage of explaining why Hegel generally describes
natural forms as actively changing into one another while also denying
that they are temporally successive. This third conception of natural
rationality is therefore Hegel's most consistent and strongest conception, in terms of which he is best interpreted.

As a whole, Hegel's understanding of the mechanism through which
natural development takes place is that all natural forms follow one
another with rational necessity, in the sense that each form actively and
continuously transforms itself into that successor which differs from it
minimally while resolving its inner contradiction (or tension). This
understanding of the mechanism of natural development discloses the
distinctive metaphysical conception of nature with which Hegel is working (but which he never states explicitly). On this conception, all natural
forms are intrinsically rational. Hegel indicates this in one of the *Philosophy of Nature*'s opening passages:

> If we want to determine what the philosophy of nature is,
> we had better separate it from that against which it is
> determined . . . In the first place we find it in a peculiar rela-
> tionship to natural science in general . . . It is itself physics,
> but *rational physics*, and it is at this point of rationality that
> we have to grasp it, and in particular to clarify its relation-
> ship to physics. (EN 1: 192–93)

More precisely, Hegel's view is that all natural forms contain an internal
locus of rationality, which propels them to resolve their internal tensions as is rationally necessary.[17] As he states: "there is reason in the
world, by which we mean that reason is the soul of the world, lives
within it, and is *immanent* in it, as its own, *innermost nature*, its universal" (EL §24 A1/56; my emphases). Hegel, then, espouses an unor-
thodox metaphysical conception of nature according to which all its
constituent forms are intrinsically rational; this is his "rationalist" conception of nature. This preliminary outline of Hegel's metaphysics of
nature leaves many questions unanswered. First, though, we must ask
how his rationalist conception compares with the metaphysical view of
nature that he takes to be presupposed in empirical science.

Rationalist and Scientific Conceptions of Nature

It is hard to tell what Hegel takes to be the metaphysical conception of
nature presupposed in empirical science, since none of his *Encyclopaedia*
is devoted to a sustained discussion of science in its own right. Despite
appraising many scientific results, the *Philosophy of Nature* says re-
markably little about the general methodology of science or its underlying assumptions.[18] Hegel's few overall statements on science are
scattered across three places in his mature system: the introduction to
the *Philosophy of Nature*, the account of "understanding" in the *Philosophy of Mind*, and two remarks on the structure of explanation
(*Erklärung*) in the *Science of Logic*. In addition, the *Phenomenology*
has a richer discussion of explanation—in chapter 3, on "Understanding"—and a longer analysis of empirical science—in chapter 5A, under
the heading "Observation of nature" (*Beobachtung der Natur*). These
latter sources must be handled cautiously, as they figure in the specific
epistemological and pedagogical project of the *Phenomenology*. Nonetheless, as a whole, Hegel's disparate treatments of science allow us to
reconstruct his understanding of the metaphysical presuppositions that
allegedly orchestrate all scientific research.

As we already know, Hegel regards science as a distinctively empirical approach to the study of nature, which reaches general conclusions on an observational basis. But he also stresses that the point of scientists' endeavor to discern universal principles or laws organizing empirical manifestations is to *explain* (*erklären*) those manifestations. Hegel associates science with the understanding, referring, for example, to "the universalised understanding which physics provides" (EN §246A/1: 201). An important aspect of the understanding is its attempt to identify imperceptible factors, primarily laws or forces, which generate and so explain perceptible givens (see EM §422–§422A/ 162–63). Scientists attempt to explain perceptible facts by postulating explanatory factors, including laws and forces, which cause and structure those facts. To explain a perceptible given in this way is to identify its *ground* (*Grund*), the nonempirical feature which is causally responsible for its existence.

In his more detailed account of scientific "observation of nature" (*Beobachtung der Natur*) in the *Phenomenology*, Hegel argues that the search for explanatory grounds advances in two stages: classification and the formulation and testing of laws. He calls these stages simply *Merkmale* (differentiae) and *Gesetze* (laws).[19] In the classificatory stage, scientists try to group empirical phenomena into natural kinds on the basis of universal properties that they instantiate. Scientists seek "the line of demarcation of what is *distinctive* of, say, elephant, oak, gold" (PhG 148/189). Yet they invariably come across new phenomena which confound their classificatory schemes: "this holding fast to passive being that remains self-identical, inevitably sees itself tormented . . . by instances which . . . invalidate the universality to which it had risen" (150/191). Scientists continually discover such counter-instances because the phenomena they observe have an intrinsically indeterminate and protean character, undergoing constant change through which they exchange one set of properties for another: each perceptible phenomenon "in a *chemical fashion*, becomes something else than it is *empirically*, confuses cognition" (149–50/190).

To preserve their belief that empirical phenomena instantiate universal properties, scientists advance to the more complex view that universal properties *themselves* change into one another:

> Reason must . . . move on from the inert determinateness, which had a show of permanence, to observe it as it truly is, namely relating itself to its opposite, disappearing. What are called *differentiae* are *passive* determinatenesses which, when expressed and apprehended as *simple*, do not repre-

sent their nature, . . . to go over into [their] opposite. (PhG
150–51/191–92)

Scientists now begin to postulate laws which explain how these universals change or "go over into their opposites." Here laws are presumed
to be underlying factors that cause universals to develop according to
given patterns. Having first identified universals that explain empirical
givens, scientists then postulate underlying laws to explain how universals change.[20] In general, for Hegel, the scientific project of explanation
presupposes a metaphysical picture of the natural world according to
which every natural entity or event has its "ground" in universals that
are themselves "grounded" in an underlying realm of laws. Hegel says
that scientists implicitly conceive of these universals and laws as the
Ursachen—causes—of what they ground (EM §422A/163). He thus
attributes to scientists a realist notion of universals and laws, according
to which these explanatory factors are really existing causes of empirical events. Moreover, according to Hegel, scientists believe that laws
constitute an imperceptible substratum, existing at a different ontological level from the universals upon which they act.

Notably, Hegel himself *shares* with scientists the realist assumption that empirical natural phenomena and events have grounds of
existence. Also like scientists, he thinks that these phenomena are
grounded in the real universal forms which they instantiate, forms that
he describes in the *Philosophy of Nature*. He shares with scientists, too,
the further assumption that these universal forms change into one another. However, he differs crucially from scientists in believing that
universals change into one another *not* as a consequence of underlying
laws, but because it is rationally necessary that they do so. The basic
difference between Hegel's and scientists' metaphysical conceptions of
universals, then, is that he explains the metamorphosis of universals by
their intrinsic rationality, whereas scientists appeal to underlying laws.[21]
We might, provisionally, gloss this difference by saying that Hegel thinks
there are *reasons* for the behavior of each natural form, whereas scientists think that this behavior has *causes*.

Perhaps, therefore, we can elucidate the difference between Hegel's
metaphysics and that of empirical science by mapping it onto the well-
known distinction between interpretive understanding (*Verstehen*),
which investigates agents' reasons for action, and explanation, which
studies the causes of events. The distinction is articulated, inter alia,
by R. G. Collingwood in *The Idea of History*. Here Collingwood is
especially concerned to demarcate history from natural science, and
thereby to establish a broader separation between the human sciences

(*Geisteswissenschaften*) and the natural sciences. According to Collingwood, history investigates events and artifacts as expressions of human thought, or as what he calls "actions," physical manifestations that are entirely directed by and expressive of thoughts. In particular, actions express general conceptions which constitute the plans or intentions adopted by human agents. The historian aims to reconstruct the meaning or point of actions by "reenacting" the thoughts that they express. Her basic activity is therefore interpretation: the interpretation of actions as to the thoughts animating them. Interpretive activity is inappropriate in the study of nature, Collingwood contends, because: "The events of nature are mere events, not the acts of agents whose thought the scientist endeavours to trace."[22] Natural entities do not think or have thoughts, which renders pointless any attempt to reenact meaning in their behavior. What is appropriate for scientists is instead to search out causes that explain this behavior, a search that is redundant in relation to history: "For history, the object to be discovered is not the mere event, but the thought expressed in it. To discover that thought is already to understand it. After the historian has ascertained the facts, there is no further process of enquiring into their cause." For Collingwood, history is interpretive and seeks reasons, whereas science is explanatory and seeks causes.

Collingwood's distinction between history and science coincides imperfectly with the distinction between Hegel's metaphysics of nature and the contrasting metaphysics that he takes to be presupposed in empirical science, but it nonetheless provides a useful point of departure for elucidating the latter distinction. After all, Hegel certainly approaches natural development by telling us the *reasons* why each natural form metamorphoses into its successor. In this sense, he appears to extend to nature the interpretive approach that for Collingwood applies exclusively within the human sciences. However, in giving reasons for (that is, interpreting) the development of natural forms, Hegel believes himself to be adducing the *grounds* of this development: he states that nature as a whole has its ground (*Grund*) in the "inner idea" constituted of all the universal forms as they mutate into one another. Thus, unlike Collingwood, Hegel thinks that by providing reasons he *is* explaining the existence and character of natural forms.[23] In this, Hegel denies any categorial distinction between interpretation and explanation, instead regarding interpretation as just one form of explanation—defined by its appeal to a specific type of explanatory factor or *Grund*, namely reasons. Hegel's notion of a *Grund*, then, embraces all types of explanatory factors, including both reasons and efficient causes.[24] Since Hegel regards reasons as a type of cause, he also believes that when we interpret human actions we are giving them a causal explanation. Contrary to the popular picture of Hegel as the "tutelary genius" behind the hermeneutic study of human activity,[25] he actually regards the study of nature and history as essentially continuous with one another. Summing up Hegel's stance on this, Alfredo Ferrarin notes that Hegel does not accept

> the division between natural sciences and *Geisteswissenschaften* (human sciences) and [he does not, as often thought] devote himself to the latter. For Hegel we do not simply have before us two different models of explanation and approaches that belong to two radically different and exclusive realms. For Hegel, nature has a life that cannot be opposed to the life of the mind . . . it is [not] alien to reason.[26]

Although Hegel sees himself, like empirical scientists, as attempting to explain the behavior of natural forms, he thinks it characteristic of scientists to seek to explain this behavior with reference to a different *type* of *Grund* from the reasons that he adduces. When scientists try to identify laws that cause change in universals, they are seeking *external* factors—external causes—which explain those universals' development.[27] According to Hegel, scientists seek external causes because they presume that the development of natural forms cannot be explained in terms of their intrinsic rationality: scientists assume that reasons are inadmissible as explanations of natural events. This suggests that empirical scientists work from a metaphysical assumption according to which natural forms cannot in any sense be considered *agents* whose behavior has meaning, but rather are *bare things* whose behavior makes up a mass of intrinsically meaningless events.

Hegel's idea that empirical science presupposes a metaphysical conception of natural forms as bare things reformulates the familiar view that modern science "disenchants" the natural world, denuding nature of the spiritual meaning and value attributed to it in ancient and medieval times, and reinterpreting it as intrinsically meaningless and valueless.[28] Hegel hints at this view of modern science in his *Aesthetics*, writing that "the modern understanding"—centrally including empirical science—

> strips the world of its enlivened and flowering reality and dissolves it into abstractions, since mind now upholds its right and dignity only by mishandling nature and denying its right, and so retaliates on nature the distress and violence which it has suffered from it itself. (VA 1: 54/1: 81)[29]

In suggesting that modern science operates with a "disenchanting" metaphysics, Hegel has no wish to reinstate the medieval view that natural forms express a hierarchy of spiritual principles emanating from God. Against both medievalism and modern science, he suggests that all natural forms develop in line with their own, intrinsic, rationality. If Hegel seeks to reenchant nature, the reenchantment he envisages is peculiarly modern. A defining feature of modernity is the emergence of the idea of reason as a formal procedure for regulating thought, in contrast to the Platonic idea of reason as the faculty for perceiving the world's substantive order.[30] The rationality that Hegel attributes to natural forms is specifically modern, consisting in adherence to the formal procedure of resolving tensions in whatever way necessary.

My discussion of the relationship between Hegel's metaphysics of nature and that (purportedly) presupposed in empirical science has been complicated, so it may help to set out more schematically how he sees the central difference between these metaphysical views. According to Hegel's rationalist view, all natural forms (and the entities that instantiate them) are intrinsically rational, or contain a locus of intrinsic rationality: they are, in some sense, rational agents whose developments are meaningful, making it appropriate to explain those developments interpretively with reference to the rationality that guides them. In contrast, according to the metaphysics presupposed in empirical science, natural forms (and entities) lack any inherent rationality that could constitute an inner principle of development. Consequently, science cannot regard these forms as agents—as beings that actively initiate their own development. Instead, science regards natural forms merely as things devoid of agency. Moreover, in denying rational agency to natural forms, scientific metaphysics must deny that those forms' behavior has any "inner" dimension—internal motivating reasons which can be investigated interpretively. According to the metaphysics of empirical science, then, the behavior of natural forms is intrinsically meaningless and is appropriately explained with reference to external causal factors. Thus, from Hegel's perspective, modern science conceives all natural forms and entities as bare things insofar as it denies them rationality, agency, and intrinsic meaningfulness.

Immediately, two questions arise from this discussion of the difference between Hegel's metaphysics of nature and that presumed in empirical science. First, one might wonder whether, in proposing to explain natural developments in terms of reasons, Hegel is resurrecting the traditional Aristotelian project of explaining this development teleologically. Second, one might reasonably protest that Hegel's conception of modern science is somewhat simplistic. Can it plausibly be maintained that the whole of empirical science—however apparently varied or so-phisticated its theories—presupposes this rather stark picture of nature as comprised of mere things? The next section addresses these questions.

Teleology and Modern Science

In proposing to explain natural developments in terms of reasons, is Hegel resurrecting the traditional teleological idea that natural forms are purposive, in opposition to the modern scientific view that these forms are inherently inert (hence requiring explanation via external causes)? In answering this question, let us first recall that Hegel distinguishes "external" from "internal" types of teleological explanation. External teleology was popularized in the eighteenth century, particularly by Christian Wolff. This form of teleology explains the character and behavior of an entity by the fact that it serves the purposes of some other entity—as when, for example, the fact that sheep grow wool is explained by the fact that this suits the purposes of human beings (EN §245A/1: 196), or, perhaps more plausibly, God. Hegel rejects external in favor of internal teleology, according to which something has its characteristics and behavior because these serve its *own* purpose(s), which constitute(s) its essential nature. On this view, each natural form is defined by a certain intrinsic purpose or developmental agenda which organizes its behavior: for example, seeds have the purpose of becoming trees, which is realized in their spontaneous development and growth. Hegel derives this conception, which he calls the "true teleological view," from Aristotle.

Given Hegel's support for Aristotelian internal teleology, many commentators have surmised that the originality of the *Philosophy of Nature* lies in its quest to synthesize Aristotelian teleology with modern scientific theory. Recently, for instance, Ferrarin has argued that Hegel believes that principles of mechanical explanation apply only within the inanimate sphere, and must be supplemented by Aristotelian principles of teleology appropriate to organisms and species.[31] According to my reconstruction of the metaphysics underlying Hegel's *Philosophy of Nature*, though, he denies that principles of mechanical explanation—referring exclusively to efficient causes—ultimately apply in any region of nature. If his view of natural forms as intrinsically rational is "teleological," then he is extending teleological explanation to the natural world in its entirety, not merely carving out a limited terrain within nature which is impervious to mechanical principles.

In any case, Hegel's view that natural forms are intrinsically rational is best seen not as a straightforward resurrection of Aristotelian teleology but as a far-reaching reformulation of it. For Hegel, natural forms act from reasons, and so carry out developmental plans, but these plans are ones that natural forms in some sense *select* on the basis of their rationality. The plans are not just given to forms in virtue of defining their essential natures. Natural forms give themselves the agendas governing their own ongoing development, rather than being governed by these agendas as something built into them at their origin. Hegel reformulates Aristotelian teleology in a Kantian way, by contending that natural forms set up their own plans for self-transformation on the basis of their inherent rationality. His view of natural forms is therefore "teleological" only in a qualified sense: namely, that he considers those forms to develop in line with plans for action which they select from rational principles. Once again, his metaphysics of nature proves peculiarly modern, resituating the ancient belief in developmental purposes within a theory on which natural forms operate according to their intrinsic, and procedurally defined, rationality. Thus, the contrast between Hegel's metaphysical conception of nature and that of empirical science is not best understood as a direct contrast between a teleological and a mechanistic view. This contrast may obtain, but only in consequence of a more fundamental disagreement as to whether natural forms are intrinsically rational or are bare things. It is in terms of this last disagreement that the difference between Hegelian and scientific conceptions of nature must fundamentally be understood.

However, a further problem that arises here is whether Hegel's account of the implicit metaphysics of science is plausible. Can science rightly be said to share any uniform set of metaphysical presuppositions at all? Perhaps the empirical character of scientific enquiry renders it entirely open-ended in content, consisting merely of a loose plurality of hypotheses and theories that undergo constant change and revision in response to observational findings. From Hegel's perspective, though, diverse scientific theories and hypotheses all remain framed against the backdrop of a common metaphysics. Scientists may (for instance) identify different laws in response to varied experiments, but according to Hegel they always conceive these laws in the same way—as acting externally on universals that lack any inherent reason to develop. Indeed, Hegel believes that scientists necessarily share this metaphysical conception of natural forms and entities as bare things, for without this conception scientists would lack any rationale for conducting their distinctive form of empirical enquiry into explanatory laws. For Hegel, then, the metaphysical assumption that natural forms are bare things orchestrates the scientific enterprise as a whole, regardless of the diversity of its hypotheses and theories.

In foregrounding the overarching *metaphysics* of science, Hegel anticipates later continental philosophical approaches to modern science, conspicuously that of Martin Heidegger. Heidegger, too, maintains that all scientific discoveries, and practical procedures of measurement and experimentation, presuppose a prior understanding of nature, which is specific to modern science. This understanding is not abstracted from observation and experiment, but regulates in advance what can be observed and how experiments are set up. Heidegger calls modern—post-Newtonian—science "mathematical" insofar as it proceeds from this prior understanding of nature, which he calls a "ground-plan" (*Grundriß*) or "projection" (*Entwurf*).[32] According to this projection, natural things are points of mass that move in a uniform, linear, way within a uniform spatio-temporal framework. "This fundamental design of nature . . . circumscribes its realm as everywhere uniform."[33] Given this projection, experimental scientific practice must center on numerical measurement, through which portions of nature's uniformity can be quantified and distinguished. Heidegger denies that any of the upheavals or revolutions that have affected modern science since its inception has altered either its mathematically projective character or the essential content of its projection. After all, as Edmund Husserl remarks in the *Crisis of the European Sciences*: "Physics, whether represented by a Newton or a Planck or an Einstein . . . was always and remains exact science."[34] In Heidegger's terms, that is, modern science remains—across all its revolutionary transformations—a projective form of enquiry that conceives nature as homogenous and thereby enables mathematically precise measurements and predictions.

Although Hegel shares Heidegger's view that modern science operates from a fundamental projection—or, in his terms, a metaphysical conception of nature—these two philosophers differ on the precise content of this conception. Whereas Hegel thinks that science conceives natural forms and entities simply as bare things, Heidegger attributes to science a considerably more complex understanding of nature, as a homogenous grid containing uniformly moving points of mass. Heidegger's account appears preferable to Hegel's, capturing more of the complexity and the distinctively mathematical orientation of post-Newtonian science. In Hegel's defense, though, we can note that the conception of natural forms and entities as bare things remains a central and defining element of science's basic projection as Heidegger describes it. Heidegger stresses that this projection includes a new—specially modern—conception of motion.

> Motions themselves are not [any longer] determined according to different natures, capacities, and forces, or the elements

of the body, but, in reverse, the essence of force is determined by the fundamental law of motion: every body, left to
itself, moves uniformly in a straight line.[35]

So, for Heidegger, one central tenet of the scientific projection is that
natural things contain no inherent principles propelling them to change;
consequently, their changes must be explained by external laws. Although Hegel's characterization of science's metaphysics as a metaphysics of bare things does not capture all its complexity, then, his
characterization does succeed in capturing one crucial and enduring
component of the metaphysics of modern science. Hegel can therefore
plausibly demarcate his metaphysics of nature from that of science by his
rejection of the idea that natural forms are bare things, and by his support for the alternative view that those forms are agents, initiating their
own developments according to the rationality inherent within them.

Science, A Priori Reasoning, and the Rationality of Nature

Having understood how Hegel distinguishes his rationalist metaphysics
of nature from the scientific metaphysics of nature as a realm of mere
things, we need to clarify how this distinction bears on his strong a
priori method, especially his practice of redescribing and incorporating
scientific descriptions into his basic theory of nature. By exploring this,
we will see how Hegel introduces his crucial claim that his metaphysics
of nature is more adequate than that of empirical science. This claim
guides the way Hegel redescribes scientific descriptions, by translating
them into more metaphysically adequate terms.

We can first note that Hegel's rationalist view of nature requires
him to construct his basic theory of nature through a priori reasoning.
Taking it that natural forms actually develop in accordance with rational requirements, a priori reasoning is uniquely equipped to produce a
theory of the activities of these forms which faithfully replicates their
real development. In thinking about nature a priori, the philosopher
diagnoses the contradiction within each form, and then makes the necessary conceptual transition to the thought of whatever resolves this
contradiction. Simultaneously, the form in question will, qua rational,
be advancing in exactly the same way. Thus the overall theory of nature
generated through pure reason will replicate the real course of natural
development. Hegel explains this, generally, in the *Science of Logic*:
"Thinking and its determinations are not something alien to the object,
but rather are its essence, or . . . *things* and the *thinking* of them . . . agree
in and for themselves, thinking in its immanent determinations and the

true nature of things forming one and the same content" (WL 45/1: 38).[36] Thus, the rationalist view of nature implies that a priori reasoning is the uniquely appropriate method for constructing a basic theory of nature.

Strong a priorism, then, is required and justified by Hegel's rationalist conception of nature. However, essential to strong a priorism is its assessment of how far natural forms that have been philosophically derived can be interpreted as identical to forms described by science. Ultimately, here, the philosopher is assessing how far forms that have been philosophically described in terms of their intrinsic rationality can be interpreted as identical to forms that empirical scientists have described as bare things. The philosopher must ascertain when scientific and philosophical descriptions refer to the same items underneath their metaphysical differences.

This formulation, though, misleadingly implies that scientific and philosophical descriptions provide equally partial perspectives upon items whose intrinsic nature exceeds the grasp of either perspective. This is not Hegel's position: he maintains that the philosophical perspective generates *better* characterizations of natural forms.

> The philosophical manner of presentation is not arbitrary, it does not stand on its head for a while because it has got tired of using its legs . . . the way of physics *is not adequate* to the concept [*den Begriff nicht befriedigt*], and for that reason we must go further. (EN §246A/1: 201–2; my emphases)

He also insists that the metaphysical "categories" employed in empirical science are "inadequate" (*Das Ungenügende*) and so must be replaced with the categories proper to philosophy (EN §246A/1: 202–3).[37] His position, then, is that "philosophical categories"—more precisely, his conception of nature as intrinsically rational—can generate true descriptions of nature's component forms, whereas empirical science can only generate descriptions of them which imperfectly capture their real character, inadequately approximating to the accuracy of philosophical accounts.[38] Natural forms are really as philosophy describes them: they only partially resemble the pictures of them painted by empirical science, which are distorted by their reliance upon an "inadequate" metaphysics that takes natural forms for mere things. Insofar, then, as Hegel includes scientific materials in his overall vision of nature, he aims to ascertain how far the features that scientists have ascribed to natural forms can be redescribed within the framework of his rationalist metaphysics so that those forms will prove identical to the ones derived within his own theory. He aims to *translate* scientific accounts into the terms of rationalist metaphysics (and, where appropriate, to reformulate scientific accounts so that they can be so translated). "Physics must . . . work into the hands of philosophy so that philosophy can translate [*übersetze*] the universalised understanding which it provides into the concept" (EN §246A/1: 201).

Yet there is a problem with Hegel's view that scientific materials can be included in the *Philosophy of Nature* only once translated into philosophical terms. This suggests that scientific materials cannot add anything to Hegel's basic theory of nature, since he allows them into that theory only to demonstrate that they are reducible to his own terms. This leaves it mysterious why he should bother appending scientific approximations to an already complete philosophical theory. Perhaps the reasons are pedagogic: by discussing scientific material, Hegel can educate scientifically literate people up to a metaphysically accurate view of scientifically described items. He does stress that philosophy should retain contact with "ordinary thinking" (EN §247A/1: 206). Yet the idea that scientific materials function merely pedagogically in the *Philosophy of Nature* hardly does justice to the way they permeate its substantive vision of nature.

For example, in discussing the idea of space, Hegel does not say that this gives an inadequate description of externality which we should leave behind. Instead, he interprets space and externality as identical to one another and refers continually to externality *as* space, even though this name presumably encapsulates scientists' inadequate understanding of externality. Moreover, Hegel refers to several empirically identified features of space (for example, its geometrical structure) to flesh out his skeletal theory of externality. He evidently believes that scientific accounts can enrich both his basic conceptions of natural forms and his detailed understandings of their features. Oddly, then, he holds both (1) that scientific descriptions reflect an inadequate metaphysics and must be reduced to rationalist terms and (2) that scientific descriptions are, on their own terms, informative and capable of enhancing rationalist accounts of nature. How can these views be reconciled?

The answer resides in Hegel's belief in the ineliminable contingency (*Zufälligkeit*) of nature. His understanding of contingency in nature belongs within a broader account of the metaphysical status of contingency elaborated in the *Logic*. This account is controversial, affirming the metaphysical necessity of contingency in a way which, some critics believe, effectively eliminates contingency by reducing it to the status of a necessity.[39] Against such readers, I want to suggest that Hegel's metaphysics successfully accommodates the reality of contingency, as evidenced especially in his treatment of the contingency that he sees as ubiquitous in nature.

According to Hegel, nature's all-pervasive contingency arises from the protracted antagonism between its material and conceptual elements:

> The *contradiction* of the idea, insofar as it is outside itself as nature, is more precisely the contradiction between on the one hand the *necessity* of its forms generated through the concept . . . and on the other hand their indifferent contingency and indeterminable irregularity. In the sphere of nature contingency and determinability from without come into their own . . . It is the *impotence* of nature, that it maintains the determinations of the concept only abstractly and exposes the detailed expression of the particular to external determinability. (EN §250/1: 215)

Natural forms retain contingent properties to the extent that their matter remains opposed to their conceptual side. The conceptual dimension of any form always acts with rational necessity, so its development, and any alterations it makes to its material side, are necessary too. But matter is inherently nonrational, hence its initially given characteristics must be merely contingent. Insofar, then, as matter has initially given characteristics, not deriving from its relation to nature's rational element, the content of these characteristics cannot be deduced a priori. Hegel insists: "The difficulty, and in many cases the impossibility, of finding clear distinctions for classes and orders on the basis of empirical observation, has its root in the impotence of nature to hold fast to the realisation of the concept" (§250R/1: 216). Philosophers must acknowledge that natural forms have contingent features inaccessible to a priori deduction, although evidently they *can* know a priori that such contingent features are invariably present. *That* there are contingent features can be established a priori, but, just because they are contingent, *what* those features are cannot be deduced. "Each case of the impotence of nature sets limits [*Grenzen*] to philosophy, and it is the height of pointlessness to demand of the concept that it should grasp—and, as it is said, construct or deduce—these same contingencies" (§250R/1: 215).

Here empirical science steps in. Unlike a priori philosophy, science can provide information about natural forms' contingent features. Because science begins with observation, it takes natural forms up just as they are *given* (EL §38R/77) and so develops descriptions of them that accommodate their contingent features. But those aspects of scientific accounts which pertain to contingencies cannot be translated into any corresponding philosophical accounts, since philosophy as such cannot access the contingent. Only those aspects of scientific accounts which pertain to natural forms' essential features can be translated into philosophical terms. For example, Hegel claims that scientists identify it as essential to birds that they inhabit the air (EN §370A/3: 190–91),[40] a claim which Hegel interprets as corresponding to his a priori thesis that different genera are defined by their relationship to different elements (§370A/3: 188). However, scientists also describe many contingent features of birds (for example, the number and variety of their species), and these descriptions find no correlate in Hegel's a priori theory. In respect of such contingencies, science provides vital information that is otherwise unavailable to philosophy. Philosophers must therefore supplement their accounts of the essential features of forms with scientific information regarding their contingencies. Like all scientific material, this information will be couched in metaphysically inadequate terms and so, presumably, distorts the reality of the contingent features it describes. In this field, though, nothing better is available—so, perforce, philosophers must incorporate the information as it is.

Hegel thus includes scientific materials in the *Philosophy of Nature* because they provide information regarding contingent features of nature. This means that he must also retain scientists' inadequate conceptions of those forms as a whole, since these conceptions orchestrate the detailed information about contingencies. For example, having argued that the scientific conception of "space" should be interpreted as referring to externality, he must retain this conception alongside his philosophical description so as to provide access to the information about contingent features of space which this conception organizes. Only by incorporating scientific conceptions into his theory *despite* their inadequacy can Hegel characterize with suitable richness the natural forms that his basic theory abstractly describes.

In this section, I have explored how Hegel's metaphysics of nature underpins the strong a priori method that he advocates. First, this metaphysics requires him to construct his basic theory of nature through a priori reasoning. Second, this metaphysics leads him to his substantive theory of nature as split between conceptual and material elements, which entails that all natural forms possess irreducibly contingent features. Hegel must therefore incorporate scientific accounts into his theory of nature wherever possible, because these accounts enable him to learn about contingencies. In this way, Hegel's adherence to strong a priorism is a necessary consequence of his fundamental metaphysical belief in natural forms which actively develop according to rational requirements.

Nature as Petrified Intelligence

Hegel thinks it best to view nature in light of his metaphysics because this allows a more "adequate" (*befriedigend, genügend*) grasp of nature's forms. However, one might think that any theory cast in terms of rationalist metaphysics, far from being more adequate than scientific accounts, will only be fantastic and false. In particular, one might reasonably suppose that natural forms can only act rationally if they consciously entertain rational thoughts or plans. In that case, Hegel's metaphysics would entail that all natural forms are conscious—a delusively anthropomorphic view. One might therefore conclude that it is not scientific metaphysics that distorts nature's being, but *Hegel's* metaphysics. Collingwood, for instance, raises broadly this concern (about anthropomorphism) with respect to a hypothetical metaphysical position that resembles Hegel's rationalist view of nature. Considering whether interpretation can rightly be extended to nature, Collingwood argues that natural developments would have to be

> processes of action determined by a thought which is their own inner side. This would imply that natural events are expressions of thoughts . . . of minds somewhat like our own inhabiting the organic and inorganic bodies of nature as our minds inhabit our bodies. Setting aside mere flights of metaphysical fancy, such an hypothesis could claim our serious attention only if it led to a better understanding of the natural world. In fact, however, the scientist can reasonably say of it "je n'ai pas eu besoin de cette hypothèse."[41]

Thus, Collingwood believes that natural forms could only act rationally if they acted from conscious rational thoughts—a metaphysical assumption that he unsurprisingly rejects as unacceptably anthropomorphic and capable of generating only uninformatively fanciful accounts of nature.

In Hegel's defense, we should note that although he believes natural forms to act according to rational requirements, he firmly denies that they are conscious of the rational requirements from which they act. Rather, he insists, natural forms act from rationality without consciously entertaining any rational thoughts. He clarifies this during a discussion of nature within his lectures on world history:

[T]he world is governed by *nous* . . . or reason—[but] not
[by] an intelligence in the sense of self-conscious reason, not
a mind as such; we must distinguish these two from one
another. The movement of the solar system follows unchange-
able laws, these laws are its [inherent] reason; but neither the
sun nor the planets which circle around it in accordance with
these laws have consciousness of them. (VG 34/23)

For Hegel, the planets revolve around the sun because this behavior is
the rationally necessary expression of the fact that the planets are partially identical with one another and partially different. But the planets
are not conscious of their partial identity and do not intend to give it
expression in their behavior. Nor can it even be said that the planets
unconsciously follow rational requirements of which they have some
kind of (structurally inaccessible) mental awareness. The planets, like all
other natural forms (animals excepted), are simply not conscious at all.

Hegel articulates the idea that natural rationality is nonconscious
through the notion of nature's "petrified intelligence" (*versteinerte
Intelligenz*). Discussing his metaphysical conception of nature in the
Encyclopaedia Logic, he notes that the view that natural forms are
conscious arouses our rightful "repugnance" because "we say that
humanity is distinguished from what is merely natural by virtue of
thinking" (EL §24A1/56). To avoid this view, he insists that intelligence
is present in natural forms in only "petrified" form. This indicates that
the intelligence of natural forms is evinced directly in their behavior.
Their rationality has no "interior," intentional, dimension, but is immediately embodied in their self-transformations. Hegel's notion of
"petrified" rationality conveys this idea that nature's rationality is poured
out completely into its external behavior.

Hegel expresses the same idea in alternative formulations. He refers,
for example, to nature as containing "objective" rather than "subjective" thought, and he suggests that it might be less misleading to say
that nature exhibits "thought-determinations" rather than thought in
the sense of intentionality (EL §24R–§24A/56). He also repeatedly suggests that, in nature, the idea is outside itself, estranged from itself (*sich
entfremdet*) (see, for example, EN §247/1: 205). For Hegel, the opposite
of being outside of oneself or self-estranged is being *bei sich selbst*, at
home with oneself. The idea—the rationality of natural forms taken
collectively—is not "at home with itself" because it is completely poured
out in its behavior, retaining no interiority. It is entirely dispersed across
the series of deeds through which natural forms continuously metamorphose into one another. At the same time, Hegel's locution that the idea

is "outside itself" in nature draws attention to the fact that rationality still *is* present throughout nature, albeit nonconsciously.

Yet Hegel's assertion that nature's rationality is petrified does not adequately address the anthropomorphism worry: it might be countered that it is only *possible* to act rationally if one entertains rational thoughts or plans. In that case, Hegel's view that natural forms act rationally commits him to seeing them as conscious, his demurral notwithstanding. Even though he explicitly repudiates anthropomorphism, then, there remains a question as to whether anthropomorphism is actually entailed by his rationalist metaphysics. Here, I want to suggest that we *can* make sense of Hegel's suggestion that natural forms can act rationally without entertaining conscious plans—by analogy to the comparatively familiar notion that living beings can act purposively without consciously upholding any purposes. In particular, it can intelligibly be claimed that living beings pursue purposes—self-preservation, growth, and reproduction—that they do not consciously entertain. This purposiveness of living beings is (arguably) directly evidenced in their behavior and formation, without these beings experiencing their purposes consciously.[42] It might be objected, again, that we cannot coherently attribute purposiveness to beings which do not and cannot consciously entertain any purposes—just as we cannot validly attribute interests to beings that are not conscious and hence are not interested in anything that happens to them. Yet, as environmental philosophers have argued, something can be in the interests of a living being if it promotes that being's good, even if the being takes no interest in this thing.[43] Living beings can therefore have interests without consciously entertaining them. As a result, they can intelligibly be said to act purposively insofar as they act, systematically, in ways that further their interests—without it being necessary that they consciously recognize those interests as purposes. By analogy, it is equally intelligible to say that natural forms act rationally insofar as they act, systematically, in ways that rational requirements dictate—without it being necessary that these forms recognize those requirements at a conscious level.

The immediate concern about Hegel's rationalist conception of nature was that rationality can only meaningfully be predicated of natural forms if they are also identified as conscious—a view which would be delusively anthropomorphic. Hegel insists, though, that natural developments are propelled by a rationality of a specially nonconscious sort. The rationality driving natural development is immediately evidenced in the structure of the natural world—in the progressive sequence of its forms. Thus, Hegel's rationalism about nature is compatible with his denial that natural forms have consciousness or intentionality (this is, after all, why his *Encyclopaedia* demarcates nature from mind).[44] His metaphysics of nature is not a form of panpsychism—that is, he does not subscribe to "the view that the basic physical constituents of the universe have mental properties."[45] Hegel's position is better categorized as "panrationalism," where rationality permeates all natural and human things without having to exist as conscious intentionality.

Since Hegel's metaphysics of nature is not naïvely anthropomorphic, he is not obviously misguided to judge this metaphysics more "adequate" (*befriedigend* or *genügend*) than science's metaphysical belief in bare things. Still, we have not begun to see why, positively, Hegel deems his metaphysics truer to the real being of nature. Only by rereading the *Philosophy of Nature* in conjunction with the rest of his system can we identify his positive arguments to this effect. Nor should we be surprised that Hegel himself failed to provide a clear and simple statement of why his rationalist view of nature is especially adequate. The issue with which he is grappling—concerning the possibility of a viable philosophical alternative to the scientific view of nature—was not only new in his time, but still remains underexplored today. The novelty of Hegel's problematic makes it impossible for him to sum up concisely and coherently his project himself.

I have argued that Hegel theorizes nature on the basis of a novel metaphysics according to which all natural forms are intrinsically rational, a metaphysics which he contrasts to the scientific metaphysics on which natural forms and entities are seen as bare things. Hegel's distinction between philosophical and scientific conceptions of nature is important, crystallizing the possibility of a form of specifically *philosophical* inquiry into nature with the potential to ground a more sustainable way of inhabiting the natural environment. To explore this possibility further, we now need to consider Hegel's substantive arguments for the claim that his rationalist metaphysics of nature is more adequate than its scientific counterpart. His mature system contains a cluster of arguments to this effect, arguments which the following chapters try to reconstruct and evaluate.

4

TWO DEFENSES OF
HEGEL'S METAPHYSICS OF NATURE

> The metaphysics of nature, that is, the essential thought of
> what is distinctive about nature, is that nature is the idea in its
> otherness.
>
> —Hegel, *Philosophy of Nature*

This chapter begins to examine the arguments contained in Hegel's system which defend his claim that his rationalist metaphysics of nature is more adequate than the scientific conception. For Hegel, we best grasp nature's real being by conceiving it not as a realm of inherently meaningless things but as a realm of intrinsically rational forms, each developing in response to requirements of rational necessity. Hegel's system can be seen to outline four main arguments supporting this claim that his rationalist conception of nature is more adequate. The first argument is that Hegel's rationalist conception can better explain natural phenomena and processes. The second is that his rationalist conception is proven uniquely true insofar as it follows necessarily from his general metaphysics of the idea. According to the third argument, the rationalist conception is uniquely faithful to the basic form of our experience of nature. Hegel's fourth argument is that the rationalist conception uniquely recognizes intrinsic value in all natural forms, deriving from their practical rationality. In this chapter I reconstruct and assess the first two of these arguments, to be called, respectively, Hegel's argument from "explanatory power" and his argument from "systematic derivation." My assessment will be negative: even in their strongest form, both arguments ultimately prove unsuccessful.

Before turning to these arguments, we must clarify more exactly what Hegel means in claiming that his metaphysics of nature is more "adequate" than that presupposed in science—the scientific metaphysics being, as he says, "inadequate," "not adequate to the concept" (EN §246A/1: 201–3). Hegel does not mean that scientific metaphysics and the accounts of natural forms generated from its perspective are wholly false. More cautiously, he holds these to be misleading relative to his rationalist view and its concomitant accounts of natural forms. This prompts the question of whether Hegel advocates an alternative science informed by his own metaphysics. He does not, or so I will argue: he thinks that a putatively alternative "science" would necessarily abandon the empirical methodology which distinguishes science and gives it privileged access to nature's contingent features. For Hegel, therefore, empirical science should continue, but its findings should succumb to ongoing reinterpretation within more metaphysically adequate, rationalist, terms.

The Limits of Empirical Science

Hegel believes his metaphysics of nature to be most adequate in that it, alone, truly captures the general mode of being of natural forms.[1] As a result, he believes, his metaphysics can generate accounts of particular natural forms that describe them as they really are. In contrast, the metaphysics presupposed in science—according to which nature consists in bare things—misrecognizes nature's general mode of being and so can generate only distorted or misleading descriptions of particular natural forms. In suggesting that these scientific descriptions are distorted or misleading, Hegel is not saying that they are wholly false. The idea that scientific accounts are misleading already hints that they contain *some* truth, or, at least, move in the direction of truth. Drawing out this suggestion, Hegel classifies scientific accounts as "representations" (*Vorstellungen*) (see, for example, EN §254A/1: 224). "Representation" is one of his technical terms, denoting conceptions that contain a pictorial, imaginary, or metaphorical element and which are therefore only partially true (as distinguished from "concepts," which are fully true). Hegel does not see scientific accounts of natural forms as "representational" in that they simply mix truth with falsity, like oil with water. Rather—as is evident in his treatment of science and contingency—he sees scientific accounts as true insofar as they identify and describe natural forms that really exist and attribute to them many detailed features that they actually possess. But, for Hegel, scientific accounts are also false insofar as they systematically misrepresent these forms and their features, casting a distorting veil over the very realities to which they point. Although scientific accounts identify and describe many actual features of natural forms, they also misleadingly portray those forms as static, nonrational, factors embodied in equally meaningless phenomena.

The question arises as to whether Hegel's belief in the inadequacy of science's metaphysics implies that he must support an "alternative" science, informed by the right metaphysical presuppositions and capable of generating correspondingly improved descriptions of natural forms.[2] This question becomes pressing in relation to any ecological appropriation of Hegel. After all, environmentalists have often maintained an ambivalent attitude to empirical science. As Freya Mathews summarizes:

> The role of science in the environmental crisis is undoubtedly ambiguous. On the one hand science acts as an advocate for the environment, identifying environmental problems and devising fixes for them. On the other hand, even the most sympathetic science [takes] . . . the view that nature is an "object" . . . to be manipulated . . . given the ecological traumas occurring on all sides, environmentalists can ill afford the ideological purity of refusing the services of science. But even as we bow to this necessity . . . we must constantly bear in mind the role of science in the genesis of the crisis, and commit ourselves . . . to the development of a genuinely biocentric science which would aim at understanding nature rather than subduing it.[3]

Hegel's diagnosis of science is similarly ambivalent: for him, science is both necessary—to describe contingent features of natural forms—but problematic—in that its descriptions are invariably inadequate. Should Hegel therefore follow Mathews in advocating an "alternative" science that would eliminate this ambiguity?

Hegel is curiously silent about the possibility of an alternative science fuelled by his rationalist metaphysics. This silence is odd as several leading scientists of his time—including Johann Ritter (1776–1810), who discovered electrochemistry and ultraviolet light, and Hans Christian Ørsted (1777–1851), who discovered electromagnetism—tried to practice just such a new, philosophically informed, kind of science.[4] These scientists—the so-called *Naturphilosophen*, who flourished from 1780–1830—were generally followers of Schelling, conducting empirical research broadly informed by Schelling's idea of nature as structured through a hierarchy of polar forces. Hegel took a fairly dim view of this tradition of *Naturphilosophie*.[5] Admittedly, his *Philosophy of Nature* includes some approving references to findings made within this tradition, such as some of Ritter's discoveries (see, for example, EN §300A/

2: 73; §302A/2: 82).[6] Mostly, though, Hegel holds that Schelling's influence has led scientists to a *worse* understanding of nature than other scientists. He inveighs against these scientists' allegedly

> crude empiricism and uncomprehended thought-forms, completely arbitrary imagination and the commonest way of proceeding according to superficial analogy, [which] have been mixed into a complete chaos, and this stew has been served up as the idea, reason, science, divine knowledge. (EN 1: 191)

Hegel thinks that scientists, influenced by Schelling's belief in a unitary force manifesting itself throughout nature at varying levels of polarity, have sought out arbitrary and superficial analogies between different natural spheres, impeding any real comprehension of those spheres in their own terms.[7] Still, even if Hegel thinks that scientific research should not be guided by Schellingian metaphysics, he might urge the institution of a science reflecting his *own*, more adequate, metaphysics. Yet he resists doing so. Why?

Crucially, Hegel thinks that science, divested of its metaphysical assumption that natural forms are bare things, would no longer be science at all. Science, for him, is defined by its empirical method of moving from observational givens to universal forms and then laws. This empirical procedure is motivated and underpinned by the scientific belief that nature is a realm of bare things. Because scientists see natural forms as nonrational, they must find empirical explanations for the behavior of these forms—by observing, experimentally, how they change. Moreover, because natural forms are not thought to develop rationally out of one another, they must be identified and described by generalizing from observable phenomena. Thus, science's empirical method is grounded in its metaphysics—without which empirical science would not exist. From Hegel's perspective, then, a supposedly alternative "science" would not really be science at all, as it would necessarily forsake the empirical method that defines science as such. Yet this empirical method is just what is valuable about science, for Hegel, enabling scientists to learn about nature's contingent features. The loss of science (or its replacement with some pseudoscientific alternative) would therefore be undesirable, and so Hegel assumes that science should continue, which it can do only by retaining its familiar character, including, above all, its metaphysical presupposition of nature as a realm of bare things. Although this metaphysics is inadequate, Hegel thinks that the proper response to this inadequacy is not to transform radically—and so, in effect, destroy—science but instead to engage in ongoing reinterpretation of scientific findings in terms of rationalist metaphysics. He does not envisage science's abolition, but its relocation within the more all-encompassing context of a philosophical form of enquiry into nature.[8]

We set out to explore the possibility that Hegel's mature philosophy develops a critique of science and proposes his metaphysical redescription of nature as the basis of a more environmentally sustainable way of life. We are now beginning to see how his work, appropriately read, realizes this possibility. Hegel criticizes scientific metaphysics, and so, too, the particular accounts of natural forms based upon it, as inadequate in that they distort or misrecognize the real character of the natural world. This distortion can reasonably be seen as the ultimate source of the destructiveness typical of the technological applications which modern science anticipates and generates, these applications being destructive because they encapsulate and embody a metaphysical conception that is not appropriate to nature as it really is. Importantly, though, Hegel's criticism of science (and, by extension, technology) is not simply antiscientific, for he does not see scientific accounts of nature as wholly false. Rather, in defining those accounts as distorting, he sees them as partially true: they do identify and describe real features of nature, but in misleading—derationalized and disenchanted—ways. Given, then, that science has a certain degree of descriptive success, Hegel considers it a worthwhile activity which should continue, but within a transformed context which sees its findings continually reinterpreted in philosophical terms.

Hegel's vision of a future recontextualization of science within philosophy of nature can be fruitful for environmentalism. Broadly, he envisages science persisting as an autonomous activity, but not governing how we inhabit the environment. Our overall way of life—including, therefore, our way of interacting with nature through technologies—should, instead, be guided by the absolute idealist interpretation of nature into which scientific results should be incorporated. Hegel's vision acquires particular relevance for environmentalism because, as we shall see later, his absolute idealist approach posits intrinsic goodness throughout nature. So, while he thinks that scientists should continue freely to research nature from their necessarily disenchanted viewpoint, he denies that their disenchanted accounts of natural forms should be decisive in regulating our interchange with nature. Instead, for him, those accounts must be reinterpreted within the framework of a rationalized, "reenchanted," view of nature which would allow us to relate to it in a more respectful and affirmative way.

To make good on these critical and constructive possibilities, Hegel must explain *why* his rationalist conception of nature is more adequate than the disenchanted metaphysics presupposed in science. We can now start to explore the main arguments that his system advances for the greater adequacy of the rationalist view. The first and most straightforward is an argument from its explanatory power.

Hegel's Argument from Explanatory Power

According to Hegel's argument from explanatory power, his rationalist view of nature has greater power than the scientific view to explain the full range of natural forms and processes, a power which indicates that the rationalist view is more adequate (for a statement of this argument, see, especially, EN §246A/1: 202; discussed later in this section).[9] This appeal to explanatory power is unexpected: defenders of empirical science could point to *science's* seemingly unparalleled capacity to generate detailed explanations of the workings of natural processes. This apparent explanatory supremacy of empirical science suggests that, actually, science's metaphysics of bare things is the most adequate account of nature. In reply, Hegel turns the point back against scientists: he claims that, appearances to the contrary, his metaphysics can better explain many natural phenomena that produce difficulties for empirical science.

Hegel's claim must be situated in its historical context. In his time, scientists had no explanatory frameworks capable of completely and satisfactorily accommodating the many recent discoveries in electricity, magnetism, chemistry, and biology. Empirical inquiry was discovering a wealth of new phenomena, but as yet had generated no stable and comprehensive frameworks for conceptualizing and explaining these phenomena. This state of flux was theoretically reflected in Kant's dismissal of chemistry as not a science but merely a practical art.[10] More optimistically, Schelling and the young Hegel saw the wealth of discoveries as exposing the need for new explanatory frameworks to be provided by the nascent field of philosophy of nature. Hegel advances a variant of this argument in chapter 5A of the *Phenomenology*: he argues that contemporary scientists cannot properly explain life, but wrongly submit it to preexisting explanatory frameworks appropriate only to the inorganic. This implies the need for a new explanatory framework that would go beyond anything available within science to accommodate life's complexity and dynamism (see PhG 154–56/196–98).[11] The problem with Hegel's argument is that science has long since expanded its explanatory capacities to cover these fields that struck Hegel and Schelling as calling for specifically philosophical explanation and conceptualization. Indeed, as historians of science have argued, the philosophy of nature—especially as developed by Schelling's scientific followers—had a significant effect in galvanizing this very expansion within science.[12] As an explanatory project, philosophy of nature emerges as less a permanent challenge to empirical science than a source of fruitful new ideas which spurred science on to expand its own explanatory range.

To show that his metaphysics has greater explanatory power than that of empirical science, then, it is not enough for Hegel to refer to the limitations of early nineteenth-century science. He needs to identify some explanatory deficiency that will continue to afflict empirical science no matter how far it develops. He needs, therefore, to pinpoint a problem within the general *type* of explanation that empirical scientists try to provide. This, as we have seen, he conceives as a type of explanation referring to external causal laws. Starting from the assumption that natural forms are nonrational, scientists strive to explain their changes with reference to laws that propel this behavior from outside. Hegel needs to identify some flaw in this whole approach to explaining the metamorphoses of natural forms.

Hegel broaches a criticism of the scientific type of explanation in the *Philosophy of Nature*:

> The inadequacy [*das Ungenügende*] of the thought-determi-nations used in physics may be traced to two very closely connected points. (a) The universal of physics is abstract or only formal; its determination is not immanent within it, and it does not pass over into particularity. (b) The determinate content is for precisely this reason outside the universal, and is therefore split up, dismembered. (EN §246A/1: 202)

Hegel's claim is that scientists can identify universal forms within particular natural entities, but they cannot derive the features of those particular entities from the universal forms within them. This is because scientists understand these forms in a purely "abstract" manner. Part of what Hegel means by this is that scientists do not regard these forms as generating their own particular instantiations, but instead envisage them as inert. This is also why scientists have to explain the change in these forms with reference to exterior laws. If, on the other hand, one were to regard these forms as dynamic, then one could also think of those forms as actively generating their particular instantiations and hence explain why the latter are as they are. Putting these points together, then, Hegel is suggesting that thinking of natural forms as related only via external laws makes it impossible to grasp how these forms can embody themselves in particular entities. Unfortunately, his own doctrine of natural contingency works against this argument. According to this doctrine, all natural forms have a contingent, material, side, the particularity of which can only be grasped empirically. This means, though, that science's practice of taking up what is empirically present actually gives it an epistemic *advantage* when it comes to describing and explaining the particular characters of natural phenomena: in contrast, philosophical attempts to derive those particular characters from universal forms are destined to be unsuccessful.

A more promising attempt to criticize science's mode of explanation can be gleaned from Hegel's sporadic discussions of what Michael Inwood calls the "dilemma of explanation."[13] Hegel's main mature statement of this dilemma is in the *Science of Logic* (under the heading "Formal and Real Ground"). He discusses the same dilemma in chapter 3 of the *Phenomenology*, and recapitulates it in the *Philosophy of Mind* (while analyzing the understanding). The dilemma is simple: according to Hegel, explanations can be either incomplete or vacuous. An explanation is necessarily incomplete if the explanatory item that it postulates is different in content from what it is supposed to explain, because in such a case "there is [invariably] . . . a logical gap between the explanatory item and the phenomenon to be explained."[14] For example, if the transformation of one natural form into another is explained by a law that is genuinely distinct from the change that it allegedly provokes, then reference to this law cannot fully explain that change, since there remains a gulf between the content of the law and that of the change. Since the content of the law differs from that of the change, reference to the law cannot fully explain why just *this* change happens as it does.[15] Hegel calls this unsatisfactory type of explanation the "formal method of explanation from a ground distinct from that which is grounded."

Hegel then suggests that one can close the logical gap between *explanans* and *explanandum* by redefining the explanatory law in terms of the very behavior or change to be derived from it. The law thereby becomes simply the "still and universal copy"—the *Abbild*—of what it explains (EM §422/163). Yet now the explanation has become vacuous: it has been reduced to a mere redescription, at a higher level of generality, of the behavior to be explained. Hegel calls this vacuous type of explanation the "formal method of explanation from tautological grounds" (alluding back to his dissection, in *Phenomenology* chapter 3, of the "tautology of explanation," which arises when scientists define laws in terms of the very phenomena they seek to explain).[16]

In claiming that explanations can be either incomplete or vacuous, Hegel may be spotlighting a genuine dilemma in the structure of explanation. Yet, if so, he seems to be identifying a dilemma besetting any explanations whatever, not only the kind of explanation from laws with which empirical science works. How, then, can his account of this dilemma support his claim that his rationalist metaphysics is more explanatory than that of empirical science? His answer to this question surfaces at the end of his analysis of "Real Ground," where he hints that the dilemma only actually arises with respect to scientific explanations. He mentions the possibility of explanations of an alternative type, which *are* complete (*zureichend*): "none [of these grounds proposed so far] is a *sufficient* ground, that is, the concept" (WL 466/2: 109). For Hegel, the only sort of ground which suffices to explain an entity's behavior is the *concept* internal to that entity (EL §121A/190–91). What does it mean to explain something's behavior from its inner "concept"? Recall that, for Hegel, we explain the development of a natural form from its concept by showing that this form contains a locus of rationality impelling it to change as rational requirements dictate. By implication, we explain a form's behavior from that form's own concept insofar as we explain that behavior with reference to the form's *reasons* for undertaking it.

Hegel's *Logic* indicates that such explanations from reasons are unique in avoiding the "dilemma of explanation"—which by implication afflicts only other, nonrationalist, types of explanation, including the scientific. But how, specifically, do explanations from reasons avoid this dilemma? First, Hegel believes that these explanations are logically complete because the content of a reason *includes* reference to the course of behavior which it justifies. For example, Hegel explains the development of externality into negativity by the fact that externality has a reason to develop into negativity: namely, that this development will resolve externality's contradiction. Here, the reason for development incorporates reference to exactly that development which it justifies. Because the content of the development is already included within that of the reason, there is no logical gap between the reason and the development that it explains. Second, Hegel thinks that explanations from reasons achieve completeness without descending into vacuity. This is because reasons do not simply redescribe the behavior that they explain. Rather, reasons present independent grounds for undertaking that behavior: specifying, for example, that externality must develop into negativity because this development will resolve its contradiction. In this way, the content of the reason *exceeds* that of the development which it explains—providing, in addition, an independently intelligible justification for that development. It is the fact that the content of reasons both includes, and yet also goes beyond (and so justifies), that of the behavior being explained which allows Hegel to conclude that explanations from reasons are uniquely capable of being both sufficient and non-vacuous. On these grounds, he believes that explanations from reasons avoid the dilemma to which all other types of explanation fall prey.

When Hegel suggests that his rationalist metaphysics is more explanatory than science's metaphysics of bare thinghood, his point is that scientific explanations must necessarily be either vacuous or incomplete because they cannot appeal to reasons.[17] This must leave him skeptical of the widespread view that science has dramatically expanded our power to explain natural events and processes. He can certainly accept that science *aims* to explain natural events, but must regard science as congenitally unable to fulfil this aim. Nonetheless, there remains a problem with Hegel's argument from explanatory power. It purports to show that his rationalist metaphysics of nature is more adequate to nature's real being than the metaphysics of science (just as science's vaunted explanatory strength has often been thought to reveal *its* descriptive superiority). Yet, having unpacked Hegel's argument, we can see that the kind of explanatory strength which he attributes to his metaphysics is insufficient to demonstrate its substantive adequacy or truth. The explanatory power of Hegel's rationalism derives simply from the formal structure of its reason-explanations, and so does not entail that it is adequate in the sense of being substantively true. The formal structure of Hegel's reason-explanations enables him to avoid an otherwise intractable logical dilemma, but this does not show that the reason-explanations he produces truly describe natural processes of development. These explanations could be logically perfect but quite disconnected from the much more messy and fragmented world of real nature. Hegel's logically complete explanations will be true of nature only if nature really is intrinsically rational—but this is precisely what has to be established. Hegel's argument from explanatory power is therefore unsuccessful, and we must seek a viable defence of the rationalist conception of nature elsewhere in his system.

Hegel's Argument from Systematic Derivation

A second argument for the greater adequacy of Hegel's rationalist conception of nature vis-à-vis the scientific conception can also be found in his mature system. I will call this his "argument from systematic derivation." According to this, Hegel's rationalist conception of nature is proven to be uniquely true because it follows necessarily from a general metaphysical standpoint (that of absolute idealism) which has, in turn, been proven uniquely true through the exhaustive critique of rival metaphysical outlooks carried out in the *Phenomenology*. In contrast, the scientific conception of nature is not supported by Hegel's general metaphysical standpoint and hence must be at least partially false.

It is important to recognize that Hegel himself does not explicitly set out this argument from systematic derivation. Rather, that argument is implied by several prominent passages in which he attributes to his system a linear form of organization.[18] By extension, the argument from systematic derivation is also implicit in the very structure of Hegel's system, to the extent that he makes this structure linear. The problem is—as we shall see—that Hegel's system becomes untenable just insofar as it obeys a linear organization, a problem that ultimately renders his argument from systematic derivation unsuccessful.

Before considering this problem, we need to reconstruct the argument as it appears in Hegel's work. One conspicuous place in which Hegel attributes a linear structure to his system is in the closing stages of the *Phenomenology*'s last chapter (chapter 8), "Absolute Knowing."[19] Earlier in this chapter, Hegel introduces his general metaphysical conception of reality, which he takes to have been proven uniquely true via the preceding phenomenological exposition. His sketch here of this general metaphysical conception of reality is frustratingly cryptic: "that which is the essence itself, namely the *concept*, has become the element of existence or the *form of objectivity* for consciousness" (PhG 485–86/583). Or: "Mind has won the pure element of its existence, the concept . . . in this self-like *form* in which existence is immediately thought [*Gedanke*], the content is the *concept*" (490–91/588–89). Cryptic as these pronouncements are, we can make sense of them with reference to my broader reading of Hegel's absolute idealism. Within this framework, Hegel can be seen to be saying that consciousness has come to understand that what objectively exists has the same "form" or structure as the self or mind: namely, the structure of "thought" or "the concept." Consciousness now holds that what objectively exists is structured by forms of thought (collectively, "the concept"), which are the objective correlates of the subjective forms of thought that are functions of the mind. Hegel thereby introduces his absolute idealist metaphysics, which he takes to have been proven uniquely true by the *Phenomenology*, all other metaphysical views or "shapes of consciousness" having been exposed as at least partially false.[20]

Speaking from within this absolute idealist standpoint, Hegel indicates that the forms of thought which structure all reality necessarily develop through a series: "The content [that is, thought] is according to the *freedom* of its *being* the self-externalising self . . . The pure movement of this externalisation, considered in relation to the content, constitutes the *necessity* of this content" (PhG 490–91/588). To say that

thought is (inherently or by its being) "free" is to say that thought acts
from rationality and therefore repeatedly "externalizes" itself, taking on
different forms in response to rational requirements.[21] These forms exhibit
"necessity" precisely because they arise in response to rational requirements. Hegel contends that the task for a philosophical system is to
describe this sequence of forms.

> Insofar as mind has won the concept, it unfolds the existence
> and movement in this ether of its life and is *science*. In it, the
> moments of its movement no longer exhibit themselves as
> specific *shapes* of *consciousness*, but . . . as determinate con-
> cepts [*Denkbestimmungen*] and as their organic self-grounded
> movement. (PhG 491/589)

To paraphrase: having come to recognize "the concept" to be all-pervasive,
mind must trace the development ("existence and movement") of the
concept, an enterprise which constitutes (philosophical) "science," the
systematic study of the "movement" undergone by forms of thought.
Our job as conscious thinkers is to reconstruct this chain of forms,
identifying the necessity that links them.

The sequence of forms that Hegel anticipates here is first described
in the *Logic*. In the *Phenomenology*, he explains that, initially, we must
trace how the forms develop in their "pure shape": "Freed from its
appearance in consciousness, the pure concept and its onward movement
depend solely on its pure *determinacy*" (491/589). That is, the forms of
thought must be considered simply in their rational interconnectedness,
as purely conceptual structures—not as instantiated in either nature or
mind. Yet the *Phenomenology* immediately adds that thought necessarily
develops through not only this series of purely logical forms but also goes
through further series as nature and mind. Hegel offers an allusive account of how pure thought comes to assume a natural guise:

> Knowing knows not only itself but also the negative of itself
> or its limit. To know one's limit is to know how to sacrifice
> oneself. This sacrifice is the externalisation in which mind
> presents its becoming mind in the form of *free contingent
> happening*, intuiting its pure *self* as time outside of it and
> equally its *being* as space. This last becoming of mind, *na-
> ture*, is its living immediate becoming. (PhG 492/590)

Broadly, Hegel anticipates that thought, having traversed a sequence of purely logical forms, will advance into a new series of forms all

of which are specifically natural—in the sense, apparently, that they involve spatio-temporality and contingency. Hegel thus takes his general metaphysical standpoint—absolute idealism—to require a theory of how nature emerges and develops as a determinate subseries of forms of rational thought. A passage from the *Philosophy of Nature* repeats this claim:

> The science of philosophy is a circle, of which each member has its antecedent and successor, so that the philosophy of nature appears as only *one* circle within the whole of the encyclopaedia, and therefore the proceeding forth [*hervorgehen*] of nature from the eternal idea, its creation [*Erschaffung*], the proof indeed that there necessarily is a nature, lies in that which precedes it. (EN 1: 192)

So, for Hegel, the detailed account of nature in the *Philosophy of Nature* presupposes that nature necessarily exists, as established in the *Logic*. Hegel directs us to EL §244, where he repeats the claim that thought first passes through the totality of purely logical forms and then necessarily adopts a specifically natural, "self-external," guise. Of course, he does not mean that nature emerges from logic in a temporal sense. Presumably, he understands nature's emergence in the same way as the other developments that we have looked at within nature—so that logical thought transforms itself into nature eternally and unceasingly (not in a single act of creation, but in an ongoing process of generation and regeneration).[22]

In all these passages, Hegel attributes a linear organization to his system, whereby it advances seamlessly from the *Phenomenology* to the *Logic* to the *Philosophy of Nature* and finally the *Philosophy of Mind*. In attributing this linear organization to his system, Hegel implicitly commits himself to arguing for his metaphysics on the grounds of its systematic derivation. Let me explain why. Hegel believes that his general metaphysics, according to which all reality is structured by forms of thought, has been proven uniquely true by the exhaustive critique of rival metaphysical outlooks carried out in the *Phenomenology*. This general metaphysics—absolute idealism—includes the view that thought's forms pass through a developmental sequence which must exist in its pure (logical) form before, at a given point, assuming a specifically natural guise. Insofar as natural forms simply *are* ("self-external") forms of rational thought, they must be intrinsically rational (albeit in a peculiarly "petrified" way). Thus, Hegel's general metaphysics necessitates his conception of all natural forms as intrinsically rational. By implication, this conception of nature is uniquely true—it is adequate to nature's real being—because it follows necessarily from a general metaphysical standpoint which itself has already been proven uniquely true.

This argument from systematic derivation is implicit in the very organization of Hegel's system inasmuch as he makes this organization linear. His implicit argument from systematic derivation has two stages, as we can now appreciate. In the first stage, Hegel defends his general metaphysics through this critique of all rival "shapes of consciousness" (that is, metaphysical views) in the *Phenomenology*. This critique aims to show that all these non-Hegelian views are, at best, only partially true. For our purposes it is not necessary to assess exactly how the *Phenomenology* accomplishes this critique: this issue has received careful examination from many scholars.[23] There are, of course, problems with Hegel's claim to criticize *all* non-Hegelian shapes of consciousness, a claim which he attempts to support through his progressive historical narrative. Bracketing these problems, I shall for now assume that Hegel's *Phenomenology* succeeds in giving a reasonably sound defense of absolute idealism, in order to concentrate on the second stage of his systematic derivation argument. In this second stage, Hegel moves on to show how pure thought necessarily "switches over" into a subseries of specifically natural forms.[24] Unfortunately, there are severe difficulties with Hegel's attempt to derive material nature from the developmental requirements of pure thought. These difficulties are reflected in the critiques of Hegel's derivation of nature advanced by Schelling and, especially, Feuerbach. They are difficulties that can be surmounted only if Hegel's system is reinterpreted in nonlinear terms—reinterpretation, however, which has the effect of making his argument from systematic derivation inapplicable.

From Logic to Nature?

We must see how Hegel explains the step by which purely logical forms "switch over" into a natural mode of existence; this will bring out the difficulties with the account of matter that he appears to endorse at this point. Understanding how logical thought goes over into nature is difficult, though, since Hegel's account of this "transition" (*Übergang*) is, infamously, one of the most enigmatic sections of his system.[25] One commentator has concluded that: "It would be difficult if not impossible to explain the transition adequately through direct interpretation of the page and a half of text Hegel devotes to it" (namely, the closing paragraphs of the *Science of Logic* and the *Encyclopaedia Logic*).[26] Despite their difficulty, though, these texts appear on close examination to support a particular interpretation of the logic/nature transition, according to which Hegel's basic argument is that logical thought generates matter in order to overcome its opposition to matter through the ensuing process of natural development.[27]

Let us examine Hegel's account of this ongoing generative process more closely. Shortly before introducing it, he describes the emergence of a form of thought which he calls the "absolute idea." The absolute idea is itself the most advanced modification of a previously described form of thought, called simply the "idea." In his *Aesthetics*, Hegel characterizes the idea as follows: "The idea is not only substance and *universality*, but precisely the unity of the concept and its *reality* [*Realität*], the concept rebuilt as concept within its objectivity" (VA 1: 143/1: 191).[28] By "concept" in this context Hegel simply means really existing rational thought, while "reality" signifies whatever is not conceptual (or, to be more exact, is not fully and explicitly conceptual). For example, Hegel regards the body as the reality of the soul, and action as the reality of an agent's plan.[29] His claim, then, is that thought now permeates or pervades—"rebuilds itself" within—all reality. At this point, though, reality can only embrace the totality of conceptual structures. So Hegel must believe that all these structures now become explicitly configured *as* forms of thought, starting to display—or to fully and properly display—the rational interconnectedness characteristic of thought. Just insofar as rationality comes to fully pervade reality in this way, Hegel calls it the "idea," as opposed to simply the "concept." The idea signifies rationality that manifests itself comprehensively within ontological structures, rather than existing in contradistinction to them.[30]

The "absolute" idea, Hegel continues, is "the concept of the idea, for which the idea as such is the object, and for which the object is itself . . . This unity, therefore, is . . . the self-thinking idea, and at this stage, moreover, it is [present] . . . *as* thinking, i.e., as *logical* idea" (EL §236/303). Thought comes to recognize itself *as* the unity of concept and reality. With this, thought has assumed the form of a *thinker*, a thinker which reflects on its own status as rationality pervading all that really exists (that is, all reality's conceptual structures).[31] At this point—having introduced the absolute or "self-thinking" idea—Hegel moves to the *Philosophy of Nature*. He claims that:

> *Considered* according to this *unity* that it has with itself, the idea that is *for itself* is *intuiting* and the intuiting idea is *nature*. But as intuiting, the idea is posited in the one-sided determination of immediacy or negation, through external reflection. The absolute *freedom* of the idea, however, is that it does not merely *pass over* into *life*, nor that it lets life *shine*

within itself as finite cognition, but that, in the absolute
truth of itself, it *resolves to release out of itself* into freedom the moment of . . . the initial determining and other-
ness, [that is] the *immediate idea* as its reflexion, or itself
as *nature*. (EL §244/307)

This elliptical passage sheds little immediate light on how Hegel understands the logic/nature transition. However, in the *Science of Logic*, he
explains that, prior to its "switch" into nature, the idea is "still logical,
it is enclosed [*eingeschlossen*] within pure thought, and is the science
only of the divine *concept*. . . . Because the pure idea . . . is so far enclosed within subjectivity, it is the *drive* [*Trieb*] to sublate this" (WL
843/2: 572). The idea exists as thought that is unified with and entirely
pervades reality, so that everything that exists is explicitly conceptually
patterned. Yet this is not an adequate mode of existence for the idea,
because, in some sense, it fails to give reality enough scope to exist in
its own way (hence, the idea is "enclosed within subjectivity," unduly
restricted by the all-pervasiveness of its conceptuality).[32] Hegel's point is
informed by a metaphilosophical assumption: namely, that concept and
reality can be properly united only if they *become* united over the
course of an ongoing process in which they advance from initial opposition to eventual unification. Hegel regards concept and reality as intrinsically opposed to one another, such that they can become united
only through the overcoming of this inherent opposition. This assumption leads him to conclude that the idea can properly exist as the unity
of concept and reality only if it first "releases" reality into a wholly
concept-independent mode of existence to be successively transcended.
Thought completely withdraws itself from the reality it had come to
fully pervade. Through this activity of withdrawal, thought transforms
reality, which in losing its structure becomes entirely material—wholly
devoid of conceptual structuration. It is with this material state that
nature begins: at first, therefore, nature's "positedness has the form of
immediacy, of being outside the idea" (EM §384A/18). Hegel does not,
then, think of matter as being created ex nihilo: instead, the ontological
structures that compose reality become material when their indwelling
rationality entirely abandons them.

This account of the logic/nature transition converges with Hegel's
substantive theory of nature, according to which nature commences
with an exhaustively material state from which it gradually advances to
matter's unification with thought. Nonetheless, it remains hard to understand how it is possible for ontological structures that are initially
*non*material to become transformed into matter. This puzzle partly in-

forms the critiques of Hegel developed by the later Schelling and by Feuerbach. Admittedly, as formulated, their critiques are misleading, resting on misunderstandings of Hegel's metaphysical project. Nonetheless, these critiques can be reformulated to yield a more apposite criticism of Hegel.

Schelling develops his critique of Hegel in his lectures from the 1830s on the history of modern philosophy. According to Schelling, Hegel's *Logic* occupies itself exclusively with what is possible. It explains *what* things must be like if they are to be possible: for example, it tells us what causes must be like, given our concept of a cause. The *Logic*, then, is an a priori examination of the implications of concepts. Crucially, therefore, it does not tell us about the "that" (*Daß*): it does not say whether there are any actual causes, or, indeed, whether any of the concepts that it explicates are instantiated. In this sense, according to Schelling, Hegel's *Logic* embodies a "withdrawal into pure thinking"[33] and is a purely "negative" study of concepts. Schelling believes that the study of actual existence requires a distinct, "positive," philosophy which starts from the sheer fact of existence, the "that" (as revealed through sensuous representation, which brings existence directly before us).[34] Hegel's key failing, according to Schelling, is that he does not recognize this distinction between negative and positive philosophy, but tries to treat existence as itself a requirement and modality of the concept. Hegel's "withdrawal to pure thought, to the pure concept, was . . . linked to the claim that the concept was *everything* and left nothing outside itself."[35] For Schelling, Hegel's confusion on this manifests itself in several ways, including, crucially, in his trying to show from conceptual requirements *that* nature exists—a fallacious enterprise, since conceptual requirements can only establish what nature would have to be like *if* it existed. Yet Schelling continues: "Hegel so little recognised the merely logical character of the *whole* of his philosophy that he declared he was stepping outside it with the philosophy of nature."[36] Hegel failed to see that conceptual requirements cannot show that nature exists. This can only be shown, according to Schelling, by deriving nature from the pure fact of existence, the "that"—which Schelling understands, ultimately, as God, as that which gives itself to us, and which is just because and in that it is.

Schelling's critique of Hegel is developed by Feuerbach (who, along with Engels and Kierkegaard, attended Schelling's lectures on the history of modern philosophy). Feuerbach redirects Schelling's critique away from theology by identifying the "that," the fact of existence, not with God but with material nature.[37] Feuerbach writes:

> The *Logic* is thinking in the element of thinking . . . Yet the thinking in the element of thinking is still abstract. Hence, it realises or expresses itself. This realised and expressed thought is nature or, in general, the real or being. Yet what is truly real in this reality? . . . Hegel has not come to *being as being*, to free and self-sufficient being, satisfied with itself. . . . Being comes from itself and through itself. . . . The essence of being *as being* is the essence of nature.[38]

That is, in treating the real existence of nature as derivative of merely logical thought, Hegel fails to recognize that real existence is just *there*, given, existing entirely through itself, as a fact. This facticity of existence, according to Feuerbach, is its materiality, which is cognitively accessible only through sensuous intuition.[39] Moreover, this facticity is the basic characteristic of nature, which Feuerbach thus conceives as an essentially material realm.

Schelling's and Feuerbach's critiques rest on a misunderstanding of Hegel. In the *Logic*, Hegel is not merely analyzing concepts but describing really existing ontological structures. His *Logic* thus already presupposes existence, describing the real conceptual structures that it actually has.[40] The transition to nature cannot therefore be seen as an invalid attempt to derive real existence, or material givenness, from mere concepts of how nature or matter are possible. Nevertheless, reconsidering Hegel's account of this transition in light, particularly, of Feuerbach's critique enables us to appreciate that there remains a problem with his account. Hegel is trying to show that really existing matter derives from a series of pure forms of thought, forms which supposedly exist as general ontological structures. In keeping with Hegel's general understanding of rational interconnectedness, matter should be understood to derive from pure thought in the sense that pure thought actively, and continuously, transforms itself into matter. For pure thought to be able to transform itself actively into matter, though, thought must actually exist in a developmentally prior mode in which it is not materially instantiated. Yet, inasmuch as forms of thought actually exist without matter, they cannot exist as structures *of* anything, for in this mode they are unaccompanied by anything extraconceptual of which they could provide the structure. This makes it impossible to see how these forms can exist in this mode—in the same way that, for example, a shape cannot exist without some material existent of which it is the shape. For ontological structures to exist, they must exist as structures *of* matter, which means that matter must at every developmental stage exist alongside those structures (as that in which they are instantiated). In turn, this makes it impossible that those structures could generate or become matter as something derivative: since ontological structures cannot exist *without* matter, they can hardly turn into matter as a developmentally secondary mode of existence.[41] Feuerbach's critique of Hegel reflects an awareness of this problem, albeit in distorted form. His critique is informed by a reasonable suspicion that Hegel cannot plausibly treat as derivative the matter which appears ontologically primordial (a primordiality which Feuerbach understands in terms of matter's givenness and facticity).

Hegel's account of the logic/nature transition is, then, deeply problematic. Notably, Hegel gets into these problems insofar as he describes and structures his system in a linear fashion, attempting within this to derive matter from prematerial forms of thought. Yet it is precisely by giving his system a linear structure that Hegel implicitly defends his rationalist conception of nature on the grounds of its systematic derivation from his absolute idealist standpoint. This defense of his rationalist conception, therefore, proves untenable together with the linear version of the system on which it depends.

Importantly, though, the problems that we have considered only affect the linear version of Hegel's system, ceasing to arise if that system is reinterpreted as having a more complex and circuitous structure. The system is, indeed, amenable to such a nonlinear reading. Hegel himself sometimes supports such a reading: consider, for example, this statement.

> When . . . we consider the Logic as the system of *pure* thought-determinations, the other philosophical sciences—the Philosophy of Nature, and the Philosophy of Mind—appear, in contrast, as applied logic, so to speak, for the Logic is their animating soul. Thus, the concern of those other sciences is only to [re]cognise the logical forms in the shapes of nature and mind, shapes that are only a particular mode of expression of the forms of pure thinking. If we take the *syllogism*, for instance . . . [it] is a universal form of all things. All things are particulars that con-clude themselves as something universal with the singular. But it is a consequence of the impotence of nature that it cannot purely present the logical forms. The magnet, for instance, is an impotent presentation of the syllogism. (EL §24A2/58–59)

This passage is ambiguous. In part, it conveys the impression that, for Hegel, thought-forms primarily exist without any concrete instantiation, in a pure and perfect state from which they only secondarily descend into the mess and imperfection of material embodiment. But partly, too, the passage makes the rather different suggestion that the *Logic* describes forms as "forms *of* all things": not, that is, as primarily noninstantiated forms, but as forms which can only exist qua instantiated, although which are in the *Logic* considered in abstraction from any of their particular instantiations in nature and mind. This second suggestion contains the germ of a nonlinear reading of Hegel's system.

Crucially, on such a nonlinear reading, the *Logic*'s role is weakened. Whereas, on the linear view, the *Logic* describes forms of thought existing unaccompanied by, and prior to, any material world, on the nonlinear view the *Logic* only describes these forms in *abstraction* from the material world. Its underlying presupposition is that these forms cannot really exist unaccompanied by, or prior to, the material world, but only as instantiated in the material structures of nature and mind. Nonetheless, the *Logic* describes these forms in abstraction—artificial isolation—from the concrete instantiations in which they are, in fact, always found. Here the interpretive shift is from a basically Platonic reading of the *Logic*, as describing a supramundane world of forms, to an Aristotelian reading, on which the forms that Hegel describes only ever exist qua concretely instantiated. Significantly, Hegel does indeed praise Aristotle for moving beyond Plato's understanding of the idea "as only abstractly identical with itself" to the better view that the idea contains "difference and determination" within it: that is, to the view that the idea is always instantiated and thereby infiltrated by the difference of its plural instantiations (VGP 2: 140/2: 155).[42]

This interpretive shift decisively alters our view of the "transition" from logic to nature, which can no longer involve the generation of matter. The move must, instead, be from the *Logic*'s merely abstract characterization of reality's basic forms to their concrete characterization as instantiated. The transition is not ontological but in epistemic perspective, as the philosopher swings from an abstract to a concrete viewpoint. This straightaway eliminates the problems in which Hegel became embroiled on his linear self-interpretation, since he can no longer be seen as attempting to derive matter from the nonmaterial. Indeed, it is interesting to note that his *Philosophy of Nature* must, instead, be read as simply starting with the description of matter, without reference to any prior requirements of the logical idea. Ironically, the nonlinear reading has Hegel *sharing* Feuerbach's critical presupposition that a world of sheer materiality is just there, given, and furnishing the starting point for philosophical reflection. Yet, unlike Feuerbach, Hegel approaches matter from the perspective of absolute idealism, seeking to find the objective conceptual structures which are contained within matter and which display intrinsic rationality. From this perspective, his *Philosophy of Nature* presses on immediately to its analysis of the paradox that structureless matter is already entirely conceptual. Hegel differs from Feuerbach not in any failure to recognize the primordial status of matter but, rather, in taking a critical approach to matter which explores the various, largely unsatisfactory, modes of its combination with thought.

It is important, too, to recognize that, on this nonlinear reading, Hegel accords primacy not to the *Logic* but to the concrete branches of philosophy (the *Realphilosophie*). Since the *Logic* describes forms in abstraction, it can be constructed only by abstracting from the concrete descriptions of those forms already furnished in the *Realphilosophie*. Hegel must first theorize the materially embedded forms comprising nature and mind before deriving his abstracted, "logical," account of those forms. In abstracting this logical account, Hegel focuses solely upon the general character that the forms of thought prove to exhibit, over and above the multiplicity of their instantiations.[43]

The claim that Hegel's system accords primacy to the *Realphilosophie* and not the *Logic* is, of course, controversial. One might object that since nature is the idea "outside itself," one must first understand the idea in its pure guise to be able to theorize nature at all (which would bear out Hegel's contention that the *Philosophy of Nature* is "applied" logic). I would suggest, though, that Hegel's procedure of reasoning a priori from nature's initially material state enables him to identify the successive conceptual forms with which matter is mixed—where these are the forms that the idea takes qua instantiated, "outside itself," in matter. From there, Hegel can extrapolate to knowledge about the idea in abstraction from these instantiations. Even if this is accepted, though, it might then be objected that granting priority to the *Realphilosophie* does not do justice to Hegel's repeated insistence on the primacy of the concept, the forms of which are, he says, "*the living spirit of what is actual*; and what is true of the actual is only *true in virtue of these forms, through them and in them*" (EL §162R/239). Yet this claim need not suggest that the forms of thought at any stage exist devoid of instantiation or actualization. All natural and mental things could be as they are by virtue of instantiating conceptual structures, without it being necessary that those structures at any stage exist in pure, noninstantiated, mode. Thus, Hegel can consistently hold both that the concept has primacy in structuring all concrete existence and that conceptual structures at no stage exist without concrete materials in which they are instantiated.

Textually, the nonlinear reading of Hegel's system is countenanced in certain of his own comments, as we have seen. More importantly, the nonlinear reading should be preferred on philosophical grounds, since it renders Hegel's system philosophically acceptable, avoiding the problematic attempt to derive matter from nonmaterial thought. On the nonlinear reading, Hegel starts by tracing the conceptual structures immanent within matter, generating from this an account of nature and then mind, and only finally abstracting the *Logic* from these prior accounts. In terms of Hegel's more specific goal of defending his rationalist conception of nature, though, my examination of his logic/nature transition has shown that his defense of the rationalist conception in terms of its systematic derivation cannot be sustained. For that defense to work, Hegel's system must exhibit a linear construction, which, however, renders that system philosophically untenable, involving it in the abortive attempt to derive matter from pure thought. If the system is given a nonlinear and more plausible reading, on the other hand, Hegel's argument from systematic derivation ceases to apply. This argument is either inapplicable or, if applicable, philosophically problematic: in neither case does it succeed.

So far, I have assessed two of Hegel's arguments for his rationalist conception of nature, reaching the conclusion that neither succeeds. The problem with his argument from explanatory power, as we saw, is that the only sort of explanatory strength he can plausibly attribute to his metaphysics is a purely formal strength at avoiding certain logical dilemmas. This merely formal explanatory strength, however, is insufficient to establish the substantive adequacy of his rationalist conception of nature. We then saw that Hegel's argument from systematic derivation is similarly unsuccessful, as it is either textually inapplicable or entails a philosophically unpalatable belief in ontological structures that exist devoid of material instantiation. We need, however, to find good arguments for Hegel's rationalist view of nature if we are to develop the important conceptual possibilities that his work opens up, possibilities for a nonobscurantist critique of science and for a metaphysical redescription of nature that is ecologically sensitive. In the next chapter, therefore, I shall explore one of the more successful arguments contained in Hegel's system, an argument which defends his rationalist conception on the grounds of its unique fidelity to our basic form of experience of the natural world.

5

SENSIBILITY AND THE ELEMENTS

As for the ancients' general thought that each body consists of
four elements . . . it should not be overlooked that the essential
significance of these names is to contain and express the determinations of the concept. . . . It is therefore quite irrelevant to refute
these conceptions empirically . . . this way of conceiving and
determining has its driving source in the energy of reason . . .
and so is raised far above mere investigation and the chaotic
enumeration of the *properties* of bodies.

—Hegel, *Philosophy of Nature*

So far, I have studied two unsuccessful arguments through which Hegel
tries to show that his rationalist metaphysics of nature is more adequate
than the scientific view. The next two chapters introduce two further
arguments which Hegel's system offers to support his metaphysics of
nature, arguments which, I shall suggest, are relatively successful and
open up fruitful ways of rethinking the natural world. This chapter
focuses on the first of these arguments, which I will call Hegel's "phenomenological" argument. Essentially, this phenomenological argument
is that the rationalist metaphysics of nature is most adequate because,
uniquely, it allows the possibility of elaborating a theory of the natural
world that remains continuous with the basic way in which we experience nature.

Hegel's phenomenological argument is complicated, and so this
chapter must be predominantly exegetical. To anticipate, I shall analyze
Hegel's phenomenological argument in the following stages. I claim that
Hegel espouses a general principle that theories are adequate to the
extent that they retain continuity with "sensible" experience (that is,
experience which is not yet conceptual). I suggest that Hegel's commit-

ment to this principle is entailed by his ideal of theoretical *Bildung*—cultivation or education—according to which theory should neither abandon nor immediately express sensible experience but *articulate* it in conceptual form. Hegel nowhere formulates this ideal of theoretical *Bildung* fully, but it is implied by his better-developed ideal of practical *Bildung*, which is structured parallel to theoretical *Bildung* (as I explain later in this chapter). According to Hegel's ideal of theoretical *Bildung*, then, a theory of nature is adequate insofar as it articulates sensible experience of nature. He analyzes the basic form which experience of nature takes under the heading of "sensation" or "sensibility" (*Empfindung*) in the "Anthropology" section of his *Philosophy of Mind*.[1] According to Hegel's analysis, sensibility presents all objects as permeated by several fundamental natural elements—light, air, and earth—which are implicitly understood to comprise an indeterminate and volatile background against which those objects emerge and into which they perpetually dissolve. Sensibility thus embodies an experience of nature as this indeterminate milieu composed of the interacting and fluctuating elements. Against the backdrop of this analysis, Hegel's theory of nature can be seen to articulate the sensible experience of nature as elemental, for his theory characterizes natural forms as composed of light, air, and earth. Furthermore, Hegel claims that only his rationalist metaphysics enables him to develop this theory of natural forms, for—uniquely—it enables him to conceptualize the dynamism and fluidity of both the elements themselves and the various natural forms that the elements compose. Hegel therefore deems his rationalist metaphysics uniquely adequate because it enables him to construct a theory of nature that resonates adequately with our basic sense of nature's elemental character.

As this summary shows, I aim to illuminate Hegel's interest in the theme of elemental nature specifically by reconstructing how his understandings of sensibility and nature feature into a unified argument that an adequate theory must characterize natural forms as both rational and as composed of the elements. Thus, I will be focusing on Hegel's conception of the elements solely in terms of its contribution to his argument for a rationalist understanding of nature that contrasts with modern science. I will therefore ignore those places where he addresses the elements outside the context of defending his rationalist conception of nature.[2] Similarly, I will largely bracket out the complex cultural background to Hegel's discussion of the elements—with the partial exception of Goethe's doctrine of color and light, which displays particular kinship with Hegel's phenomenological approach.

My reading of Hegel, as defending his metaphysics of nature partly on phenomenological grounds, raises several exegetical and philosophical questions. Exegetically, it must be acknowledged that Hegel never presents his phenomenological defense of his metaphysics of nature as a complete, interconnected, argument. Rather, when we consider together certain aspects of his thought that are usually treated in mutual isolation, we find this phenomenological argument implicit within them. More precisely, Hegel's commitment to articulating sensibility is, as I noted above, entailed by his ideal of theoretical *Bildung*, while the proximity of his actual theory of nature to his analysis of sensible experience suggests that the formation of that theory is indeed guided, at some level, by a commitment to articulating sensibility. There are, then, textual grounds to think that Hegel did at some level consider his theory of nature—as, too, the metaphysical assumptions underpinning it—to be adequate by virtue of their phenomenological resonance. This claim will become more plausible when we survey in greater detail his conceptions of *Bildung*, sensibility, and elemental nature, and appreciate how they intertwine.

Philosophically, the presence in Hegel's system of this phenomenological argument illuminates a dimension of his thought that is generally overlooked. On one standard reading, Hegel believes that philosophical thinking requires a purely rational and impersonal standpoint which breaks with sensibility. His attention to the elements shows that this standard view oversimplifies his attitude toward sensible experience. Actually, his philosophy contains strains affirming that philosophical thought must remain consonant with sensibility and establish a theory of elemental nature which retains an experiential resonance absent from the disenchanted account of nature generated by modern science. Nonetheless, proponents of the more standard, intellectualist, reading of Hegel are unlikely yet to be convinced: we need to examine Hegel's substantive discussions of sensibility and elemental nature.

Bildung and the Articulation of Sensibility

It may sound odd to claim that Hegel defends his theory of nature on the grounds that it successfully articulates the sensible way we experience nature. This might appear to position him as an empiricist—as believing that theoretical claims are only justified insofar as they are derived from sense experience (through analysis, abstraction, or induction, as he says at EL §37–§39/76–80). Hegel certainly respects empiricism for recognizing that experience is an indispensable element in knowledge: "Empiricism was the initial result of a double need: . . . first for a *concrete* content . . . and secondly for a *firm hold* against the possibility of proving any claim at all in the field [of traditional speculative metaphysics]" (§37/76). Nevertheless, he regards empiricism as ulti-mately self-defeating, insofar as he agrees with Hume that general claims cannot legitimately be derived from merely particular sense experiences. Hegel's limited support for empiricism leads him to accommodate em-pirical findings by incorporating them into his basically a priori theory of nature, thereby acknowledging that experience is essential to knowl-edge without making experience the basis of theory.[3] So, although Hegel seeks to accommodate experience within his theory of nature, he by no means endorses the empiricist view that theories of nature must be justified by derivation from sense experience.

Hegel's phenomenological argument for his theory of nature must therefore be distinguished from any empiricist approach to its justification. The phenomenological argument turns on the idea not that a theory of nature is justified insofar as it is *derived* from sensible experience but that a theory is adequate insofar as it *articulates* sensible experience's inchoate structure. The phenomenological argument thus differs from empiricism in at least two respects. First, it presupposes that sensible experience of nature has inchoate structure. It does not consist of a disconnected multitude of sensory impressions, but of impressions given internal shape and structure through principles imposed by the subject of experience.[4] Second, the fact that sensible experience of nature is internally structured in this way makes it possible to provide a theory of nature which articulates this inchoate structure, restating the struc-ture in conceptual form. Only a theory of nature that so articulates sensible experience will count as "adequate" in Hegel's eyes. Then, derivatively, only that metaphysics of nature that makes it possible to produce such a theory will count as adequate.

John Compton has noted Hegel's commitment to a phenomeno-logical justification for his theory of nature in his paper "Phenomenol-ogy and the Philosophy of Nature."[5] He situates Hegel in a tradition of philosophers who take a broadly similar approach to nature (including Aristotle, Schelling, Husserl, and Whitehead). As Compton notes, de-spite the existence of this tradition, we today "do *not* understand by 'philosophy of nature' any inclusive, continuing or compelling philo-sophical agenda."[6] To remedy this, Compton proposes an overarching rereading of this tradition of philosophy of nature, according to which it proceeds by evoking our basic prescientific understanding of nature and then reinterpreting scientific hypotheses and theories as emerging from, and remaining continuous with, this prescientific sense of nature (for example, according to the later Husserl, our basic understanding of nature is practical and rooted in the everyday life-world, with which scientific theories must be reintegrated). Underpinning this project of reinterpreting science is an assumption that scientific claims are only valid insofar as they "cohere with and extend, but [do] not negate" humanity's preintellectual understanding of nature.[7] Scientific claims that cannot be reinterpreted to "cohere" with this understanding must be revised, perhaps even rejected. Compton's analysis of the philosophy of nature captures Hegel's central view that we have a basic sensible experience of nature which an adequate account of nature must amplify. However, whereas Compton supposes that phenomenological philosophers of nature aim to reinterpret existing science so that it coheres with prescientific experience, Hegel argues that we need a basically sui generis theory of nature that coheres with sensibility.

Hegel's variation upon phenomenological philosophy of nature brings him close to the natural scientific approach of Goethe, whose doctrine of color and light, as presented in his 1810 *Theory of Colours* (*Farbenlehre*), is premised on the belief that adequate scientific theories must remain rooted in our experience of phenomena. Goethe's *Farbenlehre* was well-known in Hegel's time, and Hegel was sympathetic to it (he reformulates, and defends at length, Goethe's account of color at EN §320/2: 135–60). This makes it reasonable to suppose that Goethe's phenomenological approach to color formed a significant background influence upon Hegel's phenomenological argument for his theory of nature. In the *Farbenlehre*, Goethe famously analyzes color as arising when light, which in itself is pure, unitary, and white, interacts with darkness. Goethe thus opposes Newton's view that white light is composed of all the primary colors—more exactly, of rays of light that can be differently refracted to produce these colors. Goethe's central objection is that Newton's theory breaks with experience, portraying colors as mere epiphenomena of a reality that must fundamentally be characterized in abstract geometrical terms. Goethe holds that an adequate theory of color (as of any natural form) must, instead, grow out of the phenomena of color as perceived.

In line with this conviction, Goethe proceeds to overview the multiplicity of experienced color phenomena and trace their interrelations, endeavoring to minimize his reliance on preestablished hypotheses or theories. His aim, as Dennis Sepper explains, is to "work through the empirical givens towards the discovery of a unifying appearance or event that can be recognized in all the individual instances."[8] Goethe seeks to elicit from experienced phenomena their unifying principles—in this case, that color arises through the darkening of white light—where these principles can be found manifest *within* the phenomena as their inner organization. Insofar as these principles are manifest in phenomena, they can themselves (in some sense) be perceived: consequently, Goethe

calls them archetypal *phenomena* (or *Urphenomena*). Rather than following Newton in constructing a theory that describes light and color
as essentially different from how we experience them, Goethe aspires to
a different kind of theory, one which articulates unifying principles that
remain concretely contained within our experience of color and light.
Theory of this kind, he believes, remains congruent with experience rather
than breaking with it. In his classic statement: "The ultimate goal would
be: to grasp that everything in the realm of fact is already theory. The
blue of the sky shows us the basic law of chromatics. Let us not seek for
something behind the phenomena—they themselves are the theory."[9]

Like all those working in the tradition of phenomenological philosophy of nature as Compton has described it, Goethe believes that we
have a basic sensible experience of nature with which an adequate account of nature must remain integrated. But whereas (according to
Compton) philosophers of nature reinterpret existing science to integrate
it with phenomenal experience, Goethe thinks that we need to work
toward a new kind of science—a qualitative, concrete, science that is
properly phenomenologically grounded at the outset, arising out of rig-
orous attentiveness to perception and experience. Hegel's position is slightly
different again. He agrees with Goethe that we need a basically new, sui
generis, theory of nature to cohere with sensibility, but, for Hegel, this
theory must be a priori and philosophical, not empirical and scientific.
From Hegel's perspective, empirical science must—insofar as it remains
genuinely empirical—be necessarily committed to the metaphysics of bare
things, and therefore it cannot avoid departing from sensibility.[10] Thus,
while Hegel endorses Goethe's program of developing a new and phenomenologically resonant account of nature, he diverges from Goethe in
believing that this program can be fulfilled only at a philosophical level.

Despite his familiarity with, and considerable sympathy for, Goethe's
program for a phenomenologically integrated account of nature, Hegel
himself never explicitly or directly presents his phenomenological argument as an integrated whole. Rather, his commitment to the phenomenological argument for his theory of nature forms a central part of his ideal
of theoretical *Bildung*. Unfortunately, this ideal itself remains somewhat
underdeveloped, the shadowy underside of Hegel's better-developed ideal
of practical *Bildung*. Generally, Hegel conceives *Bildung*—culture—as
the outcome of a process of education (*Erziehung* or *Pädagogik*), and,
following earlier Enlightenment thinkers (especially Moses Mendelssohn),
he considers *Bildung* to divide between *theoretische Bildung* and
praktische Bildung (PR §197/232).[11] Most of Hegel's reflections on
education address its practical side. Yet since he thinks the two forms
of education run in parallel, an exploration of his model of practical

education can clarify his vision of its theoretical side. As I will argue, Hegel's ideal of practical education implies that theory should articulate sensible experience, which entails that an adequate theory of nature should articulate sensible experience of nature in particular.

Hegel formulates his conception of practical education in response to what he perceives as the pressing need to overcome the socially entrenched opposition between duty and desire. This belongs within a network of fundamental oppositions which he thinks philosophy must overcome—oppositions between humanity and nature, duty and desire, self and community, and finite and infinite mind.[12] Hegel thinks that the opposition between acting from duty (pure practical reason) and acting from (predominantly self-interested) sensible desires became institutionalized with the Enlightenment, receiving its highest articulation in Kant's ethics. In Hegel's early writings, particularly *The Spirit of Christianity and its Fate*, he castigates Kant for supporting this duty/desire antagonism. Hegel famously argues that whoever adheres to the moral (that is, Kantian) standpoint is unfree, because he "carries his master in himself, yet is at the same time his own servant" (GC 211/323), punitively forcing his sensible self to subserve his rational self. By the time of his mature system, Hegel's hostility to Kant has softened.[13] He now maintains, more weakly, that Kantian *Moralität* is overly demanding, since individuals can never prescind from sensible motivations to act from reason alone, action being possible only where the agent expects some sensible gratification from it:

> An action is a purpose of the subject, and it is his activity which realises this purpose; only because the subject is in even the most disinterested action in this way, i.e. through his interests, is there any action at all . . . drive and passion are the very life of the subject: they are needed if the agent is to be in his purpose and its realisation. (EM §475R/236–37)

The mature Hegel concedes that this desire for sensible satisfaction may often conflict with the requirements of morality as specified by pure practical reason. He therefore attempts to reconcile the necessity of sensible gratification with the morally binding character of rational requirements by arguing that individuals should instil their sensible urges with rationality, so that they will sensibly desire the good rather than (impossibly) yearning to pursue it from duty alone.[14] Accordingly, in the *Philosophy of Right*, Hegel claims that individuals can only act in accordance with rational requirements if their drives undergo "purification" so that they internally concur with rationality.

> Underlying the demand for the *purification of the drives* is
> the general idea that they should be freed from the *form* of
> their immediate natural determinacy and from the subjectiv-
> ity and contingency of their *content*, and restored to their
> substantial essence. The truth behind this indeterminate de-
> mand is that the drives should become the rational system of
> the will's determination. (PR §19/51)

Drives should be cultivated to concur from within with the rational
requirements which the will "determines" itself to obey.[15] This cultivation of drives is not a matter for the solitary individual: cultivation
depends upon education by appropriately rational social institutions.
For instance, by imposing marital bonds upon individuals' sexual drives
the family cultivates them into rational feelings of love, fidelity, and
commitment. Similarly, civil society establishes an all-round economic
interdependence which cultivates individuals' originally purely self-interested desires for material well-being by infusing them with a simultaneous concern to promote the general good.

   How, precisely, does Hegel understand the social cultivation/edu-
cation of drives? He tells us:

> Education [*Pädagogik*] is the art of making human beings
> ethical: it considers them as natural beings and shows how
> they can be reborn, and how their original nature can be
> transformed into a second, spiritual nature so that this spiri-
> tuality becomes *habitual* to them. (PR §151A/195)

This sketch is ambiguous between two incompatible models of education. The first may be called the "disciplinary" model, on which education coerces individuals to suppress their natural desires and act instead
as rational social norms dictate. Eventually the individual becomes
habituated to these norms—which come to comprise her "second nature"—at which point she can again be left free to act from her desires,
since these are now ingrained social norms rather than the merely natural drives she originally possessed. In this vein, Hegel states that "in
habit [*Gewohnheit*] . . . the resistance of the subject is broken" (PR
§151A/195), and, addressing the pedagogical coercion of children in
particular, contends that: "One of the chief moments in a child's education is discipline [*Zucht*], the purpose of which is to break the child's
self-will in order to eradicate the merely sensuous and natural" (§174A/
211). He seems to assume here that children's natural desires are exclusively self-interested and so must be suppressed for the child to become

fully social. As Robert Williams remarks, his model of pedagogy here appears harshly "authoritarian-penal."[16] More sympathetically, Jeffrey Reid points out that Hegel espoused this pedagogical model in reaction against the prevalent romantic model of *Bildung* (associated with Humboldt, Fichte, and Schleiermacher) as a spontaneous, instinctually driven, process of self-development personified in the "genius."[17] For whatever reasons, though, it is evident that Hegel frequently envisages education as a process of suppressing natural desires and replacing them with internalized social norms.

This disciplinary model does not account for all Hegel's comments about education. He also speaks of education as a process which should not suppress but *sublate* natural desires: children "must learn to . . . sublate [*aufheben*] their mere individual or particular wills and, moreover, . . . their sensible inclinations and desires, [so] that . . . their will may become free" (PP §21/18). The crucial reference to "subla-tion" implies that natural desires should not be eradicated to make room for social norms, but retained, although thoroughly transformed and redirected. This opens up a "developmental" model of education different from the disciplinary model. Whereas Hegel's disciplinary model envisages natural desires being progressively weakened and finally su-perseded by internalized social norms, the developmental model envis-ages those desires being reorganized around their element of latent rationality and sociality.[18]

For three reasons, we should take Hegel's developmental model as definitive. First, it is better integrated with his picture of how modern social institutions function pedagogically. For Hegel, marital relation-ships do not wipe out spouses' sexual feelings, but draw out and rein-force the proto-rational element of mutual respect and commitment immanent within those feelings.

> Marriage . . . contains *first* the moment of *natural* vitality [*Lebendigkeit*] . . . But *secondly*, in self-consciousness, the *union* of the natural sexes, which was merely *inward* (or had being only *in itself*) and whose existence was for this very reason merely external, is transformed [*umgewandelt*] into a *spiritual* union, into self-conscious love. (PR §161/200–1)

Likewise, civil society does not discipline its members to suppress and eradicate their self-interested tendencies, but encourages them to recog-nize and embrace the adherence to the common good which is already implicit in their self-interested desires. Second, the developmental model coheres better with Hegel's understanding of the desires or passions, which he insists contain an "essential," "substantial," or proto-rational core.[19] Third, the developmental model coheres better with Hegel's overriding ambition that education should overcome the duty/desire opposition. Urging that desires should be eradicated would hardly contest Kant's opposition of duty to desire—rather, it would carry that opposition through more decisively than Kant himself did.[20]

When Hegel turns to theoretical education, he again asserts the urgent need to overcome the modern culture of entrenched division (*Entzweiung*) between reason and sense, or theoretical understanding and sensible experience. One of his best-known indictments of this oppositional culture occurs in the *Aesthetics*:

> [T]his . . . battle of mind against flesh, of duty for duty's sake . . . [now appears] as the contradiction between the dead inherently empty concept, and the full concreteness of life, between theory or subjective thinking, and objective existence and experience. . . . Mental culture, the modern understanding, produces this opposition in man which makes him amphibious . . . he lifts himself to eternal ideas, to a realm of thought and freedom . . . strips the world of its enlivened and flowering reality and dissolves it into abstractions . . . But for modern culture and its understanding this discordance in life and consciousness involves the demand that such a contradiction be resolved. (VA 1: 53–4/1: 80–81)

The parallel with Hegel's concern to overcome the duty/desire antithesis strongly implies that he must urge that sensible experience be developed, *cultivated*, until its content inwardly reflects that of theoretical understanding. Again, though, he characterizes this process of theoretical education in sometimes disciplinary, sometimes developmental terms. In one place, for example, he claims that:

> Habit is part of the ethical, just as it is part of philosophical thought, since the latter requires that the mind should be formed [*gebildet*] to resist arbitrary fancies and that these should be broken and overcome to clear the way for rational thought. (PR §151/195)

This makes theoretical education like practical education in that fancies, like desires, should be "broken" and superseded by rational thinking. Yet, more carefully considered, even this passage finds Hegel advocating cultivation conceived in developmental terms. The passage recalls an argument from the *Philosophy of Mind* (EM §409–§410), according to which education enables individuals to surmount or resist the "madness" of submergence in single sense impressions. Education does this by inculcating in individuals repetitive habits that accentuate the regularities in their experience, enabling them to detect those regularities and then organize their experiences under correspondingly general concepts.[21] These educative habits initiate a process of "building up the particular or corporeal determinations of feeling into the *being* of the soul [via] . . . a *repetition* of them. . . . the external multiplicity of sensibility is reduced to its unity, this abstract unity is *posited*" (EM §410/141). Thus, education leads individuals beyond arbitrary fancies by positioning them to articulate, in general concepts, the patterns already implicit within their repeated experience. So, just as practical education cultivates individuals' sensible desires by reorienting them around their rational core, theoretical education cultivates sensible experience by leading individuals to articulate conceptually the rational core of this experience, around which its remaining purely sensible aspects are reorganized.

Hegel's analogy between theoretical and practical education reveals that he believes that theoretical culture should articulate sensible experience rather than breaking with it. This ideal of theoretical culture entails that acceptable theories will be those that articulate how we sensibly experience their objects of enquiry. By extension, an acceptable theory of nature must articulate our (implicitly rationally structured) sensible awareness of the natural world. Hegel's ideal of theoretical *Bildung* thus already implies that he is committed to the phenomenological argument for his theory of nature. This is borne out by the substantive content of his theory, which meshes closely with his analysis of sensible experience of nature—suggesting that he strove, guided by his ideal of theoretical *Bildung*, to construct a theory that coheres with sensible experience. Let us, then, explore how Hegel's theory of nature relates to his analysis of sensible experience.

The Elements in Sensibility

Hegel maintains that sensible experience of nature has an inherent structure susceptible of conceptual articulation, a structure deriving from our activity, as subjects, in organizing our experience according to determinate patterns. Hegel describes this structured sensible experience of nature under the heading of "Sensibility" (*Empfindung*) at §399–§402 of his *Philosophy of Mind*.[22] On first reading these sections on sensibility, it is not clear that sensibility has any special connection with awareness of nature. This connection will come into view after we examine the basic features of sensibility as Hegel defines it.[23]

Sensibility features in the first third of the *Philosophy of Mind*, devoted to "subjective mind." This outlines a series of developmental stages through which each individual subject passes, each stage becoming incorporated into its successors to constitute an enduring layer of mental life.[24] Sensibility is therefore an indelible stratum in the mental life of any subject, and so defines an initial, culturally invariant, way of experiencing nature. Sensible experience of nature will inevitably become infused with divergent cultural interpretations of nature but remains, to at least some extent, an underlying and basic mode of awareness which all subjects share. Hegel's developmental approach to subjectivity thus positions sensibility as the most basic way in which humanity encounters the natural world: sensibility is, he tells us, the "immediate form of my being" (VPGe 70).

Sensibility constitutes one phase within the existence of the "soul." As we saw in chapter 2, the soul is a form of subjectivity that remains embroiled with corporeality, emotions, and sensible affections. Sensibility is a fairly primitive phase in the life of the soul, in which the subject acquires dawning awareness of the external objects affecting its body. The subject does not categorize any of these objects in general terms: each object of awareness remains, for the sensible subject, entirely individual and unique: "The sensation . . . is something singularised, contingent . . . everything sensed has the form of an isolated individual" (EM §400A/74). Not being aware of any of these objects *as* objects of a given type, or indeed *as* objects at all,[25] the sensible subject cannot identify itself in contradistinction to those objects, and so becomes completely submerged in the procession of moments of awareness arising from its body: "Through sensing man posits something *in himself* . . . but . . . he posits something in his natural, immediate, singular subjectivity, not in his free, mental, universal, subjectivity" (§400A/75). We can clarify this by contrasting sensibility with "consciousness" as Hegel construes it: the conscious subject has a concept of objectivity in general and, correlatively, an at least tacit understanding of its own status as a subject. But the sentient subject does not yet have concepts; hence, all the contents of its sensations are encountered as unique. Precisely because this form of subjectivity is preconceptual, Hegel calls it "sensibility."

Although in experiencing the sensible subject does not apply any concepts strictly speaking, it does organize its experience according to certain distinctive patterns.[26] These patterns correspond to the traditional "five senses," analysis of which occupies much of Hegel's consideration of sensibility.[27] He defines the senses as "ways of sensing" (*Weisen* or *Arten des Empfindens*; see EM §401A/77, VPGe 75)—ways of being nonconceptually aware of external entities. It is, therefore, in his analysis of the five senses that we find Hegel's account of the distinctive structure of sensibility (the way it is protoconceptual and evinces inchoate rational organization).

Hegel sorts the senses into three groups.[28] The first group embraces sight and hearing, which he calls, esoterically, "the senses of physical *ideality*" (EM §401A/77). This means, he explains, that in seeing and hearing, the subject encounters external items as fully and transparently available or accessible to it. This is what Hegel means by saying that the subject encounters these items as "ideal" (*ideell*)—it takes items to exist only insofar as they stand in relationship to that subject, being available to its inspection.[29] To support this interpretation of sight and hearing, Hegel suggests that in seeing we encounter objects as pure surfaces with no depth—"In seeing we have only a surface before us" (VPGe 77)—while hearing annuls any sense of distance between perceiving subject and perceived object. The second group of senses embraces taste and smell, the senses of "*real difference*," which "are in relation to *real* corporeality . . . only insofar as it [that is, real corporeality] is in dissolution, entering into its *process*" (EM §401A/79). Broadly, in smell and taste the subject encounters external items as becoming available to it through a process by which they give up their previous self-containment. This process is, Hegel adds, "the silent, imperceptible process of the spontaneous dissipation of all bodies, the volatilization of all vegetable and animal forms." The third group of senses comprises only touch, which Hegel privileges as the most "concrete" sense.[30] Touch is the sense of "the solid reality" of bodies, of the "other subsisting for itself" (§401A/79). Through touch the subject encounters items as resistant entities with an independent existence, such that after all they can never become fully accessible to it but will always retain some residual self-containment. In touch, Hegel says, "we find the being as an achieved contradiction, thus a being for itself against us" (VPGe 79). Although the several senses reveal objects in opposed ways, they cooperate in most instances of sensation, infusing sensible experience with internal tensions.

In these rather esoteric discussions, Hegel's key aim is to analyze what subjects are really doing when they see, hear, smell, taste, or touch. He does not consider it self-evident what is going on when (for example) somebody sees: seeing demands further analysis, which reveals it to consist in nonconceptual awareness of things as fully and transparently accessible. This analysis creates a puzzle, however: in what sense can the subject be said to be aware of something *as* transparently accessible in the absence of any concept of transparent accessibility? Hegel does not directly address this issue. He appears, in fact, to presuppose that in seeing an object, or sensing it in any other way, the subject does not categorize that object in general terms, but (to beg the question) has a sense—a *Sinn*—of that object as present in a certain mode, a sense which is not equivalent to conceptual awareness. The sentient subject indeed organizes its experience according to certain characteristic patterns, ensuring that objects present themselves to it in determinate modes, but these patterns are not yet categorial or conceptual. At the same time, Hegel must understand these patterns, embedded in the senses, as approximating imperfectly to categorial structures: unless the senses were protoconceptual, their translation into conceptual terms could not count as an articulation of their inchoate contours.[31] This understanding of the senses as protoconceptual creates a pressure to see them as fully conceptual; yet Hegel's account of sensibility encourages us to resist this pressure and retain an idea of the senses as, precisely, *senses* of objects as present in certain modes.

Assuming that we can make sense of Hegel's idea of the senses as embodying certain basic, nonconceptual, patterns structuring our awareness of the world, another question arises: why is sensible experience specifically of *nature*? Nothing in Hegel's account of sensibility yet suggests any special link between sensibility and the natural world. Presumably, the sentient subject is just aware of whatever it encounters in the world surrounding it, only some of these items being natural, while many are artifacts. Why, then, have I repeatedly said that sensible experience furnishes our most basic experience of nature, rather than our most basic mode of experience of any external entities whatever? Hegel himself links sensibility to nature in several comments, referring, for example, to "the idealisation which the things of *external* nature undergo in being sensed" (EM §400A/74). He adds: "The general modes of sentience are related to the physical and chemical determinacies of the natural, the necessity of which must be demonstrated in the philosophy of nature" (§401A/77). Why does Hegel postulate this intimate connection between sensibility and natural forms or qualities? Crucially, he is not claiming that sensibility involves experience of nature in the sense of involving awareness of exclusively those items in the outer world which are natural (that is, nonartifactual). His is a significantly different claim: that the way in which the subject is sensibly aware of things—via the five senses—is a way of being aware of things *as* natural. That is, in being aware of things according to the senses, the subject is aware of those things according to a determinate sense of nature, a specific protoconceptual understanding of nature. This is an intriguing claim. To see what it means, we need to reexamine Hegel's analysis of sensibility, attending to his claim that experience structured by the five senses inherently embodies a sense of the natural elements: light, air, and earth.

Hegel deploys this argument most clearly apropos of sight. He suggests that, in being aware of something through sight, and hence in being aware of that object as fully accessible, the subject is casting that object in a certain light, imposing upon the object as it presents itself a texture of accessibility and transparency which pervades and suffuses how it appears. We can grasp this by analogy to conceptually structured awareness of objects: in being aware of something as an instance of some general type, one applies a concept which shapes the whole way that the object presents itself: conceptual awareness entirely organizes how things present themselves to us. Analogously, in sensing, the subject invests the objects of its experience with a pervasive texture or quality. In seeing, the subject invests the object with a texture of transparent openness, or full availability to inspection. Hegel maintains that this quality just is equivalent to light, which he defines as "the pure being-manifested of objects for us" (VPGe 77). He states that "sight is the sense of that physical ideality which we call light . . . It is only with this ideal element [ideellen Elemente] . . . that sight has to do" (EM §401A/78). To see objects is to be aware of them as illuminated, pervaded with a quality or texture of light.[32] Hegel refers to this quality of light as the "medium" or "element" of seeing. So, to say that light is the "element" of seeing is to say that it is a kind of glow or aura in which seeing constitutively bathes its objects of awareness.

Hegel indicates how the other senses, too, invest the objects of experience with elemental qualities. Hearing infuses objects with sound or sonority, which Hegel defines as the quality of pure self-revelation (active self-revelation as distinct from the passive transparency of light). He relates smell and taste to air. To be aware of bodies as self-dissipating is to be aware of them as located within the air, pervaded by air that passes through them, provoking their gradual dissolution. Explaining this in the Philosophy of Nature, Hegel says that air is:

> [T]he unnoticed but insidious and consuming power over the individual . . . the destruction . . . slinks in everywhere . . . just as reason insinuates itself into the individual and dissolves it. Consequently, air gives rise to odours; for odour is only this invisible, ceaseless process of what is individual with air. (EN §282–§282A/2: 36–37)

Taste and smell thus sense objects as porous and aerated, surrounded and pervaded by the corrosive air that percolates through them. Finally, touch is the sense of "earthy totality" (EM §401A/79), the sense of objects as belonging to the earth. Tactile awareness of things as resistant and independent involves a sense of them as part of the earth. Somewhat speculatively, we might say that for Hegel the objects of touch are understood to imbibe their self-contained resilience from the earth. It would then be this resilient quality which Hegel calls "earthiness" (*Erdigkeit*),[33] a quality which he takes to pervade all objects of touch.[34]

Subjects are generally aware of objects through several senses at once, and the interplay between their elements generates further qualities in experience, most saliently color. The sense of color arises, Hegel suggests, from the interplay of the quality of earthiness, which involves darkness, with the quality of transparent illumination (EM §401A/78).[35] More generally, we can think of the sentient subject as locating the objects of its awareness within a kind of elemental milieu, arising through the confluence of the several elements.

This idea of an elemental milieu invites comparison with the *Gestalt*-psychological concept of the "dispositional field," recently analyzed by Richard Boothby. He refers to Monet's quest to paint what he called the *enveloppe* suffusing individual objects, an *enveloppe* composed of elements of light and air that surround and pervade these objects.[36] Boothby defines this *enveloppe* as an "encompassing field of illumination that conditions all appearance" of objects.[37] He draws out two features of this "dispositional field" that are relevant to Hegel's analysis of sensibility. First, the field is not itself directly perceptible: individuals do not see light, but only what light renders visible. If light is the "element" of seeing, this light is never the direct object of attention but a background presence coloring and qualifying what is seen. Likewise, Hegel denies that the elements are direct objects of sensible awareness. Sight is the sense of light, but the one who is seeing does not see light as such: "Light manifests something else,—this manifesting constitutes its essence" (EM §401A/78). Hence light is, precisely, the medium or *element* of seeing, not its object.[38] Second, Boothby points out that because perception works by locating objects in a dispositional field, objects are never perceived as entirely discrete. Not being a direct object of perception itself, the dispositional field has no determinate boundaries, so that in pervading perceived objects it muddies their boundaries, interconnecting them. Again, Hegel agrees that insofar as the sentient subject bathes its objects in a common elemental milieu, it blurs the boundaries between those objects. Light, for example, is "abstract identity with self, the opposite of nature's externality emerging within nature itself" (§401A/78), so its presence introduces unity into the objects it suffuses.

In general, then, Hegel's view is that sensibility involves awareness of objects as pervaded by elemental qualities which, together, compose an indeterminate and volatile background against which those objects appear. We can now see why Hegel believes sensibility to involve a sense of nature. Because sensibility involves the sense of the natural elements of light, air, and earth, it necessarily embodies a sense of nature as a whole as the milieu constituted of the interplay between these several elements. Hegel thus defines sensible awareness as awareness of nature not because he thinks that the sentient subject encounters only those external entities which are natural, but because he thinks that it encounters all entities *as* located within nature, belonging to the terrain of the natural elements. Hegel's novel claim is that the most basic way in which we experience things is by experiencing them *as natural*, according to a preconceptual sense of nature as an elemental background to experience. Whatever additional cultural interpretations of nature (and, indeed, of artifice) individuals may imbibe, Hegel thinks that they start from a deep-lying sense of nature as elemental, as a complex and fluctuating interplay between accessibility and self-containment which suffuses objects and blurs their boundaries.

Hegel's account of sensibility may appear bizarre, but when thought over it does seem, in general terms, to capture certain features of our experience which might plausibly be seen as deep-lying and pretheoretical. Specifically, Hegel captures the sense of things as enfolded within what Monet called the *enveloppe*, an *enveloppe* composed of light, air, and earth. There is something suggestive in Hegel's idea that these elemental qualities are bound up with complex patterns of accessibility and hiddenness in things. His idea, too, that we are basically aware of things *as* natural has some plausibility: this could help to make some sense of individuals' frequently attested feeling of retaining—or being brought back into—contact with some deep-seated part of themselves through prolonged or intense contact with nature. Idiosyncratic as Hegel's analysis of sensibility might look, there are reasons to give it serious consideration as an account of the basic form of human experience of the world, even if we do not accept this analysis in detail.

I have argued that Hegel sets out to provide a theory of the natural world that articulates how we are sensibly aware of it. Having explored his analysis of sensibility in the *Philosophy of Mind*, we can see that it is this sensible experience of nature as elemental that Hegel thinks an adequate theory of the natural world must articulate. We can now explore how his theory of nature, respecting this constraint, tries to articulate an idea of the natural world as an essentially "elemental" terrain.

The Physical Elements in Nature

In the *Philosophy of Nature* Hegel proposes to articulate the sensible experience of nature as elemental by allocating a pivotal role in the composition of the natural world to the elements (*die Elemente*). He provides a description of these elements, attributing to each of them the same basic characteristics that they have in sensibility, but extending and developing his analysis of these characteristics. He also outlines how these elements become qualities belonging to all natural bodies, yet continually undermining their distinctness, driving those bodies to modify their elemental qualities in increasingly far-reaching ways in the effort to preserve some individuation. As Hegel sums up, "the determinations of the *senses* have an earlier existence [1] as properties of *bodies* and [2] still more freely as elements" (EM §380/7). In this way, Hegel's conception of the place of the elements in the *Philosophy of Nature* articulates sensible experience into a conceptual, coherently integrated, theory of natural development.

Hegel introduces the elements in the second main stage of natural development, the "Physics." In particular, the elements belong in the first phase of physical development, the "physics of universal individuality" (in the text's first edition, simply "elemental physics"). During this phase, Hegel describes various physical qualities that are not yet attached to individual bodies as properties, but are connected to the planet earth as a whole, remaining amorphous and indeterminate. He calls these "the immediate, free, physical qualities" (EN §273/2: 9). These amorphous qualities are equated with the physical elements, which make up the terrestrial atmosphere. Adhering to tradition, Hegel numbers four such elements: air, fire, water, and earth. Turning first to air, he assigns it the same character it had in sensibility: it is an insidious power of destruction eating away all bodies (§282/2: 35–36). Hegel then explains that fire and water must be understood as modifications *of* air. The corrosive, destructive, character of air must realize itself fully, at which point air transforms into fire: "Fire is air *posited* as *negative* universality or self-relating negativity" (§283/2: 38). Having then realized its ferocity, air-become-fire sinks back into a relatively neutral and passive state, becoming water (§284/2: 39–40). Air endlessly becomes fire and water before returning to existence as air, obeying a transformative cycle which Hegel identifies with meteorological processes. The fourth element, earth, is different from the other three, as it is not a modification of air. Instead, earth—or more precisely earthiness, *Erdigkeit*—is the "element of *developed* difference and *individual* determination" (§285/2: 41). Earthiness, it appears, is a quality that embodies the general nature of individuation and separateness.

Hegel has not included light among these four elements. This is because he classifies light not as a physical "element" but an immediate physical "quality"—a still more primitive form diffused throughout the entire universe. As we have seen, Hegel basically understands light as the quality within the cosmos that manifests the identity of all bodies through its perfect homogeneity and self-identity. However, light must also be considered in relation to the darkness of the individual planets, to which it is opposed. In the context of this relationship, light takes on the different guise of a quality that penetrates the darkness of the earth, rendering it manifest. Hegel concludes that light has become air, given that, for him, air is just what seeps through bodies to break down their self-containment and render them accessible. For him, air is a transformation of light:

> The element of undifferentiated simplicity [that is, air] is no longer the positive identity with self, the self-manifestation, which *light* as such is; it is only *negative universality* . . . [air is] directly active against the individual, is active and effective identity, whereas light was only abstract identity. (EN §282–§282A/2: 35–36)

Light becomes air when it enters into an antagonistic relationship with individual bodies; because light is so close to air, Hegel tends to discuss it, after all, as one element among the others, remarking, for instance, that: "Light kindles the process of the elements, stimulates it, governs it generally" (§281A/2: 33).

Hegel's view of the physical elements is arcane from a modern standpoint. But let us bear in mind that he seeks, above all, to articulate what he sees as the sensible *experience* of the elements.[39] Hegel is striving to accommodate humanity's (allegedly) basic sense that light renders individual objects manifest, that air corrodes their separateness, and that earthiness marks things out as still self-contained. He also tries to accommodate the sense that these all-pervasive elements are not themselves objects with clear boundaries, but rather are indeterminate and nebulous "physical qualities." This same concern to articulate sensibility informs his account of how the elements come to pervade and structure all natural bodies, which occupies the rest of the "Physics."

The elements, Hegel explains, are not only diffused throughout the atmosphere, but also become qualities of each individual body (EN §289/2: 54). This gives rise to a process of "the reconstruction and transformation of the physical elements through individuality. The individual body, that which is earthy, is the unity of air, light, fire, water; and the way in which they are in it constitutes the specification of individuality" (§316A/2: 117). As qualities of individual bodies, the elements take on a form different from that which they had as diffuse atmospheric forces. Individual bodies are inherently dark, so the quality of transparency or illumination that they assume gets darkened into a color. The airiness which these bodies take on gradually dissipates them, giving them smell and taste. Bodies also adopt the quality of earthiness as the embodiment of their individuation.

Although the elements are modified in becoming properties of bodies, they retain their initial indeterminacy and therefore undermine the discreteness of the bodies to which they belong. Hegel obliquely explains: "These determinations [for example, color and smell], as properties of bodies, directly relate to the universal elements, and this is the beginning of their dissolution. The power of the universal is an oppositionless penetration and infection" (EN §322A/2: 164). The elements introduce homogeneity among bodies, in response to which they reassert their separateness by further altering and qualifying their elemental properties (empirically, through chemical processes). The overall result is that bodies differentiate themselves increasingly sharply against their elemental backgrounds by investing their qualities with peculiar characteristics, up to the point where these bodies finally acquire the form of fully individuated organisms. The elements do not now disappear from the *Philosophy of Nature*, but they remain operative within life in only a subordinate manner.

Hegel's whole account of nature, and especially of its central physical stage, is structured to articulate our sensible experience that the physical elements compose a volatile milieu in which bodies are located. As Hegel himself remarks of his descriptions of elemental properties, they "recall sensibility [*sinnliche Empfindung*] . . . since they denote not merely physical properties belonging objectively to bodies, but also subjectivity, namely the being of these properties for the subjective sense [*Sinn*]" (EN §316A/2: 118). Thus, Hegel always intends his account of the place of the elements in nature to retain this coherence with sensible experience.[40]

However, Hegel's aim to articulate sensibility seems problematic in light of his commitment to theorizing nature using what I have called the strong a priori method. According to the strong a priori method, it appears that Hegel must include discussions of light, air, and earth within his overall picture of nature only insofar as he can construe them as the empirical analogues of forms that he has deduced a priori and described in correspondingly sui generis terms. For instance, according to strong a priorism he must include light only because he interprets it as identical to a form that he has already deduced and described in sui generis terms as a completely homogeneous quality manifesting the identity of all bodies.[41] Similarly, he must include air only after interpreting it as identical to a quality that actively opposes itself to individuated materials. Hegel does often seem to include the elements on this merely interpretive—and so, presumably, provisional—basis. For example, he states that: "The element of undifferentiated simplicity . . . [is] a fluidity which penetrates everything,—*air*" (EN §282/2: 36); "The elements of opposition are, first, being-for-self . . . posited as a moment of individuality, as its unrest existing for itself,—*fire*" (§283/2: 38). In both these cases, Hegel introduces his sui generis description of the form before affirming its identity with air or fire as empirically described. It seems, then, that the elements cannot feature in Hegel's basic theory, but can only be contingent, eliminable, accretions to that theory. Yet this suggests that Hegel's theory of nature cannot be said, after all, to articulate the sensible experience of it as elemental, since that theory refers to the elements only contingently, not essentially.

Nonetheless, although Hegel includes the elements in his account on an interpretive basis, they are not eliminable from the text as are the other empirically described forms that enter into his picture of nature. The elements have special status, because the experience of nature as elemental is inherent in all sensible awareness (as the most basic pattern structuring any external awareness). In contrast, all the other empirical materials included in the *Philosophy of Nature* are scientific descriptions and hypotheses that are subject to continual revision and amelioration. Consequently, those materials can only be incorporated provisionally, whereas the sensible experience of elemental nature, being invariant, can only be incorporated on a final basis. For instance, insofar as light can be interpreted as identical to "pure manifestation," this interpretation must be final, since the sensible experience of light will never change or be revised. Light and the other elements therefore feature necessarily, not contingently, within Hegel's *Philosophy of Nature*, such that reference to sensible experience *is* an ineliminable aspect of his account of nature. Consequently, Hegel's strong a priori approach does not contradict his claim to provide a theory of nature that is phenomenologically adequate.

By virtue of the phenomenological coherence of his theory, Hegel considers it more adequate than competing scientific accounts, as he stresses in assessing the modern scientific view that the physical elements are reducible to more basic chemical components. It may seem surprising that Hegel chooses to reinstate the ancient idea of the four elements at all, since this was rapidly becoming anachronistic in his own time (the period 1770–1831 witnessed the classification of most of the basic chemical elements such as oxygen, hydrogen, and potassium). Nonetheless, he deliberately rejects the view that the "physical" elements can be broken down into chemical components:

> In dealing with the physical elements, we are not in the least concerned with elements in the chemical sense. The chemical standpoint is certainly not the only one, but only a particular sphere with no right whatever to extend itself to other forms as if it were their essence. (EN §281A/2: 35)

Hegel indicates that the advantage of his view that the four physical elements are more fundamental than the elements revealed in chemical analysis is that his view remains continuous with our basic, sensible, experience of things as permeated by light, air, and earth, whereas a chemical analysis of things breaks with this experience. The "concept of a *physical* element . . . is [the concept of] a real matter, not yet dissipated into a chemical abstraction" (§281R/2: 33). The idea of the physical elements remains continuous with the "real matter" of concrete sensible experience, unlike the idea of basic chemical elements, which is "abstracted," artificially separated, from experience.[42]

Hegel concludes, then, that his theory of nature is unique in the way it articulates sensible experience, and that this renders it more adequate than any competing theory. In particular, he takes his theory of nature to be more adequate than modern scientific theories which view the physical elements as reducible to chemical constituents. In this respect, scientific theories break with sensible experience, rendering themselves inadequate. Presumably, though, this must be because scientific theories are somehow forced to break with experience by their underlying metaphysics, according to which natural forms are bare things. Conversely, it must be Hegel's rationalist presupposition that allows his theory to grasp nature's elemental character. Having seen how Hegel theorizes nature as fundamentally elemental, then, we must now ask how his rationalist metaphysics of nature enables him to construct this theory.

Rationality and Dynamism in Elemental Nature

Hegel has argued that his theory of nature is unique in the way it articulates sensible experience and that this renders it more adequate than any competing theory. In particular, he suggests, empirical science cannot generate a similarly adequate theory, because it works from a metaphysics according to which all natural forms are mere things and not in themselves rational. Hegel maintains that he can develop his phenomenologically adequate theory only through his alternative metaphysics, according to which all natural forms are intrinsically rational. He thus considers this rationalist conception of nature uniquely adequate because it allows him to formulate this theory. In this connection, he makes two specific arguments (these arguments are not fully explicit, but are implicit in some comments that Hegel makes in the *Philosophy of Nature*). First, he suggests that his rationalist conception enables him to conceptualize the elements in a phenomenologically appropriate way as indeterminate, mutable, and dynamically interrelated. Second, he suggests that his rationalist conception allows him to conceptualize bodies as struggling to individuate themselves both through and against the elements and so to accommodate our basic sense that the elements both pervade objects of experience and introduce indeterminacy into them. Let us consider these arguments in turn.

Hegel believes that we must conceptualize the elements as developing out of one another, or as, in his phrase, undergoing a ceaseless "transmutation . . . into one another" (EN §286A/2: 44). Only thus can we accommodate our sense that the elements are not stable objects but shadowy media which shade indeterminately into one another. Now, Hegel argues that we can only conceptualize the elements as transmuting into one another if we regard them as intrinsically rational. Unlike the chemical elements which "are quite heterogeneous to one another . . . [t]he physical elements . . . are universal matters particularized solely according to the moments of the concept" (§281A/2: 35). That is, each physical element adopts the form or mode of existence (the "particularization") that is required by rational necessity (the "concept") in the sense that it resolves the tension in the preceding element. By regarding the elements as intrinsically rational, then, we can understand how they develop into one another. In contrast, empirical science does not believe in nature's intrinsic rationality and therefore cannot grasp that its forms develop internally. This forces scientists to theorize the elements as chemical rather than physical: they see the qualities of bodies as inherently static, changing into one another only through external laws, and hence grasp these qualities as, precisely, chemical elements, defined by their essential separation from one another. Or, as Hegel puts it, lacking a rationalist metaphysics, scientists end up adopting "the fixed representation of the substantial and unalterable *variety* of the elements, a representation carried over by the understanding from the processes of *singularised* materials and once and for all established . . . which not only pushes aside the concept . . . Above all, *experience* itself is pushed aside [in this view]" (§286R/2: 43).

Hegel also maintains that his rationalist metaphysics enables him to conceptualize bodies as individuating themselves *against* their elemental background, and hence to accommodate our sense of bodies as both pervaded and rendered unstable by this background. When bodies incorporate elements as their qualities, this provokes the dissolution of those bodies, so that they can persist only by altering their elemental qualities to sever them from their context. Hegel alleges that we can only understand this activity of alteration if we see bodies as intrinsically rational and so driven to respond rationally to the tension that their possession of elemental qualities has introduced into them (namely, the tension that these qualities precipitate the dissolution of the bodies). Without the metaphysics of intrinsic rationality, Hegel contends, scientists cannot understand how bodies gradually attain individuation, and they assume that this individuation is a self-evident given. This assumption is, indeed, embedded in the scientific metaphysics according to which natural entities are bare things, sheer individual items. Science, Hegel concludes, feels too "much compassion for matter . . . if it wishes to proceed purely empirically, it must admit that matter passes away" into the elements (EN §282A/2: 37). Once again, Hegel thinks that only his rationalism permits the construction of a theory of nature that articulates our sense of the dynamic struggle through which its component bodies individuate themselves.

According to Hegel, any theory that articulates sensibility must be constructed on the basis of the rationalist metaphysics of nature. Only on this basis can we comprehend the dynamism of the elements and the volatility of elementally located natural bodies. By contrast, scientific accounts, embodying a metaphysical conception of nature as a realm of bare things, must regard both elements and bodies as firmly bounded items in a way that breaks with, or in Hegel's phrase "pushes aside," sensibility. In his view, this makes his rationalist metaphysics of nature adequate, as its scientific competitor is not.

Evaluating Hegel's Phenomenological Argument

Hegel has argued that his rationalist metaphysics is most adequate in that it uniquely enables him to develop a phenomenologically adequate theory of nature, which remains appropriately faithful to sensible experience. However, it is unclear why this fidelity to sensibility should make Hegel's theory—or, derivatively, his rationalist metaphysics—adequate in the sense of being true to nature's real being. Certainly, a theory which stays attuned to our sensible experience is likely to enhance *our* well being as humans, eliminating the harmful opposition of understanding to sensibility which renders us "amphibious," in Hegel's phrase. The cultural diffusion of such a theory would foster a social world in which humans can be, and feel, at home, promoting a climate of reconciliation (*Versöhnung*) rather than alienation (*Entfremdung*).[43] Hegel's vision of a more habitable culture that articulates sensibility instead of repressing it is attractive. Still, this does not prove that theories that articulate sensibility are more true to nature's real being. Indeed, defenders of science may argue that such theories are necessarily *less* true to nature's real being, because the deep-rooted sense of nature that they articulate is suffused with naïve and uncritically anthropomorphic projections. From this perspective, it is precisely science's empirical methodology, relying centrally on experimentation and intersubjective criticism and confirmation, which allows us to break with these distorting projections and gain a more accurate grasp of how nature objectively is. Hegel needs to explain why congruence with sensibility should be thought to render his theory adequate rather than distorting and chimerical.

In particular, Hegel needs to show that humanity's basic form of awareness of the natural world, as embedded in the senses, is veridical.[44] He must show that this form of awareness puts us in contact with objective structures or patterns that really obtain in nature (where these structures are not only the elements but also the objective processes of self-qualification and individuation that natural bodies undergo). If sensible experience can be shown to be essentially veridical in this way, then the conceptual articulation of its basic contours will count, precisely, as articulating its veridical element and so generating a theory of nature that is adequate in the sense of being substantively true. Hegel does gesture toward the idea that sensibility is essentially veridical by suggesting that the structures of which sentient subjects are basically aware have already been demonstrated to exist in the *Philosophy of Nature* (see EM 401A/77). This argument is circular, though, since Hegel's theory of nature is itself supposed to be made adequate by its prior consonance with sensible experience.

Hegel's *Philosophy of Mind* also hints at a different line of argument, which, although not fully developed, appears more promising. Its basic thought is that human individuals have emerged from nature (as Hegel stresses at EM §381/8) and that, consequently, their basic form of experience of nature necessarily connects with how nature really is. More specifically, Hegel's idea is that because we have emerged from nature, the system of our senses arises as a recapitulation of preexisting patterns that objectively structure various natural forms. "The different determinations which we have seen in inorganic nature are also diversified ways in which what is organic relates to the inorganic, [that is, these exist] as modifications of sentience, and for precisely this reason they are called senses" (EN §357A2/3: 137).[45] So, the system of our senses is structured in parallel to objective natural forms. Accordingly, insofar as this system is a structured cognitive system, it constrains us to perceive these objective natural forms as having essentially the structure that they actually do possess.[46] Hegel can hardly be said to have fully worked out this argument for the veridical character of sensibility. Nonetheless, his basic idea—that the human senses are continuous with nature and that this continuity means that the senses are constrained (at least in broad terms) to represent nature as it really is—seems plausible and potentially fruitful.

Since this argument for the veridical character of sensible experience is insufficiently developed, Hegel's phenomenological argument for his rationalist metaphysics of nature remains somewhat inconclusive. At best, we can conclude that his idea that sensibility must be essentially veridical because it emerges from nature is promising and that we should therefore look favorably on his overall phenomenological argument. As part of this, then, we should look favorably on his idea that science is problematically detached from sensible experience of nature, toward which it directs an inappropriate skepticism. By separating their accounts of nature from sensibility, scientists render those accounts inadequate, on Hegel's view.[47] Yet scientists are constrained into this by their metaphysical presupposition that nature is a realm of bare things. This presupposition forces scientists to attribute to particular natural forms a degree of inertia and separateness that is not present in those forms qua objects of sensibility. The inadequacy of scientific accounts, then, stems fundamentally from their underlying metaphysics, which wrongly "pushes aside" sensibility.

Although Hegel's phenomenological argument remains incomplete, then, I suggest that it does at least have positive possibilities for further development. When read as advancing this phenomenological argument, Hegel's work begins to realize its potential for criticizing modern science and proposing an alternative, specifically philosophical, redescription of nature with greater ecological sensitivity. Hegel criticizes modern science on the grounds that it presupposes an inadequate conception of nature as a realm of bare things, a conception that breaks with our basic sense of natural forms as fluid, dynamic, and elemental. Hegel assumes that this basic experience is essentially veridical, so that, in cutting itself off from sensibility, scientific metaphysics renders itself inadequate, incapable of generating accounts that are true to nature's real, elemental, mode of being. This inadequacy infects, in turn, the technological applications which scientific accounts anticipate, ensuring that these applications will tend also to be inappropriate and destructive.

Hegel's solution to these problems is to urge that scientific accounts become incorporated into his own theory of nature, a theory that remains more faithful to sensibility, emphasizing nature's dynamic and elemental character. This greater adequacy of the theory stems from its organization around the underlying metaphysical conception that all natural forms are intrinsically rational. For Hegel, this conception is more adequate than the metaphysics presupposed in science precisely because it enables him to articulate sensibility—to conceptualize nature's elemental fluidity and dynamism in terms of its intrinsic rationality. Through this phenomenological argument, Hegel can support his claim that his metaphysics of nature is more adequate—truer to nature's real, elemental, mode of being. This implies, furthermore, that Hegel's metaphysical redescription of nature could make possible correspondingly more appropriate, and less harmful, ways for us to inhabit and respond to the natural environment.

As we can see, there is ecological potential in Hegel's vision of a future in which our interchange with nature would be regulated by his metaphysical redescription of nature, within which scientific accounts would always be reinterpreted and incorporated. This ecological potential is most fully elaborated in Hegel's fourth and final main argument for his rationalist metaphysics of nature: the argument that this metaphysics is most adequate because it recognizes intrinsic goodness in all natural forms. On this point, his metaphysics of nature again differs from the standard scientific conception of nature as an essentially value-neutral domain. In proposing a future recontextualization of science within philosophy of nature, then, Hegel envisages science's value-neutral accounts of natural forms being reinterpreted within the framework of a theory that locates intrinsic goodness throughout the natural world. In his view, it is this value-rich theory that should ultimately guide and regulate our conduct with respect to nature. By examining Hegel's fourth argument for his rationalist conception of nature, we will see how the environmental relevance of his approach can be most completely developed.

6

ETHICAL IMPLICATIONS
OF HEGEL'S THEORY OF NATURE

Whatever forces nature develops and releases against man, cold,
wild animals, water, fire,—he knows means to counter them, and
indeed he takes these means from nature and uses them against
it; the cunning of his reason enables him to preserve and
maintain himself by pitting other natural things against the
powers of nature which threaten him ... However, nature itself,
in its universality, cannot be mastered in this manner, nor bent
to the purposes of man.

—Hegel, *Philosophy of Nature*

This chapter examines Hegel's fourth main argument for his rationalist
conception of nature, an argument which, again, is partially successful
and opens up a promising way of rethinking our relation to the natural
world. I will call this fourth argument Hegel's ethical argument. Essentially, the ethical argument holds that Hegel's rationalist conception of
nature is more adequate than the rival scientific metaphysics because his
rationalist conception, uniquely, allows us to recognize that all natural
forms are intrinsically good—precisely in virtue of the rationality that
it deems them to contain. Thus, Hegel believes it to be a central advantage of his metaphysics of nature that, unlike the metaphysics presupposed in empirical science, it is capable of "reenchanting" the world,
construing it as suffused with value at all points. At this point, Hegel's
approach to nature converges most closely with contemporary environmentalist concerns, suggesting the necessity for a philosophical redescription of nature which can recognize its intrinsic value and so form
the basis for a newly sustainable relationship of human beings to the
natural environment.

The detail of Hegel's ethical argument for his metaphysics is complicated, so I begin with an anticipatory summary of its main stages. First, in the *Logic*, Hegel offers a highly Kantian analysis of goodness as a general ontological structure. According to this analysis, goodness attaches primarily to action from reason and becomes—derivatively—a property of any entities or states of affairs that come to embody the effects of practical reason. This analysis implies that natural and mental forms are good in proportion as they instantiate goodness as a general ontological pattern: that is, that natural and mental forms are good in proportion as they act from, or embody the effects of action from, reason. Mapping this onto Hegel's substantive theory of natural development, we find that all natural forms instantiate goodness, and, moreover, that they do so increasingly well the higher they come in nature's ontological hierarchy. On Hegel's theory, each natural form contains a conceptual element that strives to modify and manifest itself within the material element accompanying it. In this respect, the conceptual element in each natural form is acting in accordance with the requirements of rational necessity—that is, it is acting from reason—and so is, by Hegel's definition, good. Insofar as nature's material dimension increasingly reflects its conceptual dimension, this matter derivatively increases in goodness too. In this way, Hegel's rationalist metaphysics allows him to posit (ever-increasing levels of) intrinsic goodness throughout nature.[1]

Still, why should this be thought to make Hegel's metaphysics more *adequate* to nature's being than science's underlying view that nature is an intrinsically value-neutral realm? Why think that Hegel's intrinsic goodness view is anything more than a consolatory fiction? Certain scattered comments by Hegel, taken together, suggest his reply to this question. According to this, sensible experience embodies a fundamental sense of nature's intrinsic value, which an adequate metaphysical conception of nature must articulate. Ultimately, therefore, Hegel's ethical argument intertwines with and depends upon his phenomenological argument.

Although I aim to show that much is worthwhile in Hegel's ethical argument for his metaphysics of nature, I do not see it as an unmitigated success. Ultimately, I believe, Hegel's rationalist conception of nature falls short of the phenomenological criterion of theoretical adequacy which he himself suggests. In particular, his rationalist conception, although allowing us to see all nature's component forms as intrinsically good, also entails that humans have no responsibilities to preserve or respect natural entities (as becomes apparent in Hegel's political philosophy). In this way, his account of nature's ethical status after all breaks with our allegedly fundamental sense of its intrinsic value, which is plausibly thought to incorporate a sense that natural entities, qua intrinsically valuable, are morally considerable in their own right. Hegel's ethical argument may succeed in establishing that a theoretically adequate account of nature must articulate its intrinsic value and so accommodate our sensibility, but this criterion of theoretical adequacy ultimately tells *against* the specifically rationalist metaphysics that he seeks to defend.

Exegetical questions arise with respect to my reading of Hegel as defending his rationalist conception of nature, to a significant extent, on ethical grounds. Inasmuch as he seeks to recognize intrinsic value throughout nature, Hegel shares considerable ground with many contemporary environmental philosophers, who also wish to show that many features of the natural environment are good in themselves, not solely in virtue of their relation to human feelings, interests, or desires. The proposal that Hegel has common cause with contemporary environmentalism will probably surprise environmentalists and Hegel scholars alike.[2] For a start, Hegel is not usually seen as having participated in the history of philosophical speculation on what kind of value natural entities have and whether, and in what sense, humans have moral obligations toward them. His mature system gives the immediate impression that his interest in nature was exclusively theoretical.[3] Even if one goes beyond this to reconstruct the text's understated ethical themes, then Hegel is most obviously read as endorsing the narrowly anthropocentric view that natural things have no intrinsic value but acquire value only through human beings working them over and infusing them with humanness.[4] To lend some initial plausibility to my thesis that Hegel in fact upholds intrinsic value in all nature, then, I must first outline how, despite appearances, his *Philosophy of Nature* is neither exclusively theoretical nor narrowly anthropocentric in its underlying ethical standpoint.

Ethical Complexity in the *Philosophy of Nature*

Most environmental thinkers who engage with Hegel regard his as a narrowly anthropocentric ethical standpoint, on which natural entities only acquire value when subjected to the transformative activities of human individuals. Two prominent aspects of Hegel's mature system have made this narrowly anthropocentric reading popular. First, he believes nature to be organized hierarchically, culminating in the generation of human beings, which seems to suggest that humans are radically superior to nature.[5] He plays on this connotation: "nature has . . . made its peace by shifting into something higher [that is, mind] . . . The goal of nature is to kill itself . . . to burn itself up like a phoenix in order to step forth rejuvenated from this externality as mind" (EN §376A/3: 212). That humans are radically superior to nature implies, secondly, that by modifying nature to reflect their own plans and purposes they morally improve it, investing it with their own special value. John Passmore draws out this implication in crediting Hegel with the belief that nature "exists simply in order to be overcome, to be humanized. Man offers it liberty, frees it from its fetters, only by making it human, as he does, to use a favourite example of Hegel's, when he eats plants and flesh."[6] It seems that, for Hegel, to rework and humanize nature is to make it better.[7] He appears caught up in a Fichtean vision of the future. For Fichte:

> Nature must gradually enter a condition which . . . keeps its force steady in a definite relation with the power which is destined to control it—the power of man. . . . Cultivated lands shall animate and moderate the inert and hostile atmosphere of primeval forests, deserts, and swamps. . . . nature is to become ever more transparent to us until we can see into its most secret core, and human power . . . shall control it without effort and peacefully maintain any conquest once it is made.[8]

The predilection for humanly modified over raw nature also seems to be manifested, indirectly, in Hegel's estimation of artistic over natural beauty.[9] Thus, such ethical reflections upon nature as Hegel offers appear of merely historical interest to environmentalists, exemplifying a nineteenth-century proclivity for justifying unrestricted industrialization against romantic esteem for the natural world. Unsurprisingly, environmental philosophers have tended to ignore, or quickly dismiss, Hegel's works.

Anthropocentric strands are certainly present in Hegel's thought, but they belong within a broader approach to the ethical evaluation of natural forms, which, in fact, positions those forms as having moral status in their own right. The complexity of Hegel's approach has gone generally unnoticed because it can be appreciated only given some familiarity with his substantive theory of the natural world. First, Hegel's idea that nature is organized gradually and hierarchically entails not only that human organisms—standing at the apex of the hierarchy—have the greatest value, but also that all other natural forms have intrinsic value relative to their place in the developmental scale. This means that for him humans are superior to other natural beings only in degree, not in kind: no greater gap separates humans from other organisms in value than separates organisms from physical bodies, or physical bodies from matter (and so on). Hegel sets up no dichotomy in value between humans and nature; rather, the merely quantitative superiority that he grants to humans presupposes the presence of intrinsic value throughout all nature, organic and nonorganic.[10] Moreover, insofar as Hegel postulates intrinsic value throughout nature, he cannot claim that natural entities acquire value only when transformed by human agents. Indeed, his assessment of nature as intrinsically valuable opens up the possibility of concluding that human transformative activities reduce nature's intrinsic value by disrupting the necessary hierarchy of its forms. Although, ultimately, Hegel will withstand this conclusion, his assessment of the morality of human modification of nature cannot be as unreflectively positive as his environmentalist readers have usually supposed.

Contrary to standard readings, Hegel's mature position on nature and morality is not narrowly anthropocentric, because, crucially, he maintains the intrinsic value of all natural forms. In this respect, his mature system surprisingly anticipates the preoccupations of recent environmentalists. Nonetheless, my claim that he discerns intrinsic value throughout nature still faces a further objection: namely, that his *Philosophy of Nature* nowhere explicitly states or advances this ethical thesis. The text appears exclusively concerned with the theoretical question of what forms the natural world contains and how they are most accurately described. We can only recognize that a subterranean ethical theme pervades the *Philosophy of Nature* by resituating the work in Hegel's mature system as a whole. We need to read the text in conjunction with the *Logic*, and, to a lesser extent, the *Philosophy of Mind*. In particular, we need to read Hegel's substantive theory of the natural world in light of the general conception of the good outlined in his *Logic*. On this basis it becomes apparent how his substantive theory of nature is framed by the assumption that all natural forms are good in proportion as they embody practical reason—which they do increasingly well as natural development unfolds. Let us turn to Hegel's conception of the good in the *Logic* and consider how it bears on his theory of the natural world.

Practical Reason in the World

A convincing reconstruction of the ethical subtext of the *Philosophy of Nature* must start with the acknowledgment that Hegel never explicitly states the evaluative thesis implicit behind his account of natural development. He drops occasional hints in the *Encyclopaedia* about the worth of nature—such as "we recognise the goodness of God in nature" (EL

§80A/127), or "external nature, like mind, is rational, divine" (EM §381A/ 9)—but he leaves the theoretical background to these remarks unexplained. We can only access his implicit thesis that all nature is intrinsically good when we situate his *Philosophy of Nature* in relation to the conception of the good elaborated in the closing sections of his *Logic*.

In the *Logic*, Hegel discusses the good within the broader context of his examination of the form of thought which he calls the "idea." The idea passes through three phases, existing first as "life," second as "cognition" (*Erkennen*), and last as "willing" (*Wollen*). It is with reference to the willing idea that Hegel introduces the good, arguing that the willing idea is good because it acts from rationality. This analysis suggests that the conceptual dimension which infuses all nature is good, since it acts to reshape and modify matter in whatever ways are rationally necessary to resolve the tensions internal to its previous modes of combination with matter. Hegel's evaluation of the willing idea thus implies that, through their conceptual element, all natural forms are (at least) partly good, and, indeed, become increasingly good as their conceptual element prevails over their material side, resulting in a ranking of all natural forms on a scale of ascending goodness. To appreciate how this evaluative thesis figures into the *Philosophy of Nature*, we first need to explicate in some detail Hegel's general description of the logical idea and its development, focusing on the *Encyclopaedia Logic* and the longer discussion in the *Science of Logic*.

I have argued that we should understand Hegel's *Logic* as delineating in abstract terms the ontological structures or patterns which are instantiated in the domains of nature and mind. The logical analysis of these structures or forms considers them in general, without reference to their specific modes of instantiation. As we saw previously, toward the end of his general analysis of this series of ontological structures, Hegel introduces a structure called the "idea." He defines the idea as rational thought that fully pervades and infuses all the objective structures of reality.[11] Having defined the idea as rationality existing as the governing presence within the objective world, Hegel directly infers that the idea can only fully realize its own character by existing in the guise of living organisms. As we saw earlier, he generally construes organisms as universal centers manifested within a set of thoroughly interconnected limbs and members (see, for example, EL §216/291). Hegel is arguing, then, that rationality can only fully pervade objective reality if it takes the form of universal centers that animate real items and draw them into the deeper interconnectedness characteristic of organized members. This does not amount to the (debatable) view that the entire universe consists of organic structures, for it remains to be seen how the idea as an organic structure is concretely instantiated in nature and mind.

At this point in the *Logic*, Hegel makes the further claim that all organisms are sentient (*empfindend*) (EL §216A/292), because sensibility is the automatic self-rediscovery of a universal center within the web of objects it pervades, as if these objects mirrored its image back to it. Inevitably, then, organisms possess a level of self-awareness. Sentience, though, is an inadequate type of self-awareness in Hegel's eyes, since merely sentient beings cannot grasp their character in rational, conceptual, terms. The sentience into which organisms are cast is an intrinsically imperfect form of self-awareness, pointing inexorably forward to the conceptual modes of self-awareness that would complete it.[12] This being so, originally sentient organisms have an endemic drive to remedy their deficiency by, precisely, *conceptualizing* themselves as present within objectivity, or, as Hegel puts it, by trying to "take up" the objective world into "conceptual determinations" (§226/296). He calls this the effort of organisms to "know" the world. In embarking on this sustained study of the objective world, organisms advance (indirectly) toward conceptualizing *themselves*, as the points of universality around which objective items are organized. Thus, in order to realize itself, the idea must not only assume the shape of organisms but also advance out of merely organic form to a second form as specifically cognitive organisms, or what Hegel calls simply "cognition" (*Erkennen*). Again, it should be borne in mind that this is a general ontological tendency—it remains to be seen how it is actualized by natural and human organisms.

Having argued that the idea must come to exist as cognitive organisms, Hegel now alleges that their cognitive activity must itself give way to practical activity. This is because individuals must make explicit the activity involved in their classification and categorization of objectivity, by engaging in the openly practical activity of modifying objectivity. Cognition is already active, evincing freedom, since investigators may categorize objectivity in multiple ways to suit their intellectual standpoint and requirements. So just as sensibility anticipated conceptual self-awareness, cognition anticipates properly practical activity. Individuals are driven to realize the protopractical character of cognition by starting to act on objectivity, according to their preexisting purposes. The idea—as embodied in cognitive individuals—acquires the "drive to realise itself . . . [it] aims . . . to determine the world that it finds already there according to its own purpose [*Zweck*]" (EL §233/301).

In this case, each individual's "purpose"—which is determined by the preceding course of logical development—is to rediscover itself within the world, to find in the world a reflection of itself. This logically determined requirement now becomes a purpose in the sense that it motivates individuals to the appropriate type of activity, the activity of modifying objectivity so that the organization thereby imposed upon it will reflect the agent's character back to her. But this purpose that motivates individuals into activity is rational, for the urge to find oneself in the world has been rationally necessitated by the very structure of sentient life. Agents have begun to act from rationality; or—to put it differently—their rationality has become practically effective. Hegel states that because of its new-found efficacy rationality has assumed the form of *will*, and that individuals now engage in (indeed, are essentially defined by) willing. Plainly, he equates the will with practical reason.[13] This analysis allows Hegel to conclude that the idea, as embodied in agents, has advanced from its cognitive guise into its third avatar as "willing."

At this point, Hegel introduces the domain of value into his ontology. He contends that insofar as any will motivates itself to action by its rationality, that will is good: "The will is simply the good that is self-activating" (EL §234A/302). Any such will's purpose—the goal it selects according to rationality—is also designated good: "This determinateness contained in the concept . . . and including within it the demand for an individual external actuality, is the *good*" (WL 818/2: 542). Moreover, any objective state of affairs brought about by the will and realizing its purpose is derivatively good too: "The realised good is good by virtue of what it already is in the subjective purpose" (WL 820/2: 544). Given that the will qua practical reason is good, its purposes, as well as any ensuing activities and states of affairs that realize those purposes, are also good.[14]

Evidently, Hegel is advancing a profoundly Kantian understanding of practical reason and moral worth. He himself foregrounds his Kantianism in the *Philosophy of Mind* when he discusses how the will is concretely instantiated in human agents. Here he states that the "ethical . . . consists in the will having for its purpose a universal content, not subjective, self-seeking content. But such content is possible only in thinking and through thinking" (EM §469R/228). He restates the point in reverse: "When the power . . . of self-possession and of the universal, or of theoretical or moral principles, is relaxed . . . the earthy [that is, purely individual] elements are set free—for this evil is directly present in the heart, because this, as immediate, is natural and selfish" (§408/124). This clarifies that practical rationality—that is, will—is good because its purposes necessarily display universality, or an absence of egoism. Hegel apparently presupposes an exhaustive disjunction between acting from rationality and acting from selfish, sensible desires, with rationality instituting an impartial standpoint which precludes the agent's pursuing purposes out of mere selfishness. The will as practical reason is good because it formulates its purposes from this rigorously impartial standpoint.[15]

How can Hegel reconcile this austerely Kantian conception of practical reason with his criticisms of Kant's duty/desire antagonism? As we have seen, the mature Hegel objects to Kantian *Moralität* because it is excessively demanding, since finite human individuals can only act at all insofar as they anticipate sensible gratification (see, for example, EM §475R/236–37). This is why Hegel thinks that the moral life is only possible inasmuch as desires are socially cultivated to conform internally to rational requirements. This commits him to the view that the good *human* agent cannot be one who acts from duty alone (since, after all, such human agents are an impossibility), but must be someone who acts from desires that have been cultivated to accord with the strictures of reason/duty. Nonetheless, this need not contradict Hegel's Kantian analysis of practical reason as a general ontological structure. His moral and political philosophy only outlines how this structure is instantiated in finite human beings—imperfectly, in view of their passional nature—and then fills in an account of the social institutions that can overcome this imperfection by cultivating the passions to concur with rational requirements.

To return to my main theme—the narrative of the good will in the *Logic*—Hegel has given a general analysis of the character of any being that acts from will, arguing that the will of such individuals is good since it is practically rational. However, he proceeds to diagnose an internal contradiction within the will. As we have seen, the rationally necessary purpose on which the will acts is the purpose of transforming objectivity so that it manifests the agent as a locus of rationality. But when objectivity comes to exhibit rational order just in virtue of having succumbed to modification, it also manifests the fact that this order is something it does not intrinsically possess: "This actuality . . . ranks as something intrinsically worthless [*Nichtige*] that must first receive its true determination and sole worth [*Wert*] through the purposes of the good" (WL 821/2: 545). What agents require, though, is precisely that objectivity should intrinsically exhibit rational order and so "mirror" them. In actual fact, through their activity, "this existence is determined merely as an intrinsically worthless externality, [and so] in it the good has only attained a contingent, destructible existence, not a realisation corresponding to its idea" (820/2: 544). The purpose which agents espouse is essentially unrealizable. They require a spontaneously occurring state of affairs, so necessarily cannot realize this purpose through action: their very attempt to realize this purpose means that whatever they bring about must differ in content from the purpose. Since the purpose is unrealizable, agents are irrational to espouse it; yet at the same time, they are rational to do so, since only by espousing it can they hope to realize their inchoate self-awareness. The will's purpose is "an actual [that is, actualizable] purpose and at the same time . . . merely possible [that is, unrealizable and fantastic]" (EL §234/301).[16]

According to Hegel, the irrationality of willing activity calls for the emergence of a new and different form of the idea. Essentially, agents must not simply will, but also recognize that will is already immanent within objectivity. Like a "mature person," agents must come to embrace the "providentialist" outlook according to which "the good has been reached in and for itself . . . the objective world is in this way in and for itself the idea positing itself eternally as *purpose* and at the same time bringing forth its actuality through [its] activity" (EL §235/303). At the same time as acting, agents must adopt the view that practical rationality already, independently, pervades objectivity. More precisely, they must recognize that rationality suffuses the world not passively but actively, carrying out what it purposes: "the final purpose of the world, the good, only *is*, because it constantly brings itself about" (§234A/302). Agents must come to see all objective items as inherently pervaded by practical rationality or the will. This is not an argument for quietism, since the providentialist outlook gives practical activity renewed feasibility and reasonableness. This outlook makes practical activity worthwhile again, since agents who hold to this outlook can aim to elicit the rational order that is already implicit in objectivity and is striving to emerge. Thus, the outlook which Hegel calls providentialism resolves the initial contradiction within willing activity by combining it with an outlook according to which the purpose of that activity is realizable (being complemented by a convergent dimension of willing activity within the external world).[17] Hegel is not urging that rational activity should be abandoned, but that it should be carried on from a certain optimistic standpoint. He therefore retains the idea that action is good insofar as it is done from practical reason, but adds that, to be fully rational, this action must be carried out on the further assumption that its purposes are broadly realizable.

To sum up Hegel's analysis of goodness: for him, it is a general characteristic of any practical activity that aims to transform the world to reflect the agent, an aim which is rationally necessary given the prior situation of the agent as a cognitive being. Practical activity is thus motivated by reason—which, as a motivating force, exists as will. Hegel's analysis of goodness is couched at such an abstract level that it is hard to appreciate its concrete significance. So we should bear in mind that he intends this analysis to pertain to any natural or human forms which instantiate the general characteristic of activity from reason: when any of these forms acts from reason, it is good. The question, then, is which natural forms—if any—instantiate this general structure: how does Hegel's abstract logical analysis bear on his substantive account of natural development in the *Philosophy of Nature*?

The Goodness of Nature

It is hard to work out how Hegel's abstract studies of logical structures bear on the concrete accounts of natural or human forms in his *Realphilosophie*. He occasionally hints that he understands each logical form to match up one-to-one with a corresponding natural and human form—so that, for example, being corresponds to externality (in nature) and spatial intuition (in mind), nothingness corresponds to negativity (in nature) and temporal intuition (in mind), and so forth (see, for example, WL 586/2: 257). But he does not work out these parallels accurately, leaving whole swathes of the various texts to diverge from anything in the others (for example, the *Philosophy of Mind* does not actually start with intuition at all). Moreover, some logical structures— such as contingency—are instantiated throughout nature and mind, not appearing only at one particular phase in their development. Plainly, any attempt to correlate logical with natural structures one-to-one is doomed to failure.

A further question is whether Hegel intends his analysis of practical activity and goodness to apply to any natural forms at all. Some of his language in the relevant sections of the *Science of Logic* suggests that he is discussing structures that he takes to be concretely instantiated only by the human mind. He claims, for instance, that the cognitive idea exists as: "*Thinking, mind, self-consciousness*" (WL 775/2: 487). These are all characteristics which, he always insists, are the *differentia specifica* of human beings. He adds that the discussion of cognition is the logical counterpart to the concrete account of the various stages of mind enumerated in the *Philosophy of Mind* (780–82/2: 494–96). Moreover, there seems an obvious philosophical basis for these claims. If practical reason presupposes cognition, and natural forms do not consciously entertain thoughts, then it appears that natural forms can be neither cognitive nor, in turn, practically rational. It appears that nature can instantiate only the general structures of life and sentience, but not those of cognition or will.

That conclusion would be too swift. After all, the central premise of Hegel's theory of nature is that all natural forms incessantly transform themselves in line with rational requirements. According to Hegel, the conceptual element in natural forms is the locus of their agency. In the introduction to the *Philosophy of Nature*, he refers to this conceptual element as the component of "universality" in natural forms, stating that it does not "remain . . . opposed to the individuality of things, but while it relates itself negatively against things and assimilates them to itself, it equally elicits their individuality, leaves them alone, and allows them to determine themselves freely within it" (EN §246A/1: 204). Each natural form contains elements of universality and "individuality," that is, discrete, individuated, matter. In each case, the universality strives to "assimilate" this matter, by purposefully shaping it into specific forms— "eliciting" its individuality—so that it comes to manifest universality. This purposeful activity is rational, since, as Hegel's overall account of natural development has shown, the manifestation of universality in matter is rationally necessary to resolve a tension (that, otherwise, universality is not fully present within the matter that it possesses). This element of universality or conceptuality in natural forms—acting in accordance with rational necessity to manifest itself within its material parts—appears to instantiate the logical structure of practical activity, as the activity of rationally transforming objectivity to reflect the agent. Yet one might still object that Hegel's logical analysis shows that practical rationality is only *possible* through cognitive activity, which it presupposes. His own analysis, then, seems to suggest that natural forms could only instantiate practical agency if they were conscious as well.[18] But since natural forms are not conscious, it looks as if they can instantiate the general structure of practical activity only very inadequately at best.

Does it follow, though, that because natural forms do not instantiate the structure of cognition they cannot instantiate that of practical rationality either? Hegel's idea of nature's "petrified intelligence" suggests otherwise. Although in the *Logic* he equates cognition with "mind" as the *differentia specifica* of human beings, he also says that all natural forms are "implicitly" mental (EN §251/1: 216), or are shapes in which "mind" exists, albeit "outside itself" (EM §381A/14). He identifies the protomental element in nature with the "concept" or "idea" inhabiting it (EN §251A/1: 217)—that is, with nature's conceptual element. This conceptual element exists, for Hegel, as mind that is "outside itself," "petrified"—its rationality immediately poured out in its activity, retaining no interiority. The rationality of natural forms, then, is *exclusively* practical, unaccompanied by any distinct dimension of interiority or conscious thought. In respect of this lack of interiority, nature's conceptual element fails to instantiate the logical structure of cognition. Yet, in Hegel's view, it is precisely the peculiarity of natural forms that they *do* still act according to rationality—continuously transforming themselves in line with rational requirements—despite their lack of conscious rational thoughts. For Hegel, it is characteristic of natural forms to instantiate the structure of practical rationality but not that of cognition.

More specifically, Hegel's theory of nature implies that the *conceptual* element in all natural forms instantiates the structure of practical reason, and thereby introduces some intrinsic goodness into all these forms.[19] Hegel also believes that any matter which comes to realize fully the purpose motivating its conceptual center—by qualitatively manifesting that center—is derivatively good. For example, he states that the homogeneous matter of light is good because it adequately manifests light's universality (EN §276R/2: 17). However, he passes few value judgments on specific natural forms, assuming that his readers are already familiar with his general ontological thesis that "objects . . . are what they *ought* to be . . . when their reality corresponds to their concept" (EL §213A/287). This thesis implies that the goodness of nature's material dimension increases in proportion as it progressively manifests the universality within it. Hegel's hierarchical vision of nature thus implies that all natural forms are arranged on a scale of ascending goodness. Nature's ontological progression is, simultaneously, a value-progression toward the realization of the good.

Since the material aspects of natural forms are good only inasmuch as they disclose universality, they must be bad inasmuch as they do not: "Any actual thing no doubt shows in itself what it *ought* to be, yet . . . it may equally show that its actuality only imperfectly corresponds to this concept, that it is *bad*" (WL 799/2: 518). We might conclude from this that, although matter gains in goodness as we ascend nature's ontological ladder, the gain is offset by a prevalence of badness lower down the scale, leaving nature as a whole with roughly equal quantities of goodness and badness. But this is not Hegel's position: for him, even the worst natural form has a wholly good conceptual dimension, so that even though its matter is wholly bad (not manifesting universality at all), nature still begins with an equal division of goodness and badness.[20] Goodness only preponderates ever more as nature's trajectory unfolds; hence, Hegel is implicitly committed to regarding nature as a predominantly good realm.

For Hegel, all natural forms are, to varying degrees, intrinsically good: that is, they are good not only as a function of any human interests in or feelings about them, but also in themselves, by virtue of the objective relation between their conceptual and material elements and the way this instantiates the general structure of practical reason. Generally, then, Hegel's is a broadly Kantian strategy for asserting intrinsic goodness in all natural forms. To uphold their value, he first locates goodness in practical rationality and then extends practical rationality into all natural forms. This is an unusual strategy for "reenchanting" nature, since intrinsic value has traditionally been denied to nature just

because it has been thought to lack the (practical or theoretical) rationality deemed criterial of intrinsic value. In challenging this conclusion
by extending practical rationality to nature, Hegel differs sharply from
many environmental ethicists, who revalue nature not by contesting its
nonrationality but by identifying in it qualities other than rationality
which they take as criterial of its intrinsic value. It is helpful to clarify
exactly how Hegel's account of nature's value compares with such recent approaches.

We should recall that most environmental thinkers do not believe
themselves to share any common ground with Hegel's account of nature. Instead, they associate Hegel with the view that humanity is radically superior to nature through its placement at the top of the ontological
hierarchy. Though Hegel does hold this view, the value-hierarchy at the
top of which he situates humanity already invests all nature with value.
This means that human superiority to nature is only of degree, not of
kind: on this, Hegel actually agrees with some recent environmental
philosophers who consider humans superior to animals in the extent of
their interests or capacities—just as animals exceed plants in theirs,
plants exceed minerals, and so on.[21]

However, recent advocates of intrinsic value in nature do not share
Hegel's conviction that practical rationality is the locus or criterion of
value. Alternative candidates have been proposed: life, being the subject-of-a-life, exhibition of a telic structure, or possession of interests.[22]
These varying criteria lead different thinkers to attribute intrinsic value
to different ranges of forms: higher mammals (on the subject-of-a-life
criterion), all organisms (on the life or telic structure criteria), or all
natural forms of which interests can reasonably be predicated, including
species and ecosystems (on the interestedness criterion). None of these
theories extend intrinsic value as far as natural forms that are neither
organic nor share the self-interested structure of organic life: forms such
as rivers, mountains, soils, air, or seas.[23] This divides these theories from
that of Hegel, on which intrinsic goodness suffuses *all* nature, not only
organisms or proto-organic forms. Taking intrinsic goodness to adhere
to practical reason, and then extending practical reason to all nature,
allows him to postulate goodness everywhere in it—even in nonorganic
forms such as those that he eventually identifies as chemical and electrical processes, sounds, colors, elemental qualities and rhythms, and
even the passage of time and the vastness of space. Nonetheless, Hegel
conceives natural forms to possess greater levels of value the higher
they come hierarchically, so that plants, for instance, have greater
value than the earth, and animals greater value than plants. Although
Hegel believes all natural forms to have intrinsic value, he thinks that

they do so to varying degrees, ultimately privileging the organic over the nonorganic.

This extension of (degrees of) intrinsic goodness to all natural forms is only possible for Hegel because he starts from the metaphysical view that all these forms act from requirements of rational necessity. Most environmental ethicists will not judge this seemingly baroque metaphysical view to be a viable starting point from which to revalue the environment. Yet Hegel believes his metaphysical view of nature to be more adequate than the competing scientific paradigm just *because* it gives him a robust way of positing goodness in all nature. Whereas contemporary environmental ethicists tend to believe that a viable theory of nature's intrinsic value must be minimally reliant on controversial metaphysical presuppositions, Hegel reverses this judgment: for him, the fact that his controversial metaphysical conception of nature makes possible a robust account of nature's intrinsic value actually makes that metaphysical conception especially adequate. Hegel's approach suggests that a metaphysical rethinking of nature could be extremely fruitful for environmentalism, insofar as such rethinking might encourage recognition of intrinsic value in natural forms.

I have traced how Hegel's rationalist metaphysics combines with his Kantian conception of moral worth to generate the conclusion that the natural world is predominantly good. He believes that this renders his rationalist metaphysics more adequate, above all, than that presupposed in empirical science. But why should the ability of Hegel's metaphysics to generate this ethical conclusion make it more adequate than the scientific view that it opposes? Critics might object that the unusual ethical implication of Hegel's metaphysics of nature simply confirms that this metaphysics is purely fictive, generating a fantastic view of nature that may be pleasing and consolatory but does little to illuminate nature's real character. Let us explore how Hegel could reply.

Sensibility and the Intrinsic Value of Nature

Hegel can plausibly maintain that his metaphysical conception of nature is distinguished from the scientific conception in that its rationalism enables him, given a Kantian understanding of goodness, to attribute intrinsic goodness to all natural forms. By contrast, the metaphysics which he takes to be presupposed in empirical science holds that natural forms are bare things acting only by virtue of external laws—things that are in themselves wholly value-neutral, intrinsically devoid of moral significance. From the perspective of this scientific metaphysics, natural entities can only acquire value in relation to the interests or projects of human beings. To suppose that nature can possess intrinsic value would be to project into nature in itself a value it can have only relative to us. Hegel therefore claims that his rationalist metaphysics allows him to challenge the narrowly anthropocentric assessment of nature's ethical status which is embodied in empirical science (at least when that science is understood, as by him, to presuppose a metaphysical view of natural forms as bare things). But why should this be deemed to render his metaphysics more adequate than that of science?

This important question is not one Hegel properly addresses. However, his work does contain several comments concerning the value of nature and its relation to sensible experience. When read together, these comments can be seen to sketch out an explanation of why the ethical implications of Hegel's metaphysics render it most adequate. According to the argument which Hegel's disparate comments sketch, our basic sensible (that is, preconceptual) experience of nature embodies a sense of its intrinsic value, which an adequate conception of nature must be able to articulate. Thus, Hegel supports his ethical argument—that his metaphysics is most adequate because it can identify nature as intrinsically good—with a further phenomenological argument that this makes his metaphysics most adequate because it means that it can remain continuous with our sensible experience of nature as valuable on its own terms.

Where is this argument sketched? In several places, Hegel asserts the need for a philosophical standpoint, or metaphysics, which recognizes nature's intrinsic worth. The *Spirit of Christianity* (1798–1799) exudes remarks to this effect: throughout this text, Hegel is preoccupied with the problem of human domination of nature. For example, he claims that natural beings should be recognized as having "life, rights, [worthiness of] love for itself" (GC 191/283). He contrasts such a view to the supposedly Judaic position that nature is "hostile" and "had to be mastered" (*beherrscht*) (183/275). He claims that Abraham thought that the world in itself was a "nullity" (*Nichts*)—acquiring meaning only from God, but having no intrinsic significance or value (187/279). Indeed, for Hegel, the Jews generally believed that "everything is matter . . . a stuff, loveless, without rights, something which . . . they treat as accursed and then assign to its proper place if it attempts to stir" (188/280). This is the outlook Hegel seeks to supersede, and which, in his 1801 *Differenzschrift*, he finds restated in a modern guise by Fichte: he objects that in Fichte's thought "the living is torn apart into concept and matter and nature comes under servitude [*Botmäßigkeit*]" (DS 61/82). In contrast, Hegel affirms our "[n]eed for a philosophy which would reconcile nature for the mishandling which it [also] suffers in

Kant's and Fichte's systems" (4/13). This philosophy, he continues, must be premised on a kind of reason that "forms itself into nature." To paraphrase, this new philosophy must be predicated upon a metaphysical outlook which recognizes that reason is present in nature, and hence that nature has intrinsic value—a stance that "reconciles" nature for its former mishandling. One might protest that these are isolated early pronouncements. But they are not, as evidenced in how closely they anticipate Hegel's later claims that modern culture "mishandles nature and denies its right" and that this modern denial of nature's "right"—that is, of its intrinsic worth—must be transcended by a philosophical standpoint which rejects the opposition of nature to reason (VA 1: 54/1: 81).[24]

In the *Aesthetics*, Hegel indicates that the denial of nature's intrinsic value that occurs in science and in certain post-Enlightenment philosophical views is connected to the disengagement of these views from our sensible experience. He states that these perspectives that deny nature's "right" are thinking about it "abstractly." This means, he clarifies elsewhere, that they drain nature of its color, noisiness, and qualitative richness in general (EN §246A/1: 198). Scientific and classical Enlightenment views of nature, then, represent it as lacking the qualities—including value-qualities—which we sensibly understand to be present within it. In this, scientific and Enlightenment views are "abstracted" from sensibility. Hegel's indication that the modern picture of nature is detached from sensible experience in virtue (partly) of its "disenchantment" seems to presuppose that sensibility embodies a basic understanding of nature as intrinsically valuable, as having its own "right." Hence, when Hegel affirms the need for a philosophical recognition and conceptualization of nature's intrinsic value, the implication is that this conceptualization is necessary to reintegrate philosophy with sensible experience. It would not be surprising if Hegel thought this, given that—as we saw in the last chapter—his ideal of *Bildung* commits him to the general principle that a philosophy is justified inasmuch as it retains continuity with sensible experience. But if he indeed believes that a philosophy can be adequate only if it articulates sensibility, and that it must, in particular, articulate our sensible experience of nature as valuable in itself, then he is implicitly endorsing the claim that his metaphysical conception of nature is uniquely adequate because it can articulate this experience by attributing intrinsic goodness to all natural forms.

Hegel's scattered remarks on sensibility and nature's "right" indicate that his ethical defence of his metaphysics is supported by this further phenomenological argument. Yet there seems something odd about the thought that Hegel might have held (even tacitly) to such an argument. For in believing his metaphysics to be justified by articulating a basic understanding of nature's intrinsic value, he appears to steer very near the view that moral theory must be guided by intuitions (here, certain allegedly universal and fundamental intuitions about the goodness of nature). If so, his argument is weak, for it is not obvious that we have a coherent set of intuitions about nature's ethical status, or that any such intuitions are reliable and worth accepting. Moreover, Hegel himself strenuously opposed at least one contemporary moral theory with some affinities with later intuitionism: the "ethics of conviction" of Jakob Friedrich Fries (1773–1843). Fries presented his theory as a development of Kant. For Fries, conscientious convictions provide our best guide as to the content of the moral law, so that in acting from conscience one is acting with good will, even when—as can regularly happen—one's convictions are misguided.[25] Given Hegel's acerbic response to Fries, it seems unlikely that he himself would espouse a moral theory that grants a similarly privileged status to intuitions.

In fact, though, Hegel's position on the need to articulate sensibility differs from any kind of intuitionism in two respects. First, he believes only that our sense of nature's value should receive conceptual articulation, not that all our everyday moral intuitions (or convictions) deserve a hearing. Far from it: many mundane intuitions will require substantial overhaul in light of a proper grasp of nature's ethical status. Our basic sense of nature's value holds special status among these various intuitions, for Hegel, because it is a fundamental element in all experience—not simply the internalized reflex of a contingently dominant social norm, as most intuitions are. Second, Hegel's position differs from intuitionism as he does not propose that our sense of nature's value should be straightforwardly accepted, but rather that it should receive conceptual *articulation* into a cogent metaphysical stance. As he states in the *Differenzschrift*, reason should not "renounce itself" or "become a hollow imitator of nature" but "form itself into nature out of an inner strength" (DS 4/13). That is, this new philosophy should conceptualize nature, coherently, in a way that recognizes its intrinsic value. Our basic sense of this value, being nonconceptual, is too inchoate and amorphous to provide a basis for moral judgment prior to conceptual articulation. Really, then, it is misleading to liken Hegel's position to intuitionism.

Hegel's corpus as a whole presents fragments of an argument that his rationalist metaphysics of nature is more adequate than the metaphysics presupposed in empirical science because it can recognize nature's intrinsic value, thereby articulating our basic, sensible, mode of experience. So far, my exposition has given the impression that this ethical argument for Hegel's rationalist conception of nature is wholly successful. But serious problems afflict this argument, as we now should explore.

The Morality of Transforming Nature

Problems emerge in relation to Hegel's assessment of human individuals' moral responsibility toward natural entities.[26] Incongruously, despite attributing intrinsic value to the entire natural hierarchy, he denies that humans have any duties to respect or preserve natural entities by leaving their structures intact. On the contrary, he avers that human individuals have a positive duty to mold and transform natural entities without restraint. This holds even with respect to those natural entities which Hegel situates at the pinnacle of the natural hierarchy: plants and animals. He does not believe that the relatively high value of animals generates any obligation to be a vegetarian, or that the value of plants obliges humans to treat them with care or respect. Rather, Hegel maintains that humans have a duty to transform animals and plants as extensively as they like (whether through breeding, disciplining, or outright consumption). Likewise, he believes that humans have a duty to transform natural entities of all kinds, in whichever ways they prefer. This complete denial of any duties of respect or preservation is troubling from an ecological perspective. Furthermore, Hegel's claim that humans have an unlimited duty to transform natural entities becomes problematic in terms of his *own* understanding of nature's ethical status. As I hope to show, this claim conflicts with his conception of our fundamental sense of nature's intrinsic value, which is most plausibly seen as incorporating a sense that nature's constituent entities are morally considerable in their own right. This ultimately undermines the validity of the rationalist metaphysics through which Hegel claims to articulate our moral phenomenology. Before we can explore this problem, though, we need to clarify why he maintains that human individuals have a moral duty to transform natural entities without restraint.

From the vantage point of some contemporary environmental philosophers, Hegel's denial that the intrinsic goodness of natural forms gives humans any duties to respect the entities instantiating those forms will look deeply counterintuitive. Environmental philosophers often assume that the intrinsic value of individual natural entities imposes upon humans definite duties toward those entities.[27] For Hegel, in contrast, a duty is just a course of action prescribed by practical reason, and so, since he denies that duties arise *from* the intrinsic value (or interests, rights, etc.) of others, he has no space for a notion of duties as debts owed *to* anyone or anything. This is why he can consistently affirm intrinsic value in nature and yet deny that humans have duties to natural entities. Yet Hegel's Kantian conception of duty need not stop him from postulating duties *concerning* nature. For example, practical reason might legislate the preservation of endangered species without such preservation being owed *to* those species or their members.[28] Whether such duties exist, though, and what their content is, cannot be simply read off from the evaluative axis of the *Philosophy of Nature*. For Hegel, a cogent account of human duties—including any duties concerning nature—must be embedded in a systematic theory of the human mind, which establishes how it is rational for human individuals to act.

Hegel's *Philosophy of Mind* provides this systematic theory of mind, deriving the series of necessarily interconnected phases through which the human mind develops. Crucially, the course of mental development which human individuals undergo constrains them to take a direction which precludes their acquiring duties to respect or preserve natural entities. Instead, humans are conditioned to acquire a duty to transform natural entities: individuals would actually be acting *im*morally by leaving natural entities inviolate. To understand Hegel's position, we must reconstruct the relevant portions of his account of mind. We can then see where his understanding of duty fits into this account of mind, producing the conclusion that human individuals are morally obliged to remodel nature.

In two main places in his theory of mind, Hegel explains how humans acquire duties to transform nature. The first is his account of the desire to destroy and consume natural entities, which forms the prelude to the struggle for recognition that terminates in the master and servant relationship. This account occurs at §426–§435 of the *Philosophy of Mind* (retreading the earlier account of the master/servant relationship in chapter 4 of the *Phenomenology*). Second, Hegel discusses a duty to modify natural entities which arises with the institution of private property. He introduces this, briefly, at §488–§492 of the *Philosophy of Mind*, expanding on these paragraphs in §41–§71 of the *Philosophy of Right* (making up the section entitled "Property"). Despite the popularity of Hegel's account of mastery and servitude, I shall concentrate exclusively upon his account of our duty to transform nature as sketched within his treatment of private property. To reconstruct both accounts would overcomplicate the exposition, since his mature theory of private property is itself less than straightforward. Furthermore, his account of the duty to transform nature as it arises within the context of private property represents his final, considered, assessment of the true scope of our duties concerning nature. The treatment that desirous individuals and then servants mete out to nature has only provisional legitimacy, since it takes place "in the transition between natural human existence and the truly ethical condition; it occurs in a world where a wrong is still right" (PR §57A/88). On the other hand, the *Philosophy of Right* describes the social institutions Hegel judges ideally rational and legitimate (institutions that are substantially realized in post-Enlightenment Europe). These institutions include private property and the modification of nature practiced under its rubric.[29] Thus, in offering his account of this duty to modify nature, Hegel presupposes that it has absolute validity and truly exhausts human moral responsibility concerning natural entities.

In the *Philosophy of Right* Hegel introduces private property immediately after free will. Here he presumes free will to be a familiar phenomenological datum needing no further explanation (PR §4R/37). However, he also indicates that those who do seek an explanation will find it in his *Philosophy of Mind*. This derives free will as the rationally necessary consequence of theoretical intelligence, which individuals acquire at a certain point in their mental development. Intelligent individuals originally believe themselves to acquire concepts by passively receiving stimuli from external objects. The fact is, though, that "in thinking we are necessarily active. The content of what is thought ... is something mediated, something posited by our activity" (PR §4A/36). Individuals must acknowledge their role in actively framing concepts to fit objects, and "intelligence, knowing itself as the determinant of the content ... is *will*" (EM §468/227). Will differs from "intelligence" in that it is "thinking translating itself into existence, thinking as the drive to give itself existence" (PR §4A/35). Mind takes the shape of will when its rationality becomes practical, when it starts to act from rational requirements—in this case the requirement to find conceptual organization in the entities of the external world. This transition from theoretical intelligence to free will instantiates the transition from cognition to will in the *Logic*: in both cases, cognition or intelligence transmutes into will insofar as it must realize its already implicitly practical character by starting to modify the world practically—to "translate itself into existence"—according to its own purposes.

Schematically, then, Hegel's view is that human individuals must identify rationality in physical entities, but that this involves cognitive activity, which they must acknowledge through the explicit activity of imposing conceptual organization upon objects. Human individuals become rationally obliged to transfigure objects—both their own bodies and the natural entities around them. Complicating this analysis, though,

Hegel maintains that individuals' activity in transforming objects must take place under a particular social form: the appropriation of objects (including one's own body) as private property (*Besitznahme*). This connection with private property arises in the following way. In modifying natural entities, agents are importing into them new forms of organization. Here the entire object, in both its conceptual and material aspects, becomes the material for disclosing a new form or "concept" superimposed by the human agent. In coming to exhibit such organization, an entity comes to bear witness to the agent's activity upon it and so to her will (insofar as this is evinced in her activity). "This manifestation [of will in thing] occurs through my conferring upon the thing a purpose other than that which it immediately possessed . . . a soul [that is, locus of organization] other than that which it previously had" (PR §44A/ 76). By having come to incorporate a constitutive reference back to the agent's will, this item has become a piece of her property, her presence having become encoded within its structure. Consequently, human transformation of nature necessarily takes place under the rubric of the appropriation of entities as private property.[30]

According to Hegel's account of mind, transformative activity is the rationally necessary consequence of human theoretical intelligence, making explicit the activity presupposed in the latter. Being required in response to the deficiency of theoretical intelligence, the activity of transforming nature is rational, so that in pursuing it human individuals have begun to act from practical reason. This is why they are now said to possess *will*, which Hegel continues to define as practical reason. Moreover, Hegel claims that, because it is rationally necessary for humans to transform nature, this activity is morally obligatory for them. He reaches this conclusion through his rationalistic—and still deeply Kantian—understanding of duty. According to this, action from reason is good, such that whatever practical reason prescribes is obligatory. He states that: "The good is the *essential element* of the subject's will, which thus has an unqualified *obligation* [*Verpflichtung*] in this connection . . . The essential element of the will for me is duty" (PR §133– §133A/161). Insofar as practical reason prescribes the transformation of nature through its private appropriation, then, "it is a *duty* to possess things as *property*" (EM §486R/242). Hegel's understanding of duties as courses of action prescribed by reason, conjoined with his thesis that individuals are rationally required to transform nature, produces the conclusion that any individual who strives to transform nature is acting dutifully—evincing good will.

My reading of Hegel may seem excessively Kantian. After all, as I noted before, Hegel does not believe that human individuals can act solely from reason or duty, which seems to cut against the suggestion that he establishes the absolute validity of the duty to transform nature from its rationality. But the psychological impossibility of purely rational action for human individuals affects neither Hegel's basic conception of duty nor his account of the content of duties. It only means that, in addition to outlining the content of our duties, he must also outline the series of social institutions which will cultivate desires so that these duties can be carried out. His denial that finite individuals can act from duty alone does not contradict his claim that remodelling nature is an (absolutely valid) duty, but only shows that *Bildung* is necessary for individuals to be able to discharge this duty.[31]

Having established that human individuals have the duty to modify nature, Hegel indulges in a dismaying rhetoric praising the reconstruction of the natural environment. He affirms "the absolute *right of appropriation* which human beings have over all things" (PR §44/75). This right is absolute because: "Matter is devoid of rights" (LNR §19A/ 67). Hegel also frankly declares that "man is master over everything in nature."[32] Individuals may, if they so choose, manifest their "supremacy" (*Hoheit*) over natural things by destroying them: even animals "have no right to their life, because they do not will it" (PR §47A/79). In hunting, for example (which Hegel defends), "the means whereby I take them [wild animals] in my possession, is to kill them" (LNR §20A/68).[33] Alluding to this discussion in his *Lectures on the History of Philosophy*, Hegel reasserts that nature does not "have the end in itself in such a way that we have to respect it, as the individual human has this end in himself and hence is to be respected" (VGP 3: 185/3: 87).[34]

Despite his stance in the *Philosophy of Nature* that all natural entities are intrinsically good in virtue of the goodness of their internal structures, Hegel in the *Philosophy of Right* denies that humans have any duties to respect or preserve those entities; on the contrary, he affirms our positive duty to transfigure those entities (as extensively as we please). This duty is not—and never becomes—limited or qualified by any countervailing duties of respect. As the *Philosophy of Right* unfolds, Hegel criticizes private appropriation for its still incomplete sociality, enumerating the series of progressively deepening social duties which individuals must assume. But none of these duties, which concern other human agents, ever impinge upon individuals' foundational duty to transform natural entities. Thus, Hegel's developmental account of mind, as articulated in the *Philosophy of Mind* and the *Philosophy of Right*, stipulates that it is neither rational nor good for individuals to respect natural entities in virtue of their intrinsic goodness. Rather, individuals have reason to modify these entities regardless of their degree of goodness. Anyone attracted by Hegel's ethical argument for his conception of nature, and by his phenomenological grounding for this argument, is likely to feel less than sanguine about this assessment of our moral responsibilities toward the environment. Yet Hegel's conclusion regarding these responsibilities is necessarily connected to his more basic phenomenological and ethical arguments, as we should now explore.

How Consistent Is Hegel's Account of Nature's Ethical Status?

Hegel's account of the rationality of transforming nature is thoroughly embedded in his overall theory of the development of mind and of its necessary transition from cognitive to practical (and then social) existence. As such, his rationale for the transformation of nature is firmly integrated into his encyclopaedic system; as part of this, it is bound together with his systematic theory of the development of the natural world. At the specifically ethical level, Hegel's assertion of our duty to transform natural entities is also closely intertwined with his evaluation of all nature as intrinsically good. That evaluation relies upon the premise that action from reason (which Hegel discerns throughout natural forms) is good. Yet this same premise leads him to believe it good for human individuals to act in ways that resolve their internal contradictions, and therefore to resolve the internal contradiction of theoretical intelligence by starting to modify natural entities. His accounts of the value of nature and of the scope of human responsibility to natural entities both presuppose the same metaphysics of rationality and the same attendant ethical standpoint, on which practical reason is good. Thus, while it may look incongruous that Hegel claims both that all natural entities are intrinsically valuable and that humans have no duties to respect or preserve them, really these two claims are tightly integrated within his overall system.

We may still wonder whether some inconsistency arises between these two claims. In particular, we might consider the following scenario. Suppose that human individuals, acting rationally, modify natural entities in such a deep-rooted way that those entities can no longer arise or regenerate themselves in their spontaneous form. This disrupts nature's ontological hierarchy, since it eliminates one or more of the forms which are supposed to figure necessarily within it. Yet nature's internal order is the necessary condition of the emergence of human individuals themselves—for humans emerge as the rational solution to tensions within organic life, in which natural development culminates. In dislocating nature's internal order, then, human agents appear to be acting *irrationally*, for the order that they are dislocating is the condition of possibility for their own existence. It appears that their disruption of natural order irrationally erases the very condition that makes it possible. Doesn't the possibility of this scenario reveal that, after all, Hegel ought not to affirm our duty to modify nature without restraint?

He avoids this problem by denying that the scenario *is* possible. Certainly, he agrees that we can modify natural entities in deep-seated ways. He distinguishes between modifying entities in relatively superficial ways—by merely adding new structures to those they already possess—and altering these entities internally, at a deep level. This involves penetrating inside their existing structures to rearrange the relations between their constituent elements.

> Matter . . . is never without an essential form, and it is only by virtue of this form that it is something. The more I appropriate this form, the more I come into *actual* possession of the thing. The consumption of foodstuffs [for example] is a penetration and alteration of their qualitative nature by virtue of which they were what they were before they were consumed. . . . In face of the free will, the thing does not retain any distinct property for itself. (PR §52R/82–83)

Hegel calls this process the "formation" (*Formierung*) of entities, through which "the effects which I have on [a natural thing] do not remain merely external, but are assimilated by it" (§56R/86). He adduces the breeding of new types of animal and plant and the conversion of soil into fertile land, but gestures toward a potentially infinite range of methods by which natural entities can be internally altered.

However, Hegel denies that this alteration can affect the *forms* that the entities being acted upon instantiate. For example, he denies that we can alter "elemental" forms such as air and water (PR §46R/77, §56A/86)—we can only alter isolated portions of these elements:

> [T]he genus and the elemental are not as such the *object of personal individuality*; in order to become such an object and be taken possession of, they must first be individualized (a breath of air—a drink of water). With regard to the impossibility of taking possession of an external genus as such, or of the elemental, the ultimate consideration is not the external physical impossibility of doing so, but the fact that the person, as will . . . is at the same time immediate individuality; hence he is also related, as a person, to the external world as to individual things [*Einzelheiten*]. (§52R/82)

Modify particular entities as deeply as we will, no amount of such modification can touch the universals or forms (the "genera") which these particular entities instantiate. It is therefore impossible for the activities of finite human individuals to impact upon the internal order of nature, according to Hegel. This looks a naïve view, in light of the thoroughgoing reconstitution which the environment has undergone since the early 1800s. But Hegel's belief in the impermeability of nature's internal order is philosophically grounded in his overall metaphysical conception of nature. For him, the order of natural forms is rationally necessary, generated not in time, through contingent physical processes, but "within the inner idea" (EN §249/1: 212). As such, this order is invulnerable to any contingent actions that human individuals may carry out: regardless of those actions, the order itself will be endlessly regenerated through the sheer force of rational requirements. Thus, the very fact that natural order is rationally necessary means that it cannot be disrupted by human activities, so that individuals are at no risk of negating the conditions of their own possibility, however radically they interfere with the natural entities around them.

Hegel's claims that we have an unlimited duty to transform nature and that all its forms are intrinsically good continue to prove consistent. Indeed, beyond this, these claims are deeply intertwined, both relying upon the same rationalist metaphysics and the same rationalist understanding of good action. Let me clarify further how Hegel's rationalist standpoint binds these two claims together. Unusually, his revaluation of nature extends to it a property—practical rationality—which is traditionally assumed to be the prerogative of human beings and to be opposed to matter as its superior counterpart. In assuming that nature needs to possess this property to have value, Hegel uncritically accepts that matter and rationality are hierarchically ranked opposites, presupposing that, whereas matter is discrete and inert, rationality is synthesizing and active, in a way defining it as intrinsically valuable whereas matter is not. Hegel revalues nature by rescuing it from (what he sees as) the sphere of mere matter, instead conceiving nature as saturated with rationality.[35] Rather than simply repeating the view that matter and rationality are distributed between nature and humanity, Hegel duplicates the traditionally hierarchical split between these poles *within* the natural world. In this, he fails to interrogate either the firmness of the traditional distinctions between rationality and matter or the validity of the grounds on which intrinsic value has traditionally been accorded only to rationality.

Above all, in failing to question the historical ascription of unique value to rationality, Hegel is failing to question the very basis on which humanity has traditionally been allotted a value denied to nature. Thus, his strategy for revaluing nature remains paradoxically dependent upon the same narrow anthropocentrism which that revaluation sets out to complicate and mitigate. This makes it inevitable that his account of nature should climax in an account of the generation of human individuals as practically rational to an unparalleled degree. It also makes it inevitable that Hegel should deny that the less perfect—more material, "petrified"—rationality of nature can ever limit the obligations practical reason imposes upon human agents. His assertion that humans have the duty to modify natural entities without restraint only makes explicit a presupposition—that human rationality sets the standard of intrinsic value—which, implicitly, has been in force all along behind his revaluation of nature.

However, there *is* an inconsistency between Hegel's rationalist conception of nature and the phenomenological basis upon which he defends it. His rationalist conception entails our lack of moral responsibility to preserve or respect natural entities—which, arguably, conflicts with the moral sensibility that Hegel implies us to have. As I have argued, he believes that we need a conception of nature which articulates our sense of its intrinsic value; he contends that his rationalist conception fulfills this role because it discerns goodness in all natural forms. Yet by articulating our sense of nature's intrinsic value in terms of its rationality, he generates an understanding of its goodness which entails that we have no responsibilities to protect, preserve, or respect natural entities. This conclusion clashes with the sense of nature's intrinsic value from which Hegel begins, insofar as that sense of intrinsic value is plausibly thought to include, or imply, that nature's constituent entities are morally considerable in their own right.

To say that a natural entity is morally considerable is to say, as Mary Anne Warren explains, that "we may not treat it in just any way we please: we are morally obliged to give weight [to it] in our deliberations . . . because [it has] moral importance in [its] own right."[36] Now, there seems to be a conceptual connection between the idea that natural entities are valuable in themselves and the idea that these entities deserve moral consideration: that in deliberating on what to do, we must take into account how our actions will affect these entities, for their own sake. If natural entities are intrinsically valuable, this fact must bear upon our deliberations. These deliberations cannot consistently refer only to our own needs in resolving contradictions, but must also make independent reference to natural entities in virtue of the value intrinsic to them. Admittedly, just as our basic sense of nature's intrinsic value is (for Hegel) quite incipient and amorphous, so our sense of nature's moral considerability must be correspondingly incipient and amorphous too. Nevertheless, it seems inconceivable that one could have the sense of intrinsic value without an attendant sense that this value implies the need to take natural entities into account, for their own sake, in deciding how to act.

The way in which Hegel articulates our sense of nature's intrinsic value—in terms of its practical rationality—results in his denying that humans have any duties to respect natural entities, thereby violating the sense of nature's moral considerability that seems integral to our sense of its intrinsic value. But since Hegel believes that a metaphysical conception of nature is only adequate if it can articulate sensibility, his rationalist conception of nature turns out, by his own standards, to be inadequate. The rationalist conception falls foul of his own phenomenological criterion of adequacy. Although he claims that his rationalist conception is more adequate than the scientific view of nature because it better articulates sensibility, it transpires that his rationalist conception itself breaks significantly with experience and so cannot be deemed adequate.

Assessment of Hegel's Ethical Argument

Let me review Hegel's ethical argument and its central problem. He argues that his rationalist view of nature is uniquely adequate because it allows him to attribute intrinsic goodness to all natural forms, deriving from their practical rationality. Although he only sketches it out obliquely, his underlying assumption is that this makes his metaphysics of nature adequate because it means that this metaphysics articulates our basic sense of nature's intrinsic value. Yet, by Hegel's own phenomenological criterion, his rationalist view of nature is inadequate: since it entails that humans have no duties to respect natural entities, it fails to accommodate fully our fundamental sense of nature's intrinsic value.

This problem does not render Hegel's ethical argument worthless. On the contrary, I think, this argument establishes a plausible set of criteria that an adequate conception of nature must meet—even though, ironically, these criteria invalidate the specifically rationalist conception that Hegel supports. He suggests that we have a basic sense of nature's intrinsic value, which an adequate view of nature must articulate conceptually. We need not embrace his further belief that his particular conception of natural forms as intrinsically rational provides this articulation. Nonetheless, he does provide grounds for denying that the scientific understanding of nature is capable of articulating our ethical sensibility. As Hegel suggests, science presupposes that natural forms are bare things, a view which entails that the whole of nature is intrinsically value-neutral. In arguing that an adequate metaphysical view of nature must remain attuned to our ethical sensibility, Hegel provides grounds for thinking that we need an alternative, specifically *philosophical*, conception of nature, distinct from this scientific conception. In particular, he provides grounds for thinking that an adequate philosophical reconceptualization of nature must reject its interpretation as a domain of bare things. Without this, it will be impossible to see nature in itself as anything other than value-neutral. The argument for articulating sensibility tells, in addition, against Hegel's own rationalist conception of nature, but it remains important in opening up the project of a philosophical rethinking of nature which *could*, in some way, accommodate our sense of its intrinsic value. In the conclusion to this book, I shall assess the prospects for such a project as it has arisen through my reading of Hegel's *Philosophy of Nature*.

CONCLUSION

Hegel's Project of a Philosophy of Nature

This conclusion has two aims. First, I want to bring together the strands of my interpretation of Hegel's *Philosophy of Nature* to provide a comprehensive outline of how his arguments constitute one interconnected defence of his theory of the natural world. Second, I wish to indicate how Hegel's arguments, although not fully successful in defending the actual theory of nature that he presents, nevertheless have the important outcome of opening up the philosophy of nature as a project. I hope to suggest that the lasting achievement of Hegel's *Philosophy of Nature* lies not in its specific theory of nature but in its opening up of this project, conceived as the project of redescribing natural forms in terms of a metaphysics of nature which is distinct from that presupposed in empirical science, and which is adequate in virtue of its phenomenological and ethical richness. In view of the deficiencies in Hegel's defence of his own theory of nature, this broader project of a philosophy of nature needs ultimately to be rearticulated outside the parameters of his work. It is beyond the scope of this book to explore in any detail what shape this incipient project might assume. More modestly, I will point toward some possible directions for future inquiry, based on my appraisal of the strengths and weaknesses of Hegel's own formulations.

First, let me bring together the strands of my reading of the *Philosophy of Nature*. I began by intervening into the controversy over the work's methodology, outlining three interpretations of this methodology: what I called the strong a priori, weak a priori, and a posteriori interpretations. I argued that strong a priorism, as Hegel construes it, is more cogent than is generally appreciated, since it neither deduces nor absolutizes scientific findings but constructs a sui generis theory of nature in terms of which scientific findings can provisionally be reinterpreted. In contrast, weak a priorism cannot but falsely absolutize scientific findings, and it should therefore be rejected as an interpretation of Hegel's approach. In contrast again, the a posteriori interpretation of Hegel *is* philosophically tenable—but, as I argued, we should still prefer the strong a priori interpretation, because this enables us to develop a fruitful metaphysical reading of Hegel, according to which he aims to give a realistic description of forms of thought that structure, and are instantiated throughout, the domains of nature and mind. This reading is fruitful insofar as it allows us to explore the possibility that Hegel develops a basic theory of nature's organizing conceptual structures, a theory that is couched in the sui generis terms of absolute idealism and is potentially capable of grounding a critique of modern science.

Rereading Hegel's *Philosophy of Nature* in strong a priori terms, we find it presenting a basic theory of nature as the scene for the gradual unification of its two constituent elements, thought and matter. This theory reflects Hegel's absolute idealist metaphysics: it describes all natural forms as forms of objective thought which are instantiated in, or combined with, matter in progressively improving ways. Hegel's basic theory of nature also reflects his absolute idealist view that objective forms of thought are intrinsically rational. This view underpins his claim that his theory of nature is more adequate than contrasting scientific accounts (which must therefore be recontextualized and reinterpreted in his terms). Hegel takes his theory to be more adequate because it reflects his more adequate metaphysical conception of natural forms, according to which they are intrinsically rational. However, this metaphysical conception of natural forms as intrinsically rational might well be thought *less* adequate than the contrasting metaphysical conception presupposed in empirical science, according to which natural forms are bare things. This is because Hegel's rationalist metaphysics of nature seems to suffer from a delusive anthropomorphism. Averting this worry, he stresses that the rationality of natural forms is specifically "petrified," nonconscious, and entirely poured out into their behavior.

Hegel's mature system sketches four main arguments defending his claim that his rationalist conception of nature is more adequate than the scientific conception. He suggests, unsuccessfully, that his rationalist metaphysics of nature has the greater explanatory power, and, again unsuccessfully, that this metaphysics is proven uniquely true by its systematic derivation from his analysis of abstract forms of thought in the *Logic*. Hegel also advances two comparatively successful arguments:

what I have called his "phenomenological" and "ethical" arguments. According to his phenomenological argument, his rationalist metaphysics is more adequate because, uniquely, it enables the elaboration of a theory of nature that remains continuous with our basic, sensible, experience of nature as elemental. Only the rationalist view of nature allows Hegel to conceptualize the dynamism and flux that we sense to characterize the elements and the natural forms that they compose. He also argues that his rationalist metaphysics is more adequate because it allows him to conceptualize intrinsic value in all nature, stemming from its practical rationality. Hegel therefore takes his metaphysics to be more true to nature's real being than the metaphysical belief in bare things that is presupposed in empirical science, because it allows us to recognize both the intrinsic value and the elemental dynamism of natural forms, thereby generating a theory of nature that remains appropriately consonant with sensibility.

Nonetheless, as I have suggested, neither Hegel's phenomenological nor his ethical arguments entirely succeed. His phenomenological argument is incomplete: he fails to explain fully why sensible experience should be considered veridical in the first place. Moreover, Hegel's ethical argument cuts against the rationalist metaphysics of nature that he wishes to defend. Even though this metaphysics enables Hegel to assign intrinsic goodness to all natural forms, it also obliges him to deny humans any moral responsibilities to respect natural entities. This is because Hegel's rationalist criterion of goodness entails that humans should so act as to resolve contradictions, which means, given his substantive account of mind, that they should act so as to transform all kinds of natural entities without restraint. Here Hegel's rationalist metaphysics compels him to break with the sense of nature's moral considerability that is reasonably seen as essential to our sense of its intrinsic value. His rationalist conception of nature falls short of his own standards of metaphysical adequacy.

Reviewing Hegel's overall defense of his rationalist metaphysics and theory of nature, we must conclude that this defense is only partially successful. Yet, although Hegel's claims and arguments do not entirely cohere, his *Philosophy of Nature* remains important as the place where he works out and articulates a distinctive approach to the study of nature. Over and above his specific arguments, Hegel can be seen to be engaged in defining philosophy of nature as a project, a definite way of thinking about the metaphysical and ethical status of the natural world. Centrally, this project involves redescribing natural forms on the basis of a specifically philosophical metaphysics of nature, a metaphysics that is held to be adequate in virtue of both its continuity with sensible experience and its recognition of nature's intrinsic value. So conceived, the philosophy of nature differs significantly not only from empirical scientific inquiry, but also both from the philosophy of science and from more traditional, prescientific, modes of cosmological enquiry. Unlike the philosophy of science, Hegel's philosophy of nature fundamentally aims to generate a sui generis theory of nature and not merely to justify, clarify, or reorganize scientific accounts (although part of his remit is, subsequently, to reinterpret scientific accounts in philosophical terms). Moreover, unlike traditional cosmological inquiry, Hegel seeks to redescribe nature guided by phenomenological and ethical criteria of theoretical adequacy: this confers on his approach a distinctive potential for powerful *critical* engagement with modern science.

In respect of this critical potential, the philosophy of nature as Hegel articulates it can make a crucial contribution to environmentalist projects. As I have stressed, his work makes possible a sustained diagnosis of environmental problems as deriving, ultimately, from the defective metaphysical presuppositions that underlie modern empirical science as a whole. According to Hegel, science is unified—despite its variety and its ever-increasing sophistication—by the basic and enduring metaphysical assumption that nature is a realm of bare things. From Hegel's perspective, this metaphysical conception of nature is inadequate, and so, by implication, is bound to issue in correspondingly inadequate accounts of natural forms and correspondingly damaging technological applications. In particular, for Hegel, empirical science's metaphysics of nature is inadequate insofar as it is separated from our basic sense of nature as dynamic, elemental, and intrinsically valuable—instead offering a misleading portrayal of natural forms as inert and inherently value-neutral. Given this inadequacy at the level of its metaphysical presuppositions, it is unsurprising that modern science should typically generate technologies that are poorly attuned to the real character of nature, on which they tend to exert destructive or damaging effects.

Hegel's projection for a specifically philosophical form of inquiry into nature implies a novel solution to environmental problems, which would repay further investigation. Implicit within his mature work is a vision of a future recontextualization of scientific findings within a specifically philosophical theory of nature. Thus, Hegel in no way recommends the abandonment of science or its supersession by some spurious alternative. Rather, for Hegel, scientific research should continue, because its findings are informative; yet, paradoxically, these findings are always misleading as well, which makes it necessary that they succumb to ongoing reinterpretation in terms of a more adequate philosophical theory of nature. From Hegel's point of view, it is this philosophical theory that should be authoritative in informing our interactions with nature; this should ensure that those interactions would assume a relatively benign and environmentally sensitive form.

Despite the ecological potential of Hegel's proposal for a specifically philosophical form of study of nature, his particular, rationalist, philosophical theory of nature is insufficiently supported by his own arguments, as we have seen. Yet since these arguments fall short at determinate points, reconsidering these weak points allows us to identify alternative directions in which the philosophy of nature could be developed beyond Hegel's original formulations. First, then, it has transpired that Hegel's rationalist metaphysics is inadequate ethically because it revalues nature by extending to it characteristics—conceptuality and rationality—which have traditionally been regarded as unique to humanity. Rather than revaluing nature qua material, Hegel revalues nature by redescribing it as containing conceptuality in addition to matter. In this way, he sets out to "rescue" nature from the sphere of (what he presumes to be) intrinsically worthless matter. Hegel's revaluation of nature thereby depends upon—and, ultimately, reinstates—the narrowly anthropocentric view that nature is valuable only insofar as it resembles or approximates to humanity. To avoid this continuing tendency to privilege humanity over nature, the nascent discipline of philosophy of nature needs to begin to revalue nature *in* its materiality—questioning the stability of the distinction between matter and rationality, and rediscovering neglected dimensions of agency, dynamism, and self-organization within materiality itself. A revaluation of material nature along these lines would problematize, rather than take for granted, the preeminent value of rational humanity, and could therefore accommodate human duties of respect for nature in a way that Hegel's excessively rationalist perspective cannot.

Second, Hegel's phenomenological argument for his rationalist metaphysics has proved to be incomplete insofar as he has not fully explained why sensible experience should be considered veridical—or, therefore, why a theory of nature that articulates sensibility should be considered to be true to nature's real being. Nonetheless, Hegel's discussion of sensibility does open up a positive line for further inquiry, indicating that sensibility should be considered veridical because human beings emerge from nature and consequently possess a system of senses that recapitulates, and accurately reflects, the patterns of organization that objectively structure preexisting natural forms. Insofar, then, as the philosophy of nature aims to produce a theory of nature that remains congruent with sensibility, it needs to include as one of its central elements a phenomenological examination of how the contours of our sensibility reflect our embeddedness in the natural world.[1] The philosophy of nature should incorporate reflection on the status of humans as ecologically situated beings with senses that develop in parallel to objective natural forms—senses which should therefore be considered to be veridical, and to merit theoretical and metaphysical articulation.[2]

Despite the limitations of Hegel's own thinking about nature, his work opens up the philosophy of nature as an important project and suggests several promising ways in which this project could be extended and developed so as to contribute to the revaluation of the natural environment. Yet, in affirming the kinship between Hegel's approach to nature and that of contemporary environmental thought, I may still appear to have been guilty of anachronism. This is especially so as Hegel's critical perspective upon modern science and the disenchantment of nature remains largely implicit within his work, emerging only when the claims of his *Philosophy of Nature* are carefully reconstructed in light of his entire system. However, by reconstructing the *Philosophy of Nature* in this way, I hope to have brought out a critical and protoenvironmentalist strain of thought which is really present within Hegel's work. Certainly, this strain of thought does not exhaust Hegel's philosophy. Yet it is precisely the inexhaustible richness of this philosophy which permits us to reread it in light of current ecological concerns, and to recover its neglected project of redescribing nature in a reenchanted and phenomenologically resonant way. We can, and should, rediscover Hegel as a thinker who seeks to recognize agency, rationality, and intrinsic value in nature, and who therefore has a significant contribution to make to the contemporary task of reappraising the metaphysical and ethical status of the natural world.

NOTES

Introduction: The Problem of Hegel's Philosophy of Nature

1. It may immediately be objected that Schelling, not Hegel, originates the project of philosophy of nature. I discuss this issue on p. xvii.

2. Terry Pinkard, *Hegel: A Biography* (Cambridge: Cambridge University Press, 2000), pp. 562–63.

3. Alexandre Kojève, *Introduction to the Reading of Hegel*, trans. James H. Nichols, Jr. (Ithaca: Cornell University Press, 1969), p. 146.

4. On the standard charge that a priori theories of nature must be fantastic, see, for example, Karen Gloy and Paul Burger, eds., *Die Naturphilosophie im Deutschen Idealismus* (Stuttgart-Bad Cannstatt: Frommann-Holzboog, 1993), p. viii; Habermas, *Knowledge and Human Interests*, trans. Jeremy J. Shapiro (London: Heinemann, 1978), p. 24.

5. That is, natural forms lack rationality, agency, and intrinsic meaning; see chapter 3.

6. Importantly, though, Hegel does not believe that natural forms are conscious: for him, they exhibit a specifically nonconscious or "petrified" rationality, as I will explain.

7. Whenever I refer to Hegel's "rationalist" view/conception/metaphysics of nature, this denotes his view that all natural forms act rationally (otherwise expressed, that all natural forms are intrinsically rational). Thus, I do *not* mean that Hegel uncritically endorses reason in a traditional Enlightenment fashion, nor do I mean that he practices metaphysics in a pre-Kantian (Leibnizian or Spinozist) sense.

8. David Kolb, *The Critique of Pure Modernity: Hegel, Heidegger, and After* (Chicago: University of Chicago Press, 1986), p. 91.

9. Jeffrey Reid, "Hegel and the State University: The University of Berlin and Its Founding Contradictions," *Owl of Minerva* 32: 1 (2000): 11.

10. As they are, for example, by David Farrell Krell, who satirically portrays Hegel as a dualistic and somatophobic figure in his philosophical novel *Son of Spirit* (Albany: State University of New York Press, 1997).

11. Inasmuch as Hegel's *Philosophy of Nature* supports a metaphysical reading of his mature system, it is no coincidence that, inversely, nonmetaphysical readings of Hegel tend to minimize the salience of nature in his thought; for example, Robert Pippin states that: "Hegel concentrates on the basic idealist issues and usually stays far away from Schelling's romantic philosophy of nature" (*Hegel's Idealism: The Satisfactions of Self-Consciousness* [Cambridge: Cambridge University Press, 1989], p. 66). (For clarification of what I mean by "metaphysical" and "nonmetaphysical" readings, see chapter 1, "Metaphysical Disputes in the Interpretation of the *Philosophy of Nature*.")

12. See, respectively, Allen Wood, *Hegel's Ethical Thought* (Cambridge: Cambridge University Press, 1990), and Alan Patten, *Hegel's Idea of Freedom* (Oxford: Oxford University Press, 2000).

13. If this picture of Hegel seems surprising, consider Sebastian Gardner's similar interpretation of German Idealism as a whole, on which it opposes Spinozist naturalism by theorizing what Gardner calls our "objectual" relation to value: that is, our relation to "value as in some sense an object of experience," embodied above all in nature (Gardner, "German Idealism," in *Proceedings of the Aristotelian Society* Supplement 76 [2002]: 221).

14. "Mind" is, of course, the English translation of Hegel's term *Geist*, which can also be translated as "spirit." Whereas "mind" captures better the rational, conceptual, and thinking aspects of *Geist*, "spirit" better captures its cultural, historical, and collective dimension. I use "mind" in some contexts and "spirit" in others, depending on which aspects of *Geist* feature most prominently in the relevant parts of Hegel's philosophy.

15. Robert Wicks, "Hegel's Aesthetics: An Overview," in *The Cambridge Companion to Hegel*, ed. Frederick Beiser (Cambridge: Cambridge University Press, 1993), pp. 352–58.

16. As Jon Stewart suggests with reference to Hegel's figuration of reason as a "disease" in the *Phenomenology of Mind*, Hegel "is very aware of the pernicious aspects of reason, and thus is best seen not as the last *Aufklärer* but rather as a forerunner of the so-called 'irrationalist tradition' " ("Hegel and the Myth of Reason," in *The Hegel Myths and Legends*, ed. Jon Stewart [Evanston, Il.: Northwestern University Press, 1996], p. 307).

17. A well-known representative of this approach is Michael J. Petry; see his introduction to his translation of the *Philosophy of Nature*, 3 vols. (London: Allen and Unwin, 1970). I discuss other authors associated with this approach in chapter 1.

18. Prominent examples of this primarily historical approach to the *Philosophy of Nature* are Otto Breidbach, *Das Organische in Hegels Denken: Studie zur Naturphilosophie und Biologie um 1800* (Würzburg: Königshausen und Neumann, 1982); Dietrich von Engelhardt, *Hegel und die Chemie: Studie zur Philosophie und Wissenschaft der Natur um 1800* (Wiesbaden: Pressler, 1976); Rolf-Peter Horstmann and Michael J. Petry, eds., *Hegels Philosophie der Natur: Beziehungen zwischen empirischer und spekulativer Naturerkenntnis* (Stuttgart: Klett-Cotta, 1986); Michael J. Petry, ed., *Hegel und die Naturwissenschaften* (Stuttgart: Frommann-Holzboog, 1987); Michael J. Petry, ed., *Hegel and Newtonianism* (Dordrecht: Kluwer, 1993).

19. See, for example, John W. Burbidge, *Real Process: How Logic and Chemistry Combine in Hegel's Philosophy of Nature* (Toronto: University of Toronto Press, 1996); Stephen Houlgate, ed., *Hegel and the Philosophy of Nature* (Albany: State University of New York Press, 1998); David Farrell Krell, *Contagion: Sexuality, Disease, and Death in German Idealism and Romanticism* (Bloomington: Indiana University Press, 1998); and the articles on "Logic, Nature, and Empirical Science" in *Owl of Minerva* 34: 1 (2002–2003). See also Brigitte Falkenburg, *Die Form der Materie* (Frankfurt: Athenäum, 1987).

20. On this conflict between present-centered and past-centered approaches to interpretation, see Richard Rorty, "The Historiography of Philosophy: Four Genres," in *Philosophy in History*, ed. Richard Rorty, J. B. Schneewind, and Quentin Skinner (Cambridge: Cambridge University Press, 1984), pp. 49–53. Quentin Skinner famously defends the past-centred approach in "Meaning and Understanding in the History of Ideas," *History and Theory* 8 (1969): 3–53.

21. Hans-Georg Gadamer, *Truth and Method* (1960), 2nd ed. rev., by Joel Weinsheimer and Donald G. Marshall (London: Sheed and Ward, 1989), pp. 265–85.

22. Brian Fay, *Contemporary Philosophy of Social Science* (Oxford: Blackwell, 1996), p. 144.

23. Michelet employed Hegel's Jena notes on philosophy of nature from 1805 to 1806, as well as materials relating to his lectures in Heidelberg (1818) and Berlin (1819–1820, 1821–1822, 1823–1824, 1825–1826, 1828, 1830). See John N. Findlay, foreword to the *Philosophy of Nature*, trans. A. V. Miller (Oxford: Clarendon Press, 1970), pp. vi–vii.

24. *Naturphilosophie Band I: Die Vorlesung von 1819/20*, ed. Manfred Gies (Napoli: Bibliopolis, 1982); *Vorlesung über Naturphilosophie Berlin 1821/22, Nachschrift von Boris von Uexküll*, ed. Gilles Marmasse and Thomas Posch (Frankfurt: Peter Lang, 2002); *Vorlesung über Naturphilosophie Berlin 1823/24, Nachschrift von K. G. J. v. Griesheim*, ed. Gilles Marmasse (Frankfurt: Peter Lang, 2000). For a helpful overview of the relationship between the versions of Hegel's *Encyclopaedia*, his various lecture courses on nature, and the surviving student transcripts, see Wolfgang Bonsiepen, "Hegels Vorlesungen über Naturphilosophie," *Hegel-Studien* 26 (1991): 4–54.

25. John Burbidge, *Real Process*, pp. 7–8.

26. George R. Lucas, "A Re-Interpretation of Hegel's Philosophy of Nature," *Journal of the History of Philosophy* 22 (1984): 103. A representative statement of this view of Hegel can be found in Joseph L. Esposito, *Schelling's Idealism and Philosophy of Nature* (Lewisburg, PA: Bucknell University Press, 1977), p. 9.

27. See Schelling, *Ideas for a Philosophy of Nature*, trans. Errol E. Harris and Peter Heath (Cambridge: Cambridge University Press, 1988). Schelling's other main publications on nature were *Von der Weltseele, eine Hypothese der höheren Physik zur Erklärung des allgemeinen Organismus* (1798) and *Erster Entwurf eines Systems der Naturphilosophie* (1799).

28. However, the early German Romantics—Novalis and Schelling above all—saw art (and, later, religion) as the medium for the reenchantment of nature,

rather than philosophical theory as for Hegel. See, for example, the selections in *The Early Political Writings of the German Romantics*, ed. Frederick C. Beiser (Cambridge: Cambridge University Press, 1996).

29. See, especially, Andrew Bowie, *From Romanticism to Critical Theory* (London: Routledge, 1997); Philippe Lacoue-Labarthe and Jean-Luc Nancy, *The Literary Absolute: The Theory of Literature in German Romanticism*, trans. Philip Barnard and Cheryl Lester (Albany: State University of New York Press, 1988); Charles Larmore, *The Romantic Legacy* (New York: Columbia University Press, 1996).

30. I also ignore the question of Hegel's rejection of evolution (EN §249/ 1: 212–15; of course, Hegel was not rejecting specifically Darwinian evolution). I sidestep this issue because I regard Hegel's denial of evolution as a merely contingent, inessential, feature of his account of nature: this follows from my broader view that Hegel only ever accepts or rejects scientific findings and theories on an interpretive, provisional, basis (see chapter 1). For discussion of Hegel and evolution, see: Wolfgang Bonsiepen, "Hegels kritische Auseinandersetzung mit der zeitgenössischen Evolutionstheorie," in *Hegels Philosophie der Natur*, ed. Horstmann and Petry, pp. 151–71; Otto Breidbach, "Hegels Evolutionskritik," *Hegel-Studien* 22 (1987), pp. 165–72; Martin Drees, "Evolution and Emanation of Spirit in Hegel's *Philosophy of Nature*," *Bulletin of the Hegel Society of Great Britain* 26 (1992): 52–61.

31. See, on this, Dieter Wandschneider, *Raum, Zeit, Relativität: Grundbestimmungen der Physik in der Perspektive der Hegelschen Naturphilosophie* (Frankfurt: Klostermann, 1982).

32. Some scholars have attempted to reconstruct Hegel's overall view of natural development: Errol E. Harris, "The Philosophy of Nature in Hegel's System," *Review of Metaphysics* 3 (1949–1950): 213–28; Thomas Kalenberg, *Die Befreiung der Natur: Natur und Selbstbewußtsein in der Philosophie Hegels* (Hamburg: Meiner, 1997); Robert Stern, *Hegel, Kant, and the Structure of the Object* (London: Routledge, 1990). However, they have not recognized Hegel's basic theory that nature progressively unifies its conceptual and material elements.

1. A Priori Knowledge in Hegel's Philosophy of Nature

1. Hegel does, of course, think his own philosophy scientific (*wissenschaftlich*) in that it provides a systematically organized body of knowledge: accordingly, he designates his work the "system of science" (*System der Wissenschaft*). However, his philosophy is not scientific in the sense of being *empirical*. For clarity, I use "science" here—and throughout—to mean only modern empirical science. So, when I refer to Hegel's approach to nature as nonscientific or distinct from that of science, I am not denying his systematicity, but claiming that his approach is nonempirical.

2. Given this broad understanding of how natural science is empirical, Hegel occasionally includes under the heading of natural science not only modern science but also some ancient and medieval natural philosophy. Nonetheless, he ultimately sees modern science as distinctive in its sustained attention to the

empirical, reflected in its experimental method (PhG 151/192–93; VGP 3: 175–76/3: 77–78).

3. Throughout my exposition I use "natural forms" to refer to the patterns or ontological structures embodied in perceptible natural events and entities (so, I use "natural structures" interchangeably with "natural forms'). I use "natural entities" or "natural phenomena" to refer to the particular events and entities instantiating these general structures.

4. In the introduction to the *Science of Logic*, Hegel again urges us to adopt—rather than merely pretend to employ—a philosophical approach that derives each logical category in a necessary series, a derivation which he describes as the "deduction" (*Deduktion*) and "leading out" (*Ableitung*) of categories (WL 55/1: 51). (Miller translates both terms as "deduction.")

5. On Hegel's inconsistency, see also Martin Drees, "The Logic of Hegel's Philosophy of Nature," in *Hegel and Newtonianism*, ed. Michael J. Petry (Dordrecht: Kluwer, 1993), p. 97; Thomas Webb, "The Problem of Empirical Knowledge in Hegel's Philosophy of Nature," in *Hegel-Studien* 15 (1980): 177. As Webb puts it, Hegel vacillates between saying that "empirical phenomena . . . merely illustrate the necessary and autonomous development of the natural categories" and that these phenomena are "constitutive of the content of the categories of nature themselves" (p. 177).

6. Hegel, *Vorlesung über Naturphilosophie Berlin 1823/24*, p. 72.

7. For example, Gerd Buchdahl states that the idea that Hegel's approach was basically speculative "bear[s] little relation to the truth of the matter, and [is] certainly not supported by a reading of Hegel's actual writings" ("Hegel on the Interaction between Science and Philosophy," in *Hegel and Newtonianism*, ed. Petry, p. 61).

8. Ernan McMullin, "Philosophies of Nature," in *The New Scholasticism* 43 (1969): 50.

9. Milic Capek, "Hegel and the Organic View of Nature," in *Hegel and the Sciences*, ed. Robert S. Cohen and Marx W. Wartofksy (Dordrecht: David Reidel, 1984), p. 109.

10. Habermas, *Knowledge and Human Interests*, trans. Jeremy J. Shapiro (London: Heinemann, 1978), p. 24. The worry, then, is that "Hegel was vainly and anachronistically competing with the natural sciences" (Ivan Soll, *An Introduction to Hegel's Metaphysics* [Chicago: Chicago University Press, 1969], p. 136).

11. As John J. Compton sums up, "hallowed misunderstandings . . . have Hegel either totally *ignoring* empirical facts and regularities or else claiming somehow to *derive* them deductively from the notion of nature" ("A Comment on Buchdahl's 'Conceptual Analysis and Scientific Theory in Hegel's Philosophy of Nature,' " in *Hegel and the Sciences*, ed. Cohen and Wartofsky, p. 37).

12. John Findlay, *Hegel: A Re-examination* (London: Allen and Unwin, 1958), p. 24.

13. Webb, "The Problem of Empirical Knowledge," p. 171.

14. This does not contradict my earlier claim that the overall organization of Hegel's theory is systematically ambiguous. My point is that the discussion of light is one place where Hegel openly constructs and describes part of

his theory in strong a priori terms. This discussion is therefore especially helpful for elucidating what strong a priorism involves, although it cannot as such resolve the wider dispute between strong and weak a priori readings.

15. Thomas Kalenberg also explores, with reference to light, how Hegel's proofs of "identity" involve provisional, contingent, interpretations of scientific material (Kalenberg, *Die Befreiung der Natur*, pp. 207–12).

16. Hegel adds that: "Philosophy must proceed on the basis of the concept, and even if it demonstrates very little, one has to be content with that. It is an error on the part of the philosophy of nature to want to face up to all appearances . . . Whatever is known through the concept is clear for itself and stands firm however, so that philosophy need not be disturbed if not all appearances are yet explained" (EN §270A/1: 281).

17. For some attempts at this, see Errol E. Harris, "The *Naturphilosophie* Updated," *Owl of Minerva* 10: 2 (1978): 2–7; Daniel O. Dahlstrom, "Hegel's Appropriation of Kant's Account of Teleology in Nature," in *Hegel and the Philosophy of Nature*, ed. Houlgate, pp. 177–82; Liberato Santoro-Brienza, "Aristotle and Hegel on Nature: Some Similarities," *Bulletin of the Hegel Society of Great Britain* 26 (1992): 13–29.

18. Stephen Houlgate agrees that "the philosophy of nature does not deduce the necessity of [for instance] *space* as such. It deduces the necessity of *externality*, and we find in experience that space is what most obviously corresponds to such externality" ("Logic and Nature in Hegel's Philosophy," *Owl of Minerva* 34: 1 [2002–2003]: 115).

19. Petry, Introduction to *Philosophy of Nature*, pp. 11–177.

20. Petry, Introduction to *The Berlin Phenomenology*, pp. xiii–xiv. See also Petry's "Hegel's Dialectic and the Natural Sciences," *Hegel-Jahrbuch* 19 (1975): 452–56.

21. Falkenburg, "How to Save the Phenomena: Meaning and Reference in Hegel's Philosophy of Nature," in *Hegel and the Philosophy of Nature*, ed. Houlgate, p. 130.

22. See Gerd Buchdahl, "Conceptual Analysis and Scientific Theory in Hegel's Philosophy of Nature (with Special Reference to Hegel's Optics)," in *Hegel and the Sciences*, ed. Cohen and Wartofsky, pp. 13–36; "Hegel's Philosophy of Nature and the Structure of Science," in *Hegel*, ed. Michael Inwood (Oxford: Oxford University Press, 1985), pp. 110–36.

23. Buchdahl, "Hegel on the Interaction between Science and Philosophy," p. 70.

24. Burbidge states: "Experience alone can show what phenomena actually occur" (*Real Process*, p. 164).

25. Hegel states: "Objects that are chemically differentiated are explicitly what they are only in virtue of their difference. Hence, they are the absolute drive to integrate themselves through and into one another" (EL §200A/278).

26. According to Burbidge, this development exemplifies a pattern that recurs whenever we think logically. First we define a concept and specify it (Hegel calls this the moment of "understanding"), then we identify a limitation in this specification (the moment of "dialectic"), then we devise a new specification

to correct this, which we again find limited, and finally we grasp all our limited conceptions as a whole (the "speculative" moment). This whole picture becomes a fresh concept for definition and specification (Burbidge, "Hegel's Conception of Logic," in *The Cambridge Companion to Hegel*, ed. Beiser, pp. 91–92).

27. Burbidge, *Real Process*, p. 105.

28. For Burbidge, this excessiveness of empirical phenomena is ontologically grounded in the "impotence" (*Ohnmacht*) of nature to correspond perfectly to logic. For Hegel: "It is the *impotence* of nature, that it maintains the determinations of the concept only abstractly and exposes the . . . particular to external determinability" (EN §250/1: 215).

29. Burbidge, *Real Process*, p. 164.

30. Ibid., p. 162.

31. Ibid., p. 198.

32. Ibid., p. 201.

33. As it happens, the "natural" category of chemical process is identical in content to the logical category of chemism, although it arises from reflection on empirical electricity rather than on the logical category of mechanism (*Real Process*, p. 114).

34. Ibid., p. 201.

35. Ibid., pp. 208, 207. Burbidge at one point suggests that natural categories are a priori *as well as* a posteriori, because they provide the starting points for organizing empirical materials (ibid., p. 131). But categories, like any items of knowledge, are a priori or a posteriori in virtue of how they are justified. Since natural categories are justified through their derivation from the empirical materials that they unify, they must be a posteriori. They may *appear* a priori when viewed in abstraction from their empirical context of justification, but really their justification renders them a posteriori—as Burbidge admits: "Of course the references . . . to real process have been justified on the basis of a posteriori considerations. . . . So I am using 'a priori' here not in any absolute sense" (ibid., p. 244). Elsewhere, he revealingly comments that, for Hegel, "philosophy about the real world is an a posteriori discipline" ("Challenge to Hegel: Contraries and Contradictories in Schelling's Late Philosophy," in *Hegel on Logic and Religion* [Albany: State University of New York Press, 1992], p. 69).

36. Burbidge, *On Hegel's Logic: Fragments of a Commentary* (Atlantic Highlands, NJ: Humanities Press, 1981), p. 4.

37. Ibid., p. 204.

38. Metaphysical readings of Hegel are defended in Frederick Beiser, "Introduction: Hegel and the Problem of Metaphysics," in *The Cambridge Companion to Hegel*, ed. Beiser, pp. 1–24; Michael Inwood, *Hegel* (London: Routledge, 1983); Michael Rosen, "From *Vorstellung* to Thought: Is a 'Non-Metaphysical' View of Hegel Possible?," in *G. W. F. Hegel: Critical Assessments*, ed. Robert Stern, 4 vols. (London: Routledge, 1993), vol. 3, pp. 329–44; Stern, *Hegel, Kant, and the Structure of the Object*; Thomas Wartenberg, "Hegel's Idealism: The Logic of Conceptuality," in *The Cambridge Companion to Hegel*, ed. Beiser, pp. 102–29.

39. The first nonmetaphysical interpreter was Klaus Hartmann, who regards Hegel as a "category theorist" who propounds a "scheme of ideas" but "engages in *no metaphysical commitment*" (*Studies in Foundational Philosophy* [Amsterdam: Rodopi, 1988], pp. 417, 420). See Hartmann's classic statement, "Hegel: A Non-Metaphysical View," in *Studies in Foundational Philosophy*, pp. 267–87. Terry Pinkard develops this interpretation in *Hegel's Dialectic: The Explanation of Possibility* (Philadelphia: Temple University Press, 1988).

40. Henry Allison, *Kant's Transcendental Idealism* (New Haven: Yale University Press, 1983), pp. 10–13.

41. See Pippin, *Hegel's Idealism.*

42. But see Kenneth Westphal, *Hegel's Epistemological Realism* (Dordrecht: Kluwer, 1989).

43. Patten, *Hegel's Idea of Freedom*, pp. 203, 24.

44. Wood, *Hegel's Ethical Thought*, p. 4.

45. Wartenberg points this out in "Hegel's Idealism," p. 120.

46. Wartenberg calls Hegel's metaphysics "conceptualism": a conceptualist "holds that concepts are the most basic objects in reality and the things that there are have reality only insofar as they reflect the structure of these concepts" ("Hegel's Idealism," p. 103). Wartenberg stresses that these concepts are primarily not items in the mind but blueprints for the development of finite beings: "Reality must contain the developmental plan of its own existence just as the seed does . . . 'the idea' is simply the developmental plan for all that exists" (p. 109). Wartenberg shows that Hegel envisages these objective concepts on the model of Aristotelian substantial forms, which really embody and manifest themselves in finite phenomena. However, Wartenberg downplays Hegel's distinctive view that these forms are logically interconnected to constitute a rational sequence. Precisely because of their rationality, Hegel calls these forms *thought*-forms (or the "idea"). We need to recognize Hegel as a metaphysical thinker or "absolute idealist" in that he believes all reality, natural and human, to instantiate a sequence of conceptual forms that exhibit a distinctively *rational* interconnectedness.

47. See EL §41A/67–68; EN §246A/1: 200; and the preface to the second (1831) edition of the *Science of Logic* (WL 36/1: 26, 39/1: 30).

48. Pippin, *Hegel's Idealism*, p. 7.

49. As Frederick Beiser remarks, "It is necessary to be extremely cautious in claiming that absolute idealism permits the absolute [that is, the "idea"] to exist independent of the knowing subject . . . [rather] the absolute comes to its fullest realization, organization, and development only in the . . . knowing subject" (*German Idealism: The Struggle against Subjectivism, 1781–1801* [Cambridge, MA: Harvard University Press, 2002], p. 13).

50. In the *Science of Logic*, Hegel distinguishes his logic from traditional metaphysics on the grounds that traditional metaphysics deployed categories uncritically without first investigating *how* they could be true of reality, or of what he prefers to call the "reasonable" (*Vernünftig*) (WL 64/1: 61–62).

51. Scholars often balk at seeing Hegel as critical of science itself; Kenneth Westphal, for example, states that: "Hegel seeks to discredit not science,

but those philosophical perspectives which are overawed by science and have come to worship it" (*Hegel's Epistemological Realism*, p. 96). Likewise, David Lamb sees Hegel as critical of philosophical empiricism but not of empirical science: "Hegel is not critical of observational and empirical procedures within the sciences" (*Hegel: From Foundation to System* [The Hague: Martinus Nijhoff, 1980], p. 102). Here Hegel scholars show themselves oddly dislocated from current ecological concerns about science.

52. Christopher Belshaw, *Environmental Philosophy: Reason, Nature, and Human Concern* (Chesham, Buckinghamshire: Acumen, 2001), p. 26. As Belshaw notes, premodern technological interventions were relatively localized and transient, tending to accommodate themselves to available natural materials.

53. According to Max Horkheimer, modern science conceives nature as uniform stuff or matter grasped in purely quantitative, mathematical, terms. Because scientific theories thereby disenchant nature, they inherently lend themselves to technological applications, and, moreover, specifically to technological applications of a kind which dominate the perceptible, qualitative, natural world. See Horkheimer, *Eclipse of Reason* (1947) (New York: Continuum, 1974), pp. 105–9. Herbert Marcuse agrees that scientific rationality, in defining nature as stuff, defines it as manipulable, thus anticipating the practical domination of nature. This is the "*internal* instrumentalist character of scientific rationality by virtue of which it is *a priori* technology, and the *a priori* of a *specific* technology . . . of domination" (*One-Dimensional Man* [Boston: Beacon Press, 1964], pp. 157–58).

54. See Genevieve Lloyd, "Feminism in History of Philosophy," in *The Cambridge Companion to Feminism in Philosophy*, ed. Miranda Fricker and Jennifer Hornsby (Cambridge: Cambridge University Press, 2000), pp. 245–63.

2. The Development of Nature: Overcoming the Division between Matter and Thought

1. See chapter 1, note 7.

2. This brevity arises, of course, because Hegel wrote the *Philosophy of Nature* as an outline for use in lecturing.

3. For now, I leave unexplained in what sense nature "progresses" or "develops." Hegel denies that natural development is temporal, but this leaves considerable ambiguity (explored in chapter 3). I also postpone until chapter 3 proper examination of Hegel's puzzling idea—introduced below—that natural stages follow one another *necessarily* (and, in particular, with *rational* necessity).

4. As Karl-Heinz Ilting notes, "Hegel . . . wants to show that we can present these shapes [of nature] as a developmental process in the course of which what he calls the "idea" [that is, the unity of matter and concept] or the 'absolute idea' increasingly comes forth" ("Hegels Philosophie des Organischen," in *Hegel und die Naturwissenschaften*, ed. Petry, p. 367). Gilles Marmasse characterizes the tension between concept and matter as a tension between nature's "inwardness" and "externality" in his foreword to Hegel's *Vorlesung über Naturphilosophie Berlin 1823/24*, p. 34.

5. For simplicity I use a terminology slightly different from Hegel's own: I call "consciousness" what he calls "consciousness as such," which he locates within a *wider* category of "consciousness" that also includes "self-consciousness" and "reason" (see EM xxi).

6. Petry's bilingual translation of EM §377–§482 as *Philosophy of Subjective Spirit* includes the 1825 lecture transcripts by Griesheim and Kehler as additions. I refer to these whenever they augment Hegel's main paragraphs.

7. Hegel's claim that nature is originally wholly "external" is elaborated further in his concrete study of nature's first form, externality, which he equates with empirical space (see EN §254–§257, and below). See also EL §140A/210—"nature is what is external generally."

8. Consequently, he regularly uses the terms "externality" and "matter" interchangeably: see, for instance, EN §252A/1: 218–19, §262A/1: 243, VG 47–8/55.

9. This will be borne out by Hegel's detailed account of nature's first form, externality: see "Sensuous Consciousness/Material Externality." Moreover, EL §20 criticizes the concept of externality as it figures in "sensuous consciousness," which Hegel explicitly treats as the subjective correlate of objective externality in nature (as I explain below). It is therefore reasonable to take EL §20's critical point as applying to the objective externality of nature as well.

10. However, the *Phenomenology* begins immediately with sense-certainty, which does not arise from any preexisting soul. Consequently, the subject of sense-certainty has no inherited corporeal content to access. In the *Phenomenology*, therefore, sense-certainty's vaunted richness proves entirely illusory, whereas in the *Philosophy of Mind* Hegel *does* think that a certain rich corporeal content is available to sensuous consciousness.

11. Charles Taylor argues that Hegel makes a similar case apropos of "sense-certainty" in the *Phenomenology*. Here again, consciousness is attempting to know purely singular objects. But, Taylor claims, a subject of knowledge must be able to say what it knows: sayability is a criterial property of knowing (Taylor, *Hegel*, p. 141). The position of sense-certainty is that one can merely say "this" and point to what one means by "this." But, Taylor claims, if I am to point to anything, that thing must have a definite scope, and I therefore have to use general terms to approach it. The problem with Taylor's reading is that he imports into Hegel the assumption that knowledge must be *sayable*. Hegel's weaker argument—in the *Philosophy of Mind* and the *Phenomenology*—is just that knowledge must be able to *pick out* the object it claims to know. Pippin reads Hegel as advancing this weaker argument in the *Phenomenology*: see *Hegel's Idealism*, p. 119.

12. Hegel's reinterpretation of space and time contrasts intriguingly with Kant's view of them. Unlike Kant, Hegel sees space and time as objective features of the world, not merely forms of intuition (on this, see also Vittorio Hösle, "Raum, Zeit, Bewegung," in *Hegel und die Naturwissenschaften*, ed. Petry, p. 258). Hegel also considers space and time to be (in part) forms of thought or universals. Kant, on the other hand, thinks of space as a whole the constituent units of which are parts and not instances of a universal. Hegel

claims, though, not that spatial units instantiate a universal but that they merge to *become* a universal. On Hegel's views on space and time, see, among others, John W. Burbidge, "Concept and Time in Hegel," *Dialogue: Canadian Philosophical Review* 12: 3 (1973): 403–22; Edward Halper, "The Logic of Hegel's *Philosophy of Nature*: Nature, Space, and Time" in *Hegel and the Philosophy of Nature*, ed. Houlgate, pp. 29–49; Richard Dien Winfield, "Space, Time, and Matter: Conceiving Nature without Foundations," in *Hegel and the Philosophy of Nature*, ed. Houlgate, pp. 51–69.

13. Hegel's earlier association of sense-certainty with space and time in the *Phenomenology* reinforces the connection between sensuous consciousness and nature's first stage (see PhG 59–66/82–9). In the *Phenomenology*, Hegel defines the object of sense-certainty—the "this"—as possessing the joint aspects of "here" and "now." Although in the *Philosophy of Mind* he criticizes his earlier association of sense-certainty with space and time, he simultaneously continues, obscurely, to connect them (see PSS §418A/3: 299–303).

14. Hegel clarifies that the "thing" remains a singular, external, being, referring to it as that which "as a singular in its immediacy has *multiple predicates*" (EM §419/160).

15. To help understand Hegel's point, let us bear in mind how it recasts his internal critique of perception in the *Phenomenology*. There perception is defined as the awareness of individual things through their universal properties. By implication, though, the perceiving subject is aware of a thing *only* as the collection or amalgamation of its properties—as a mere "also" or "medium" (PhG 73/100). Yet if the perceiving subject insists that it is aware of the thing as something substantive underlying its properties, then the subject has relapsed into sense-certainty's unsatisfactory view of the object as a bare "this" a simple singularity or "one" (*Eins*).

16. "Material bodies" are not the same as matter *in general*, that is, the fundamental element that threads through all of nature. However, Hegel calls material bodies "material" because these bodies are the form that matter assumes when it maximally differentiates itself from thought: material bodies are the purest form of matter.

17. Hegel relates his view of material bodies to that of Newton, for whom material bodies possess impenetrability and mass. Hegel reinterprets these characteristics, respectively, as the body's negativity and the quantity of material units that it negates (EN §261R/1: 237). Hegel's often hostile relationship to Newton is deeply controversial. See on this, inter alia, Karl-Norbert Ihmig, *Hegels Deutung der Gravitation. Eine Studie zu Hegel und Newton* (Frankfurt: Athenäum, 1989), and the essays in Petry, ed., *Hegel and Newtonianism*. Behind much of this controversy lurks the question of whether Hegel attempted to prove a priori that there can be only seven planets in his *Philosophical Dissertation on the Orbits of the Planets* (1801). Bertrand Beaumont argues against this in "Hegel and the Seven Planets," in *The Hegel Myths and Legends*, ed. Jon Stewart, pp. 285–88; see also Cinzia Ferrini, "Features of Irony and Alleged Errors in Hegel's *De Orbitis Planetarum*," *Hegel-Jahrbuch* (1991): 459–77.

18. On the one hand, gravity is "the acknowledgement of the nullity of the self-externality of matter, its lack of independence, its contradiction" (EN §262R/1: 242). On the other hand, the gravitational "unity is a mere ought [*Sollen*], a yearning . . . never reached" (§262A/1: 243).

19. Initially consciousness tries to do this by reconceiving the inner essence as a set of *laws*. Through this, the understanding can view appearance as manifesting essence, since essence is redefined as a set of laws with the same determinate content as the appearance that they produce. The law is the "still and universal copy" (*Abbild*) of the appearance it is held to engender (EM §422/163). Hegel rejects this because it fails to understand appearance as genuinely derivative of essence, instead continuing to take the character of appearance as given and merely redefining laws to suit. "The determinateness of law as law does not progress to subjectivity . . . absolute negativity is not posited, for both sides are only connected by the law" (PSS §422A/3: 311). In *Phenomenology* chapter 3, Hegel criticizes the understanding's conception of laws on identical grounds— namely, that it is tautologous or vacuous (PhG, 95/126), merely redescribing the appearance that it purports to derive. This criticism is central to his analysis of the "tautology of explanation," on which see chapter 4 in this volume.

20. Actually, there are further complexities within Hegel's approach to light and the elements: see chapter 5.

21. Life occupies a somewhat equivocal place in Hegel's mature theory of forms of consciousness. He muses on whether it constitutes a third form of consciousness, with understanding comprising merely the point of transition between perception and consciousness of life (PSS §423A/3: 311–12). He is most usefully understood as simply seeing consciousness of life as a *fourth* form of consciousness.

22. In its rational intelligibility, the living object has finally come to resemble the conscious subject, which precipitates the subject's transition to self-consciousness. In contrast, in the *Phenomenology*, Hegel classified life not as the final object of consciousness but as the first type of object to which the already self-conscious subject starts to relate (in its initial phase as "self-certainty"). On this earlier account, the subject that has become self-conscious begins to desire, and in desiring it necessarily desires living objects. Yet it seems more logical for Hegel to claim— as in the *Philosophy of Mind*—that the subject must define its object as living *before* becoming self-conscious, for it is only because its object is living that the subject can identify itself within that object and so gain self-consciousness.

23. One might think that the nature/consciousness analogy undermines this: as consciousness goes through successive conceptions of reality, perhaps, the *Philosophy of Nature*, too, traces successive ways of thinking about nature. This objection misunderstands the *structural* character of the parallel between stages of nature and consciousness.

3. The Rationality of Nature

1. See introduction, note 7.

2. "Whereas the scientist sees the world as a congeries of external phenomena, linked together by external laws, the philosopher of Nature is . . . aware of the Idea immanent in it; he sees Nature as implicit or potential mind. . . . The

difference between *Naturphilosophie* and empirical science, therefore, is one of viewpoint" (Errol E. Harris, "Hegel and the Natural Sciences," in *The Spirit of Hegel* [Atlantic Highlands, NJ: Humanities Press, 1993], p. 133).

3. "What differentiates the two sciences [philosophy of nature and empirical science] is the metaphysics of both" (Hegel, *Vorlesung über Naturphilosophie Berlin 1823/24*, p. 73).

4. Hegel often speaks of "contradictions" in presenting the transitions between natural forms (whether philosophically or empirically described). For example, negativity is said to be a contradiction (EN §258R/1: 230), as are material bodies (§262R/1: 242), physical bodies (§298/2: 67), electrical processes (§324R/2: 168), and animals insofar as they are sentient vis-à-vis their environment (§359R/3: 141; see also WL 770/2: 481). Hegel uses additional terms as synonyms for "contradiction," notably "tension" (*Spannung*) and "dialectic." He describes the contradiction within electrical processes as a "tension" (EN §324–§324A/2: 166–68), finding "tension" within, also, the meteorological process (§287/2: 48) and sentient animals (§357/3: 136). Again, he claims that chemical processes embody a "dialectic" (§336A/2: 222) and insists that "the dialectic . . . asserts itself in all the particular domains and formations of the natural . . . world. In the motion of the heavenly bodies . . . Similarly, the physical elements prove themselves to be dialectical, and the meteorological process makes their dialectic apparent. The same principle is the foundation of all other natural processes" (EL §81A/130).

5. Hegel famously asserts that there are contradictions in the world as well as in thought, and that Kant denied the possibility of contradictions in the world merely out of misplaced "tenderness" for mundane items (EL §48R/92).

6. Priest, *Beyond the Limits of Thought* (Cambridge: Cambridge University Press, 1995), p. 5.

7. Findlay, *Hegel: A Re-examination*, p. 77. David Kolb helpfully summarizes the different positions in the controversy surrounding Hegel's notion of "contradiction" in *The Critique of Pure Modernity*, pp. 45–6. As Kolb explains, the most common view is that Hegel "was not careful enough about formal logical terms and used 'contradiction' when he meant only contrary concepts or conceptual tensions of various types" (p. 45). A second view is that Hegel attempted to structure his system around strict contradictions but failed. A third view is that he actually succeeded in structuring the system around strict contradictions. An important motivation for this third view is the thought that without strict contradictions Hegel cannot get his system to unfold with the necessity he claims for it. I suggest below, however, that Hegel's quasi-technical notion of necessity makes it unnecessary that his system devolve upon strict logical contradictions.

8. See note 4 to this chapter.

9. Accordingly, I sometimes also speak of "tensions" rather than contradictions, following Hegel's practice of using these terms interchangeably.

10. According to Findlay, Hegel's transitions are not necessary at all, but merely "plausible" in light of empirical knowledge (Findlay, *Hegel: A Re-examination*, pp. 74, 353). However, Hegel himself emphasizes the necessity of his transitions, which puts the onus on us to find an interpretation that accommodates this emphasis.

11. Forster, *Hegel's Idea of a Phenomenology of Spirit* (Chicago: University of Chicago Press, 1998), p. 186. Strictly, Forster says that B must depart less from A than any other *known* shape, but this makes B's necessity dependent on our ignorance of (or inability to imagine) alternative shapes that depart from A even less. Since this ignorance may well be culturally or psychologically contingent, Forster's view risks making B's "necessity" no necessity at all (on this, see Wendy L. Clark and J. M. Fritzman, "Reducing Spirit to Substance: Dove on Hegel's Method," in *Idealistic Studies* 32: 2 [2002]: 91). The problem can be solved by simply saying that B necessarily follows A if it departs from A as minimally as is compatible with its resolving A's contradiction.

12. Clark and Fritzman also suggest ("Reducing Spirit to Substance," p. 92) that one cannot readily tell which of two different shapes departs least from a predecessor, since they might introduce modifications that are different but equally extensive. Hegel seems to believe, however, that forms never introduce equal levels of modification, but always gain complexity one characteristic at a time. (This, at least, is implied by his view of nature as a hierarchy of complexity.)

13. In 1819–1820, Hegel says: "Space is self-contradictory and makes itself into time" (*Naturphilosophie Band I*, p. 16).

14. Examples can be multiplied. Later, for instance, Hegel says that light is "posited" as air (EN §282A/2: 36), air posited as fire (§283/2: 38), fire "subsides" into water (§283A/2: 39), and that all these elements constantly "transmute" into one another (§286A/2: 44). Moreover, Hegel often passes between forms by saying that the first "is" the second: for example, motion "is" matter (§261/1: 237), density "is" cohesion (§294/2: 61), cohesion "is" sound (§299/2: 69), etc. Since, as Judith Butler notes, Hegel generally uses the word "is" to mean "becomes," these apparent statements of identity actually tell us that each form actively *becomes* its successor. See Butler, *Subjects of Desire: Hegelian Reflections in Twentieth-Century France* (New York: Columbia University Press, 1987), p. 18.

15. Karl-Heinz Ilting objects that this transformative conception of natural forms is "nonsense" in "Hegels Philosophie des Organischen" (p. 369), but he does not clarify why he thinks this or what he means.

16. See Richard Dien Winfield, "Space, Time, and Matter," p. 60.

17. This rationality is what Hegel calls nature's "drive" to "make itself simple" and eliminate its inner contradictions (*Naturphilosophie Band I*, p. 11).

18. As part of this, Hegel says little about the epistemology of natural science. As Petry comments, he "was interested first and foremost in what had been discovered, and . . . was very largely indifferent to the various procedures by means of which such knowledge had arisen. Throughout the whole of the *Philosophy of Nature*, the entire extent of this systematic survey of the multitudinous facts and theories of early nineteenth-century science, there is hardly any mention . . . of the epistemological issues which many still regard as the heart and soul of any . . . philosophy of science" ("Hegel, Francoeur, and Pohl," in *Hegels Philosophie der Natur: Beziehungen zwischen empirischer und spekulativer Naturerkenntnis*, ed. Horstmann and Petry, p. 21).

19. Hegel alludes back to this division in the *Philosophy of Nature*, stating that the "universal" that scientists seek in nature comprises "forces, laws, and genera" (EN §246/1: 197).

20. The idea that universals change may seem odd, but it makes sense if we start from Hegel's own metaphysics, on which nature's basic forms continually change into one another (for example, negativity continually changes into material bodies), while being incessantly regenerated from preceding forms (as negativity is regenerated out of externality).

21. So, in saying that Hegel sees scientists as realists, I do not mean that realism, per se, is the aspect of scientific metaphysics to which he objects. On the contrary, as I read him, Hegel *shares* scientists' commitment to realism, but disagrees with how scientists *conceive* of real universals, as inherently inert and thing-like.

22. R. G. Collingwood, *The Idea of History*, ed. T. M. Knox (Oxford: Clarendon Press, 1946), p. 214.

23. Hegel's conviction on this underpins his important claim to give *better* explanations of how natural forms develop than empirical science (see chapter 4). This claim presupposes that philosophical and scientific approaches to nature are both engaged in the same explanatory enterprise.

24. It is sometimes denied that reasons can be causes because reasons justify actions whereas causes have no normative dimension. Presumably, Hegel believes that in identifying the reasons for some natural development we postulate a special sort of cause which *does* carry normative significance. This recalls the Aristotelian idea that a thing's purpose or function both causally explains its development and simultaneously establishes that that development is good. If Hegel does believe that all natural developments have reasons, then, he must posit normativity throughout nature (as he does, affirming that insofar as they act from reason all natural forms are intrinsically good: see chapter 6).

25. Martin Hollis, *The Philosophy of Social Science: An Introduction* (Cambridge: Cambridge University Press, 1994), p. 143.

26. Alfredo Ferrarin, *Hegel and Aristotle* (Cambridge: Cambridge University Press, 2001), pp. 201–2.

27. The suggestion that scientists conceive laws as external causes does not seem obviously correct as an account of the typical metaphysical commitments of empirical scientists. Ultimately, though, whether scientists believe in ontologically real laws exerting continuous causal influence upon universals is not essential to Hegel's account. His key point is that scientists consider natural forms as inherently nonrational and therefore explain their behavior with reference to external causal factors of some sort. Whether these external factors are identified as laws does not affect this central point.

28. The idea of nature's "disenchantment" (*Entzauberung*) derives of course from Weber, who famously argues that in modernity "there are no mysterious, incalculable forces that come into play, but . . . one can in principle, master all things by calculation. This means that the world is disenchanted" ("Science as a Vocation" [1919], in *From Max Weber: Essays in Sociology*, ed. H. H. Gerth and C. Wright Mills [New York: Routledge, 1948], p. 139).

Appropriating Weber's terminology, Charles Taylor has examined how the Romantic generation preceding Hegel took modern science to have "disenchanted" nature (Taylor, *Hegel*, pp. 7–11).

29. Similarly, in the *Philosophy of Nature*, Hegel writes that "as [through science] thoughts penetrate the limitless multiformity of nature, its richness is impoverished, its springtimes die, and the play of its colours fades. That which in nature was rustling with life, falls silent in the quietness of thought; its warm abundance, which shaped itself into a thousand intriguing wonders, withers into arid forms and shapeless universalities, which are like a murky northern fog" (EN §246A/1: 198).

30. On the ancient and medieval "substantive" conception of reason versus the modern "procedural" conception, see Charles Taylor, *Sources of the Self* (Cambridge: Cambridge University Press, 1989), pp. 121–22, 168.

31. Ferrarin, *Hegel and Aristotle*, pp. 201–33.

32. Hence, Heidegger uses the word "mathematical" in an unusual sense, to mean "projective': establishing templates, prior to experience, for what can be known.

33. Heidegger, "Modern Science, Metaphysics, and Mathematics" (1962), in *Basic Writings*, ed. David Farrell Krell, 2nd ed., rev. (London: Routledge, 1993), p. 291.

34. Husserl, *The Crisis of the European Sciences and Transcendental Phenomenology* (1954), trans. David Carr (Evanston, IL: Northwestern University Press, 1970), p. 4.

35. Heidegger, "Modern Science," p. 287.

36. Hegel therefore claims that our thinking renders nature's "universality" present for us, or "overgrasps" the thinking embedded in it (EL §24A1/57).

37. This reference to "categories" might suggest that Hegel wants only to change how we *think* about nature (nonmetaphysically), not to redescribe nature's real structure. Since Hegel is best interpreted as a metaphysical thinker, though, his phrase "philosophical categories" is best read as referring to the metaphysical conceptions of nature that inform his descriptions of it, conceptions that center on the idea of nature's intrinsic rationality.

38. One might think that Hegel could disagree with the metaphysics of science without disputing the truth of any particular scientific claims. But since he believes that the metaphysics thoroughly informs and infiltrates those particular claims, his disagreement with the metaphysics obliges him to judge particular scientific claims inadequate too.

39. For discussion, see John W. Burbidge, "The Necessity of Contingency," in *Art and Logic in Hegel's Philosophy*, ed. Warren E. Steinkraus and Kenneth I. Schmitz (Atlantic Highlands, NJ: Humanities Press, 1980), pp. 201–17; Dieter Henrich, "Hegels Theorie über den Zufall," *Kant-Studien* 50 (1958–1959), pp. 131–48; Stephen Houlgate, "Necessity and Contingency in Hegel's *Science of Logic*," *Owl of Minerva* 27: 1 (1995): 37–49.

40. Hegel is referring to the view that species should be classified ecologically, promoted especially by the biologist G. E. Trevinarus (1776–1837).

41. Collingwood, *The Idea of History*, p. 217.

42. The idea that living beings follow purposes "blindly"—nonconsciously—finds another important articulation in Schopenhauer's philosophy (although for Schopenhauer, unlike Hegel, the "blindness" of life's purposiveness makes it nonrational). On Schopenhauer's view on this, see Christopher Janaway, "Will and Nature," in *The Cambridge Companion to Schopenhauer*, ed. Janaway (Cambridge: Cambridge University Press, 1999), p. 149.

43. See Paul W. Taylor, *Respect for Nature: A Theory of Environmental Ethics* (Princeton: Princeton University Press, 1986), pp. 60–4.

44. Actually, for Hegel, nature's conceptual structures lack consciousness precisely because they are not fully manifest in their material parts. Hegel sees consciousness, basically, as the concept's self-rediscovery within material parts that it fully pervades (see chapter 6).

45. Thomas Nagel, "Panpsychism," in *Mortal Questions* (Cambridge: Cambridge University Press, 1979), p. 181.

4. Two Defenses of Hegel's Metaphysics of Nature

1. Hegel does not, as such, say that by "adequacy" he means truth or correspondence to how nature independently is. My interpretation of his "adequacy" as truth is supported by my overall interpretation of him as attempting to describe nature's real structures (an interpretation supported by his work, as I have argued).

2. Hegel and Schelling are regularly associated with the project of an "alternative" science: for example, William Leiss refers to "the long hidden motif of Romantic *Naturphilosophie* . . . the idea of a 'new' science and technology cleansed of the stain of domination" (*The Domination of Nature* [New York: Braziller, 1972], p. 200).

3. Freya Mathews, "Fertility Control in Wildlife," *Habitat* 19: 1 (1991): 9–12. Quoted in Val Plumwood, *Environmental Culture*, pp. 246–47.

4. On *Naturphilosophie*, see, especially, Andrew Cunningham and Nicholas Jardine, eds., *Romanticism and the Sciences* (Cambridge: Cambridge University Press, 1990); Barry Gower, "Speculation in Physics: The History and Practice of *Naturphilosophie*," *Studies in History and Philosophy of Science* 3: 4 (1973): 301–56; Stefano Poggi and Maurizio Bossi, eds., *Romanticism in Science: Science in Europe, 1790–1840* (Dordrecht: Kluwer, 1994); Robert J. Richards, *The Romantic Conception of Life: Science and Philosophy in the Age of Goethe* (Chicago: University of Chicago Press, 2002); H. A. M. Snelders, "Romanticism and Naturphilosophie and the Inorganic Natural Sciences 1797–1840: An Introductory Survey," *Studies in Romanticism* 9 (1970): 193–215.

5. Throughout, I use "*Naturphilosophie*" to refer specifically to these broadly Schellingian scientists, distinguishing their essentially scientific project from Hegel's essentially philosophical project by calling the latter "philosophy of nature." Despite the artificiality of this distinction (since "philosophy of nature" in German is *Naturphilosophie*), it allows me to mark a crucial theoretical disjunction.

6. Hegel still endorses these findings only provisionally, insofar as he reinterprets them within the terms of his own metaphysics. This reinterpretation

is necessary because Schellingian and not Hegelian metaphysical views generally informed the researches of the *Naturphilosophen.*

7. This accusation dates back to Hegel's criticisms of the *Naturphilosophen*'s arbitrary formalism in the *Phenomenology*: see H. S. Harris, *Hegel's Ladder,* vol. 1 (Indianapolis: Hackett, 1997), pp. 48–52.

8. As Pinkard sums up: "Hegel was simply not willing to yield any pride of place to the natural sciences with regard to the authority to interpret the world, but he was also by no means willing or inclined to write off the natural sciences merely as illusions" (*Hegel: A Biography,* pp. 565–66).

9. Varying this line of argument, Robert Stern sees Hegel as offering a holistic metaphysics which better explains many phenomena that resist explanation in the atomistic or reductionist terms of science: see Stern, *Hegel, Kant, and the Structure of the Object,* pp. 77–8, 105–6.

10. Kant, "Metaphysical Foundations of Natural Science," in *Philosophy of Material Nature,* trans. James W. Ellington (Indianapolis: Hackett, 1985), pp. 7–8.

11. See, on this, Robert Stern, *Hegel and the Phenomenology of Spirit,* pp. 106–9.

12. Thomas Kuhn famously argued that Schelling's influence contributed to the discovery of the principle of energy conservation: see Kuhn, "Energy Conservation as an Example of Simultaneous Discovery," in *Critical Problems in the History of Science,* ed. M. Clagett (Madison: University of Wisconsin Press, 1959), pp. 321–56. Kuhn's account is criticized and complicated in Kenneth Caneva, "Physics and *Naturphilosophie*: A Reconnaissance," *History of Science* 35 (1997): 35–107.

13. Hegel himself does not use this phrase. Inwood introduces it in *Hegel,* pp. 59–64. My exposition of the dilemma is indebted to Inwood.

14. Inwood, *Hegel,* p. 63.

15. In the *Science of Logic,* Hegel mainly illustrates this type of explanation by attempts to derive multiple aspects of some phenomenon—for instance, punishment—from a single one of its aspects, for example, deterrence (WL 465/ 2: 107). This illustrates how the disparity of content between ground and grounded undermines the attempt to derive the latter from the former. Nietzsche argues similarly about punishment: see *On the Genealogy of Morality,* trans. Carol Diethe (Cambridge: Cambridge University Press, 1994), pp. 56–8.

16. On the "tautology of explanation," see also Kalenberg, *Die Befreiung der Natur,* pp. 38–45; Pippin, *Hegel's Idealism,* pp. 134–35.

17. Hegel can extend this criticism to traditional teleological explanations. These can become logically complete only by becoming vacuous (as when a seed is said to become a tree because it has the *telos* of becoming a tree, or opium to send people to sleep because of its dormitive powers). That Hegel can criticize teleological explanations confirms, again, that he does not accept teleology wholesale, but only incorporates a teleological element into his overall rationalist approach.

18. Of course, Hegel famously denies that his system is linear, characterizing it as a "circle of circles" (EL §15/39). Ultimately, I believe this circular

characterization is correct (as this chapter will argue). My point is only that in *some* passages Hegel describes, and sets out to structure, his system in a linear way—passages which imply a particular argument for his metaphysics of nature.

19. On the structure of this chapter, see Mitchell H. Miller, Jr, "The Attainment of the Absolute Standpoint in Hegel's *Phenomenology of Spirit*," in *The Phenomenology of Spirit Reader: Critical and Interpretive Essays*, ed. Jon Stewart (Albany: State University of New York Press, 1998), pp. 427–43.

20. Most simply, a "shape of consciousness" is a way in which subjects are "conscious" of reality, that is, a way in which they conceptualize it. Thus, a shape of consciousness can equally be referred to as a conception or view of reality, or as a metaphysical view. Such conceptions do not belong to single individuals, but are shared by the majority of individuals in any given historical epoch.

21. Freedom and rationality (and, indeed, morality) are reciprocal terms for Hegel, as for Kant: see Patten, *Hegel's Idea of Freedom*, ch. 3; and, on Kant's "reciprocity thesis," see Henry Allison, *Kant's Theory of Freedom* (Cambridge: Cambridge University Press, 1990), ch. 11.

22. As Hegel states: "The world is created, is now being created, and always has been created; this becomes apparent in the guise of the conservation of the world" (EN §247A/1: 207).

23. See, inter alia, Karl Ameriks, "Recent Work on Hegel: The Rehabilitation of an Epistemologist," *Philosophy and Phenomenological Research* 52: 1 (1992): 177–202; Michael Forster, *Hegel and Skepticism* (Cambridge, MA: Harvard University Press, 1989); Michael Inwood, "Solomon, Hegel, and Truth," *Review of Metaphysics* 31: 2 (1977): 272–82; Robert Solomon, "Hegel's Epistemology," in *Hegel*, ed. Michael Inwood, pp. 31–53; Kenneth R. Westphal, "Hegel's Solution to the Dilemma of the Criterion," in *The Phenomenology of Spirit Reader*, ed. Jon Stewart, pp. 76–101. As Forster and Westphal particularly stress, Hegel's concern to prove his metaphysical standpoint uniquely true is motivated by his engagement with the ancient scepticism of Sextus Empiricus: see his *Outlines of Scepticism*, ed. and trans. Julia Annas and Jonathan Barnes (Cambridge: Cambridge University Press, 2000). Hegel discusses Sextus Empiricus in "On the Relationship of Scepticism to Philosophy" (1802), in *Between Kant and Hegel: Texts in the Development of Post-Kantian Idealism*, rev. ed., ed. and trans. George di Giovanni and H. S. Harris (Indianapolis: Hackett, 2000), pp. 311–62.

24. The notion that thought "switches over" into nature comes from the *Philosophy of Mind*: "The *first* way in which . . . the logical idea reveals itself, consists of the idea's switching over [*umschlagen*] into the immediacy of external and individualised existence. This switching over is the becoming of nature" (EM §384A/18).

25. Hegel at one point denies that the move to nature is a "transition" since nothing arises through it that was not already present in logical thought (WL 843/2: 573). Yet, simultaneously, he speaks of the "transition" to "*another sphere and science*" (843/2: 573).

26. Alan White, *Absolute Knowledge: Hegel and the Problem of Metaphysics* (Athens, OH: Ohio University Press, 1983), p. 89.

27. Rival accounts of this "transition" abound: see, among others, William Maker, "The Very Idea of the Idea of Nature," in *Hegel and the Philosophy of Nature*, ed. Houlgate, pp. 8–9; Dieter Wandschneider, "Nature and the Dialectic of Nature in Hegel's Objective Idealism," *Bulletin of the Hegel Society of Great Britain* 26 (1992): 30–51; Dieter Wandschneider and Vittorio Hösle, "Die Entäusserung der Idee zur Natur und ihre zeitliche Entfaltung als Geist bei Hegel," *Hegel-Studien* 18 (1983): 173–99. Broadly, for Maker and Wandschneider, the idea in grasping itself as a whole necessarily grasps itself as limited (since all determination is negation); it must, therefore, pass beyond itself to start categorizing what exceeds it: see Wandschneider, "Nature and the Dialectic of Nature," pp. 33–4; Maker, "The Very Idea of the Idea of Nature," pp. 8–9.

28. Hegel adds that: "The idea is what is true in and for itself, the absolute unity of concept and objectivity . . . its real content is only the presentation that the concept gives itself in the form of external existence [*Dasein*]" (EL §213/286). Previously, I have argued that Hegel understands the idea as a comprehensive ontological structure; now, however, he appears to treat the idea merely as one form of thought *within* the wider totality of logical forms. His claim, though, is that the idea is that form in which thought openly pervades all its own structures. That is, the idea is specific just in that it embraces, overarches, and folds itself back into all other forms of thought; as such it *does* remain ontologically comprehensive.

29. Inwood, *A Hegel Dictionary*, p. 94.

30. Joseph McCarney elucidates Hegel's terms "idea" and "concept," pointing out his signal failure to use the terms in the differentiated way he proposes; see McCarney, *Hegel on History* (London: Routledge, 2000), pp. 51–5.

31. This seemingly perplexing transition to thought's existence as a thinker is explained in the sections of the *Logic* that describe the idea's successive forms, a succession culminating in its assuming "absolute" form. I interpret these sections of the *Logic* in chapter 6, "Practical Reason in the World."

32. As Philip Grier comments, "at the culmination of the *Science of Logic*, the . . . Absolute Idea . . . which has been declared to be fully concrete and something *actual*, is nevertheless declared to be enclosed within pure thought" ("Abstract and Concrete in Hegel's Logic," in *Essays on Hegel's Logic*, ed. George di Giovanni [Albany: State University of New York Press, 1990], p. 64). Grier concludes that for Hegel the absolute idea is actual and concrete only within thought, not yet within reality.

33. Schelling, *On the History of Modern Philosophy*, trans. Andrew Bowie (Cambridge: Cambridge University Press, 1994), pp. 134, 145.

34. See Stephen Houlgate, "Schelling's Critique of Hegel's *Science of Logic*," *Review of Metaphysics* 53 (1999): 101.

35. Schelling, *On the History of Modern Philosophy*, p. 134.

36. Ibid., p. 135.

37. Kierkegaard also builds on Schelling's critique, claiming that: "Abstractly viewed, system and existence cannot be thought conjointly, because in

order to think existence, systematic thought must think it as annulled and consequently not as existing." See Kierkegaard, *Concluding Unscientific Post-script* (1846), ed. and trans. Howard V. Hong and Edna H. Hong (Princeton: Princeton University Press, 1992), p. 197. Here Kierkegaard redefines existence as the givenness to itself of each individual subject, which he calls "the existing spirit *qua* existing" (p. 191) or the "individual human being" (p. 193). Meanwhile, Feuerbach's materialist/naturalist critique of Hegel is reprised by the young Marx in "Economic and Philosophical Manuscripts" (1844), in *Marx: Early Writings*, trans. Rodney Livingstone and Gregor Benton (Harmondsworth: Penguin, 1975), pp. 383–84, 397–400.

38. Feuerbach, "Provisional Theses for the Reformation of Philosophy" (1843), in *The Young Hegelians: An Anthology*, ed. Lawrence S. Stepelevich (Atlantic Highlands, NJ: Humanities Press, 1983), pp. 166–67.

39. Ibid., p. 164. On Feuerbach's related defense of "sense-certainty" against Hegel, see Martin J. De Nys, " 'Sense-certainty' and Universality: Hegel's Entrance into the *Phenomenology*," in *G. W. F. Hegel: Critical Assessments*, vol. 3, ed. Stern, pp. 108–30.

40. Alan White also defends Hegel from Schelling's critique, but by arguing that Hegel is a non-metaphysical category theorist who never attempts to derive factual existence (White, *Absolute Knowledge*, pp. 24–5). For a broadly similar view, see Klaus Brinkmann, "Schellings Hegel-Kritik," in *Die Ontologische Option*, ed. Klaus Hartmann (Berlin: De Gruyter, 1976), pp. 117–210. In contrast, Stephen Houlgate defends Hegel, as I do, by arguing that even in the *Logic* he gives an "ontological account of the basic structure of being" ("Schelling's Critique of Hegel's *Science of Logic*," p. 126). Similarly, R.-P. Horstmann defends Hegel as offering an "objective," not a merely "subjective," logic: see Horstmann, "Logifizierte Natur oder naturalisierte Logik?," in *Hegels Philosophie der Natur*, ed. Horstmann and Petry, pp. 290–308. For a defense of Schelling's reading of Hegel, see Andrew Bowie, *Schelling and Modern European Philosophy: An Introduction* (London: Routledge, 1993), ch. 6.

41. One might defend Hegel by arguing that pure thought precedes matter in only a logical sense. Thus, no actual or literal emergence of matter from thought need be envisaged, and thought can be viewed as always existing accompanied by matter. However, as I have suggested in chapter 3, this merely logical reading of Hegel does not do justice to his pervasive tendency to conceive transitions in terms of active developments. To be sure, these developments must be understood as ongoing and eternal rather than temporally specific. But the ongoing, eternal, character of the process by which pure thought becomes or generates matter does not affect the fact that this generation is only possible if thought actually exists in a developmentally prior, noninstantiated, mode. Rather, the eternity of this generation entails that thought must always persist in its pure and developmentally prior mode, from which its material instantiation will be never-endingly regenerated.

42. In this connection, Hegel criticizes Aristotle for failing to "logically abstract the universal idea" (VGP 2: 136/2: 151). Having first described the forms qua concretely instantiated, Aristotle failed then to stand back and describe those forms in abstract logical terms. Consequently, Hegel claims, Aristotle's

logic only offers canons for subjective thinking, but fails to describe forms of thought that are embodied in the world.

43. My claim that Hegel prioritizes the concrete over the abstract might seem to undermine my view that his basic theory of nature is a priori. Yet the abstraction of the *Logic* from the *Realphilosophie* need not imply that the *Realphilosophie* itself is derived, through prior abstraction, from empirical accounts of the world. Hegel can consistently derive nature's basic forms a priori—describing them as levels of thought/matter unification—and then abstract his account of the purely conceptual aspects of these forms by considering them in artificial isolation from their accompanying material aspects.

5. Sensibility and the Elements

1. *Empfindung* can also be translated as "sensation" (as does Petry in *The Philosophy of Subjective Spirit*), but I think that "sensibility" better conveys the structured character of the experience in question, whereas "sensation" evokes an entirely structureless reception of impressions (as in Hume's theory of impressions and ideas). A possible problem with translating *Empfindung* as "sensibility" is that Hegel himself uses *Sensibilität* to designate animals' merely physiological capacity to sense, which, for him, does not yet count as full sensible experience (EN §354/111–26). Hegel juxtaposes *Sensibilität* with *Irritabilität* and *Reproduktion* as the three aspects of physiological shape—a taxonomy widely accepted in his time, instituted by Albrecht von Haller (1708–1777). Since this notion of *Sensibilität* plays no role in Hegel's discussion of *Empfindung*, it need introduce no confusion here.

2. Such as Hegel's discussion of "earth" as the "universal individual" in the *Phenomenology* (PhG 177–80/223–26), on which see John Sallis, *Force of Imagination: The Sense of the Elemental* (Bloomington: Indiana University Press, 2000), pp. 176–78. Discussions of the elements recur throughout Hegel's mature thought: see PR §247/268 on earth and seas; his *Aesthetics* relates the elements to the individual arts (VA 2: 622/2: 255–56). I suggest, though, that all these passages are best approached in light of Hegel's more sustained discussions of the elements in the *Philosophy of Nature* and *Philosophy of Mind*.

3. As Robert Stern points out, Hegel often treats it as axiomatic that our original access to the world is experiential (see, for example, EL §7R/31), but never translates this into an endorsement of empiricism as an epistemological position (Stern, "Going beyond the Kantian Philosophy: On McDowell's Hegelian Critique of Kant," *European Journal of Philosophy* 7: 2 [1999], p. 252).

4. Hegel follows Kant in maintaining that experience (*Erfahrung*) is only possible through the subject's imposition of structure onto its sensory impressions. But whereas for Kant the subject imposes forms of intuition and categories of the understanding upon the givens of sensibility, for Hegel the subject also, more basically, imposes patterns upon its impressions *at* the purely sensible level. Hence, in Hegel's view, sensibility—the reception of sensory impressions—already evinces internal structure *prior* to any (further) imposition of forms of intuition or categories. See also note 26 to this chapter.

5. John J. Compton, "Phenomenology and the Philosophy of Nature," *Man and World* 21 (1988): 65–89.

6. Ibid., p. 66.

7. Ibid., p. 80.

8. Dennis L. Sepper, *Goethe Contra Newton: Polemics and the Project for a New Science of Color* (Cambridge: Cambridge University Press, 1988), p. 73.

9. Goethe, "Selections from *Maxims and Reflections*," in *Scientific Studies*, ed. and trans. Douglas Miller (Princeton: Princeton University Press, 1988), p. 307.

10. For Hegel's argument to this effect, see chapter 4, "The Limits of Empirical Science."

11. See Ardis B. Collins, "Hegel on Language, Citizenship, and the Educational Function of the Workplace: The Marxist Challenge," *Owl of Minerva* 32: 1 (2000): 34. Hegel's division stems from Mendelssohn's 1784 essay "On the Question: What Is Enlightenment?," in *What Is Enlightenment? Eighteenth-Century Questions and Twentieth-Century Answers*, ed. James Schmidt (Berkeley: University of California Press, 1996), pp. 53–7. Mendelssohn, however, differentiates theoretical *Aufklärung* from practical *Cultur*: see James Schmidt, "A *Paideia* for the 'Bürger als Bourgeois': The Conception of 'Civil Society' " in Hegel's Political Thought," *History of Political Thought* 2: 3 (1981): 478.

12. Taylor, *Hegel*, p. 36.

13. The mature Hegel makes several laudatory comments about Kant: for example, "I should do my duty [*Pflicht*] for its own sake . . . In doing my duty, I am with myself and free. The merit and exalted viewpoint of Kant's philosophy are that it has emphasized this significance of duty" (PR §133A/161). And, in his *Philosophy of History*: "That which is just and ethical, however, belongs to the essential, universal will, which has being in itself, and in order to know what is truly right one must abstract from inclination, drive, desire as the particular; one must therefore know what the *will in itself* is. For benevolent, charitable, sociable drives remain drives, to which various other drives are opposed" (VPG 442/524). On Hegel's Kantianism, see also Pedro Ramet, "Kantian and Hegelian Perspectives on Duty," *Southern Journal of Philosophy* 21: 2 (1983): 282–83, 293.

14. Patten, in *Hegel's Idea of Freedom*, pp. 56–7, outlines Hegel's Aristotelian solution to the reason/passion conflict.

15. In this respect, Hegel's mature ethics remains after all continuous with the *Spirit of Christianity*, in which he alleges that "love," the spontaneous virtue of the passions, renders the strictures of morality palatable and averts sadomasochistic enslavement to oneself.

16. Robert R. Williams, "Reason, Authority, and Recognition in Hegel's Theory of Education," *Owl of Minerva* 32: 1 (2000): 53.

17. Reid, "Hegel and the State University": 6, 17.

18. Hegel makes this explicit in discussing the educative function of art, which, he comments, purifies the drives by "dividing pure from impure in the passions" (VA 1: 50/1: 75)—sifting out and accentuating the passions' implicitly "universal" and "essential" content.

19. See PR §19/51. Hegel justifies this insistence in the *Philosophy of Mind* by tracing the conceptual structures pervading every layer of mental life.

20. I have stressed why I believe Hegel to be ultimately committed to the developmental model because he is frequently associated exclusively with the disciplinary model in the secondary literature: see Michael George and Andrew Vincent, Introduction to *The Philosophical Propaedeutic*, trans. A. V. Miller (Oxford: Blackwell, 1986), pp. xx–xxi; Inwood, *A Hegel Dictionary*, pp. 68–70; Millicent Mackenzie, *Hegel's Educational Theory and Practice* (London: Swan Sonnenschein, 1909), pp. 59–65. Scholars typically construe Hegel as a "disciplinarian" because the scheme of progression from natural desires to social norms to renaturalized norms exemplifies his favored ontological pattern of progression from unity to division to higher unity. However, this ontological pattern is equally instantiated by what I call the "developmental" form of education, involving progression from "immediate" natural desires to the accentuation of the rational nucleus within those desires and lastly the successful reorientation of the desires around their rational element.

21. See Kirk Pillow, *Sublime Understanding: Aesthetic Reflection in Kant and Hegel* (London: MIT Press, 2000), pp. 147–57.

22. An expanded account of sensibility is also found in the transcripts of Hegel's 1827–1828 lectures on mind by J. E. Erdmann and F. Walter, published in 1994 as *Vorlesungen über die Philosophie des Geistes: Berlin 1827/1828*.

23. Confusingly, sensibility (*Empfindung*) occurs not only in the *Philosophy of Mind* as characteristic of human beings, but also in the *Philosophy of Nature* as characteristic of all animals, including humans (EN §358/3:138–40). This animal *Empfindung* is not the same as animals' merely physiological *Sensibilität*, mentioned above in note 1 to this chapter. In the *Philosophy of Mind* Hegel considers sensibility as paving the way for humans' further cognitive capacities (including the capacity to articulate sensible awareness conceptually).

24. As Hegel comments, all the stages of mind "are essentially only as moments, states, determinations within the higher stages of development" (EM §380/7).

25. Murray Greene notes that the sentient soul has no "awareness of an objective outer world as source or locus of the content found" (*Hegel on the Soul: A Speculative Anthropology* [The Hague: Martinus Nijhoff, 1972], p. 82).

26. Greene explains that, "although the sentient soul obtains its first filling through a 'finding,' nevertheless Hegel wants us to understand that there is an essential moment of activity in sentience . . . [which] is not the faculty of pure receptivity and passivity in the way *Sinnlichkeit* is for Kant" (*Hegel on the Soul*, p. 84).

27. Admittedly, this analysis is largely in the addition to EM §401, but reliance on this addition is justifiable, since it amplifies the main body of Hegel's text and is confirmed by the transcripts of Erdmann and Walter.

28. Hegel says, "why we have exactly the familiar *five* senses— . . . the rational necessity of this must be proved [*nachgewiesen*] in a philosophical consideration. This is done when we grasp the senses as presentations of the

moments of the concept. These moments are . . . only *three*. But the five senses reduce quite naturally to three classes of senses" (EM §401A/77).

29. Hegel's adjective *ideell* is multifaceted. As Inwood explains, a thing can be *ideell* for Hegel in any of four senses: (1) it exists only through itself, (2) it exists in unrealized form, (3) it exists only through something else, upon which it depends, (4) it exists only as part of a greater whole, upon the existence of which it depends (Inwood, *A Hegel Dictionary*, p. 127). Hegel's use of *ideell* in EM §401A applies sense (4): qua visible and audible, items are held to exist only insofar as they belong within an overarching relationship of availability to the perceiving subject.

30. Hegel reverses the Platonic valuation of sight over touch, according to which touch introduces a proximity and indeterminacy between subject and object which diminishes objectivity. Yet Hegel's reversal of the traditional hierarchy remains within its terms of evaluation, since for him sight misleadingly reduces the distance between subject and object by depicting objects as fully accessible. See Cathryn Vasseleu, *Textures of Light: Vision and Touch in Irigaray, Levinas and Merleau-Ponty* (London: Routledge, 1998), pp. 12–17.

31. The protoconceptuality of sensibility emerges in Hegel's *Aesthetics*: " 'Sense' [*Sinn*] is this wonderful word which is used in two opposite meanings. On the one hand it means the organs of immediate apprehension, but on the other hand we mean by sense: the meaning, the thought, the universality of the thing. And so sense relates on the one hand to the immediate externality of existence, on the other to its inner essence" (VA 1: 128–29/1: 173).

32. I take the phrase "texture of light" from Vasseleu, although she uses it to indicate that light is material and tactile, making things visible by physically touching the eyes, so that touch is always "implicate[d] . . . in vision" (*Textures of Light*, p. 12). Although Hegel construes light as nonmaterial, "texture" still captures how light thoroughly pervades and suffuses objects of visual sensibility for him.

33. Hegel introduces the concept of *Erdigkeit* in EN §285/2: 113.

34. This understanding of earthiness as self-contained, turned in on itself, is upheld elsewhere in Hegel's system. For example: "When the power . . . of self-possession and of the universal, or of theoretical or moral principles, is relaxed . . . the earthy elements are set free—for this evil is directly present in the heart, because this, as immediate, is natural and selfish" (EM §408/124). These "earthy elements" are the self-centered aspects of individual personality.

35. Here Hegel's approach has marked kinship with the first part of Goethe's *Farbenlehre*, which elucidates how color appears in visual perception, among the "innate conditions for sight" (Goethe, "Theory of Color" [1810], in *Scientific Writings*, p. 168). Likewise, Hegel is attempting to elicit how the sense of color necessarily arises within subjective experience.

36. In a letter of 1890, Monet states his aim to "render what I'd call . . . the *enveloppe* above all, the same light spread over everything" (*Monet by Monet: Artists by Themselves*, ed. Rachel Barnes [Devon: Webb and Bower, 1990], p. 50).

37. Boothby, *Freud as Philosopher* (New York: Routledge, 2001), p. 19.

38. Similarly, Hegel remarks: "We cannot hear sound as such, but only ever a determinate, higher or lower tone" (EN §276A/2: 19). Generally, he stresses how the elements only ever manifest themselves "in relation to particular objects" and cannot be directly grasped themselves (§286A/2: 44).

39. Burbidge agrees that "in analysing the universal forms of individuating [the elements] he [Hegel] was not talking about science, but about the most general characteristics of our *experience* of the world" (*Real Process*, p. 127).

40. Again, Hegel's claim that the objective elements always point back to sensibility recalls Goethe's *Farbenlehre*. Goethe first examines what he calls "physiological" colors, colors which are "wholly, or largely, a property of the observer, of the eye"—these include, for instance, after-images and experiential effects of adaptation to light or darkness ("Theory of Color," in *Scientific Studies*, p. 168). Goethe goes on to study colors as present in external objects, but avers that the physiological colors remain the "basis for [his] entire theory." By studying external colors in relation to physiological colors, and crystallizing the same principles from both sets of phenomena, Goethe aims for a theory of external colors that stays attuned to sensible experience.

41. See chapter 1, "How Cogent is Strong a Priorism?"

42. In 1823–1824, Hegel particularly objects to how empirical science generates "universals" (that is, conceptions of natural forms) which "abstract" from how natural phenomena are present in sensible intuition (*sinnliche Anschauung*) (*Vorlesung über Naturphilosophie Berlin 1823/24*, pp. 73–4).

43. On the concept of reconciliation and its importance in Hegel's social philosophy, see Michael Hardimon, *Hegel's Social Philosophy: The Project of Reconciliation* (Cambridge: Cambridge University Press, 1994).

44. Hegel's concern to show that sensible experience is veridical is stressed in John McDowell, *Mind and World* (Cambridge, MA: Harvard University Press, 1994), esp. pp. 43–5.

45. Hegel also comments: "What belongs to nature as such lies behind mind; certainly, mind has within itself the whole content [*Gehalt*] of nature, but the determinations of nature are in mind in a thoroughly different way than in external nature" (EM §381A/14–15).

46. See also Greene, *Hegel on the Soul*, p. 96.

47. This may sound odd given science's distinctively empirical method, but we must recall that Hegel uses "sensibility" technically, to refer to our basic sense of nature as elemental. Thus, for him, it is precisely through its empirical method that science produces accounts of nature that are separated from sensibility. This is because empirical method is itself underpinned by science's metaphysics of nature, which already breaks with sensibility at a deeper level.

6. Ethical Implications of Hegel's Theory of Nature

1. In environmental ethics, the notion of "intrinsic" value is used in several ways: (1) noninstrumental value; (2) nonrelational value, deriving solely from a thing's intrinsic properties—this usage stems from G. E. Moore, "The Conception of Intrinsic Value," in *Philosophical Studies* (London: Routledge

and Kegan Paul, 1960); (3) objective value, which really exists and is not solely a function of valuations made by humans. For this taxonomy, see John O'Neill, "The Varieties of Intrinsic Value," *Monist* 75: 2 (1992): 119–37. Environmental ethicists primarily want to establish nature's "intrinsic" value in sense (3). So does Hegel: he assigns nonrelational goodness to the conceptual element in natural forms and relational goodness to their material element (since this becomes good solely through the activity of the conceptual element upon it). Both types of natural goodness are "intrinsic" in sense (3), *objective*. Accordingly, whenever I refer to Hegel's thesis that all natural forms are "intrinsically good," I mean that he considers them objectively valuable, their existence and character being good in themselves, not only in relation to the feelings or projects of human beings.

2. There are exceptions: Leiss, for instance, observes that "the general tendency of *Naturphilosophie* [was] an attempt to transcend the attitude that nature existed only as an object of domination for man, an attitude that the philosophers of nature regarded as having become prevalent as a result of the enthusiasm generated by the natural sciences" (*The Domination of Nature*, p. 89).

3. Correspondingly, most scholars treat the *Philosophy of Nature* as purely theoretical. For some exceptions, see Manfred Gies, "Naturphilosophie und Naturwissenschaft bei Hegel," in *Hegel und die Naturwissenschaften*, ed. Petry, pp. 74–6; Elaine P. Miller, "The Figure of Self-Sacrifice in Hegel's *Naturphilosophie*," *Philosophy Today* 41 Supplement (1997): 41–8; Mark C. E. Peterson, "Animals Eating Empiricists: Assimilation and Subjectivity in Hegel's Philosophy of Nature," *Owl of Minerva* 23: 1 (1991): 49–62, and "The Role of Practical and Theoretical Approaches in Hegel's *Philosophy of Nature*," *Owl of Minerva* 27: 2 (1996): 155–65. Fritz Reusswig studies the environmental aspect of Hegel's social theory in *Natur und Geist: Grundlinien einer ökologischen Sittlichkeit nach Hegel* (Frankfurt: Campus, 1993).

4. This quintessentially nineteenth-century view is forcefully expounded in Fichte, *The Vocation of Man* (1800), trans. Peter Prauss (Indianapolis: Hackett, 1987), and John Stuart Mill, "Nature" (1874), in *Nature and Utility of Religion*, ed. George Nakhnikian (New York: Bobbs-Merrill, 1958).

5. For an ecological critique of this view, see Val Plumwood, "The Ecopolitics Debate and the Politics of Nature," in *Ecological Feminism*, ed. Karen J. Warren (New York: Routledge, 1994), p. 69.

6. John Passmore, "Attitudes to Nature," in *Environmental Ethics*, ed. Robert Elliott (Oxford: Oxford University Press, 1995), p. 135. Similarly, Beat Wyss claims that Hegel finds no value at all in wild nature, only advocating its cultivation (Wyss, *Hegel's Art History and the Critique of Modernity*, trans. Caroline Dobson Saltzwedel [Cambridge: Cambridge University Press, 1999], pp. 53, 146, 149). Wyss relates this to the scorn for natural scenery in Hegel's diary of a 1796 walking holiday. John O'Neill, too, credits Hegel with the view that natural entities have value only insofar as humans find their own powers reflected in them (O'Neill, "Humanism and Nature," *Radical Philosophy* 66 [1994]: 21–9).

7. Elaine Miller finds in Hegel the even stronger thesis that "nature has a value only as known, conceptualized nature" ("The Figure of Self-Sacrifice,"

p. 42). She relates this to Hegel's early—and unpleasantly magisterial—poem about commanding and beating his dog: "Distichs on a Pet Dog" (1798), in *Miscellaneous Writings*, p. 140.

8. Fichte, *The Vocation of Man*, p. 83.

9. Environmental thinkers regularly indict Hegel for preferring artistic beauty: see, for example, Bruce V. Foltz, *Inhabiting the Earth: Heidegger, Environmental Ethics, and the Metaphysics of Nature* (Atlantic Highlands, NJ: Humanities Press, 1995), p. 171; Passmore, "Attitudes to Nature," p. 135.

10. One sees this in EM §381: although Hegel at first introduces mind as if it differed absolutely in kind from any natural form, he clarifies that (1) mind only distinguishes itself from nature across a gradual series of stages, and that (2) nature itself becomes increasingly mind-like across the sequence of its stages. Hence, "the transition of nature to mind is not a transition to something wholly other, but only a coming-to-itself of the mind which is outside itself in nature" (EM §381A/14).

11. See chapter 4, "From Logic to Nature?"

12. This does not contradict the idea that Hegel's project is to articulate sensibility: rather, it reflects his belief that sensibility is protoconceptual and so fully realized only in its conceptual articulation.

13. As is again apparent when Hegel avers that because children and animals are not rational, they lack will (PR §10A/45; EM §468A/228).

14. Here Hegel echoes Kant's view that, as Christine Korsgaard expresses it, "the good will is the only unconditionally good thing, [which] means that it must be the source and condition of all the goodness in the world; goodness, as it were, flows into the world from the good will, and there would be none without it." See Korsgaard, "Two Distinctions in Goodness," in *Creating the Kingdom of Ends* (Cambridge: Cambridge University Press, 1996), p. 259.

15. Hegel's equation of practical reason, free will, and goodness means that for him much of what ordinarily counts as "free will" is no such thing, but is mere *Willkür* (arbitrariness), the capacity to select from among pregiven desires. Hegel's term "will" (*Wille*) may therefore strike modern readers as curiously restricted. On his *Wille/Willkür* contrast, see PR §15–§17/48–50.

16. In the *Science of Logic*, Hegel calls this the "finitude" of the purpose—the fact that it *cannot* be realized, and hence stands always over against the world. The purpose therefore remains an "ought" (*Sollen*), for whose realization the agent strives endlessly, doomed to make "infinite progress" (EL §234/302). Hegel is alluding to Fichte's idea that agents, insofar as they take themselves to be ontologically separate from the world, can only strive endlessly—with no possibility of satisfaction—to overcome their limitation by the world. See Fichte, "Some Lectures Concerning the Vocation of the Scholar" (1794), in *Early Philosophical Writings*, ed. and trans. Daniel Breazeale (Ithaca: Cornell University Press, 1988), p. 152.

17. Hegel adds: "Another way of regarding [its] defect is that the *practical* idea still lacks the moment of the *theoretical* idea" (WL 821/2: 545); "The reconciliation consists in the will's returning—in its result—to the presupposition of cognition; hence the reconciliation consists in the unity of the theoretical and practical idea" (EL §234A/302). So, the will "returns" to cognition insofar

as it again supposes that rationality is to be found, potentially, within objectivity as it is prior to being affected by willing activity.

18. Cf. the possible objection to Hegel's conception of nature as intrinsically rational discussed in chapter 3, "Nature as Petrified Intelligence."

19. This implicit account of nature's intrinsic goodness is compatible with the idea that, ultimately, human beings instantiate practical activity more perfectly, because they consciously entertain the rational purposes from which they act and therefore better instantiate the whole complex of logical relations between cognitive and practical activity. However, Hegel's account of nature's intrinsic goodness does place a question mark over the ethical status of the earliest natural forms—externality, negativity, and material bodies—as these do not yet contain any conceptual element distinct from their materiality. At the same time, these forms still change from rational necessity and so too must be good, acting from practical reason. Presumably, Hegel believes that it is because these forms are (immediately) conceptual that they can transform themselves as reason dictates. At the physical stage, this conceptual element, which is the locus of nature's practical rationality/goodness, becomes more independent. Hence, Hegel can take the physical stage to exemplify the overall way that intrinsic goodness penetrates the natural world.

20. In Hegel's theory this form is, evidently, externality (empirical space), whose discrete material constituents do not manifest at all the universality with which they are fused.

21. See, especially, Lawrence Johnson, *A Morally Deep World* (Cambridge: Cambridge University Press, 1991).

22. See, respectively, Kenneth E. Goodpaster, "From Egoism to Environmentalism," in *Ethics and Problems of the 21st Century*, ed. Kenneth E. Goodpaster and Kenneth M. Sayre (Notre Dame, IN: University of Notre Dame Press, 1979); Tom Regan, *The Case for Animal Rights* (New York: Routledge, 1983); Paul Taylor, *Respect for Nature*; Johnson, *A Morally Deep World*.

23. Other environmental philosophers have sought moral standing beyond the organic or quasi-organic, notably through either Aldo Leopold's "land ethic" or deep ecology. However, Leopold's land ethic—on which, famously, "A thing is right when it tends to preserve the integrity, stability, and beauty of the biotic community. It is wrong when it tends otherwise" (*A Sand County Almanac* [New York: Oxford University Press, 1949], pp. 224–25)—arguably extends moral standing to the biotic community understood, again, as quasi-*organic*. Deep ecology affirms the moral status of all natural entities by adopting a strong holism which denies firm ontological boundaries between things, so that we cannot distinguish ourselves from the world and can realize ourselves only by promoting the self-realization of the world too. Critics have noted that this approach remains anthropocentric and, indeed, egoistic, appealing to our concern for our own well-being: see Clare Palmer, *Environmental Ethics and Process Thinking* (Oxford: Clarendon Press, 1998), pp. 204–11.

24. As Jere Paul Surber notes, the *Differenzschrift* remains in the background to Hegel's later thought: it "provides what can . . . be called a 'metaphilosophical' viewpoint which seems to remain constant throughout the rest of his [Hegel's] life." See Surber's introduction to *The Difference between the*

Fichtean and Schellingian Systems of Philosophy (Arascadero, CA: Ridgeview, 1978), p. v. The *Differenzschrift* establishes that an adequate philosophical system must meet certain criteria and, above all, overcome the Enlightenment's subjectivity/nature opposition.

25. So Fries argues in his *Handbuch der praktischen Philosophie* (1818). Hegel's notorious, not wholly fair, polemic against Fries prefaces the *Philosophy of Right* (PR 15–16); he more rigorously attacks the "morality of conscience" at PR §135–§140/162–184.

26. Remember that, throughout, I understand natural "entities" to be the particular phenomena which instantiate universal forms or structures.

27. For Paul Taylor, for example: "To say that an entity has inherent worth [that is, intrinsic value] is to say that its good (welfare) is deserving of the concern and consideration of all moral agents and that the realization of its good is something to be promoted and protected as an end in itself." See Taylor, "Are Humans Superior to Animals and Plants?" *Environmental Ethics* 6 (1984): 150–51.

28. Such putative duties "concerning" nature are not the same as the duties that Kant classifies as duties "with regard to" nature. Kant adduces the duty to treat animals kindly so as to develop one's power to empathize with other human individuals. The content of this duty of kindness to animals refers *directly* only to humans, animals being involved only derivatively insofar as the duty of empathy with fellow humans calls indirectly for a certain mode of conduct towards animals: see Kant, *The Metaphysics of Morals* (1787), ed. and trans. Mary Gregor (Cambridge: Cambridge University Press, 1996), pp. 192–93. In contrast, the content of what I call duties "concerning" nature refers directly to nature.

29. Lest this repeated connection of private property with the modification of nature seem odd, we should remember that, for Hegel, property has an unusually active dimension: "Behind the seeming thinglike fixedness that property has as an object of the will, lies . . . the movement, the . . . process of the active preparation of nature, with which it gets transformed into an object of the will" (Joachim Ritter, *Hegel and the French Revolution: Essays on the Philosophy of Right*, trans. Richard Dien Winfield [Cambridge, MA: MIT Press, 1982], p. 132).

30. I am omitting much of the complexity of Hegel's justification of private property. Unfortunately, my simplified account makes it look as if Hegel offers a linear, individualistic, justification of private ownership as the necessary consequence of labor upon objects (Jeremy Waldron interprets Hegel broadly on these lines in *The Right to Private Property* [Oxford: Clarendon Press, 1988], pp. 351–60). Actually, Hegel thinks that private property already presupposes a determinate sociohistorical context of mutual recognition among human individuals. A thing can successfully incorporate one individual's will only if others recognize it as doing so—otherwise those others will simply reappropriate that thing for themselves. As Michel Rosenfeld explains: "Recognition as a property owner . . . involves an act of forbearance whereby the recognizing person refrains from interfering with the recognized person's enjoyment

of her possessions" ("Hegel and the Dialectics of Contract," in *Hegel and Legal Theory*, ed. Drucilla Cornell, Michel Rosenfeld, and David Gray Carlson [New York: Routledge, 1991], p. 242).

31. One might doubt that "duty" is the apposite notion here, noting that Hegel focuses more on our *right* (liberty) to modify nature. Yet it is clear from the broader systematic context that our activity in modifying natural entities instantiates the general ontological structure of action from practical reason, that is, from (good) will or duty. This is not incompatible with a right to private property: one must have the right to do one's duty (see EM §486R/242).

32. Marginal note to the *Philosophy of Right*, cited in Ritter, *Hegel and the French Revolution*, p. 134.

33. Admittedly, Hegel views destruction as a poor way of appropriating things compared to forming them (LNR §21/70).

34. Some commentators note the *Philosophy of Right*'s central preoccupation with the "rational domination of nature" (Ritter, *Hegel and the French Revolution*, p. 136); see also Peter Stillman, "Property, Freedom and Individuality in Hegel's and Marx's Political Thought," in *Nomos 22: Property*, ed. J. Roland Pennock and John W. Chapman (New York: New York University Press, 1980), pp. 137–40; Waldron, *The Right to Private Property*, pp. 356–57.

35. As Manfred Gies says, Hegel frees nature from "servitude" by viewing it as implicitly identical to mind (Gies, "Naturphilosophie und Naturwissenschaft bei Hegel," pp. 74–6).

36. Warren, *Moral Status: Obligations to Persons and Other Living Things* (Oxford: Oxford University Press, 1997), p. 3. Warren refers to Kenneth Goodpaster's definition of moral considerability as meaning "that something falls within the sphere of moral concern, that it is morally relevant, that it can be taken into account when moral decisions are made" (Goodpaster, "On Being Morally Considerable," *Journal of Philosophy* 75 [1978]: 63). Goodpaster differentiates moral considerability from moral significance, which means "how far [a thing] should be taken into account, its relative weighting in situations of moral conflict."

Conclusion: Hegel's Project of a Philosophy of Nature

1. For an example of what such an examination might look like, see David Wood, "What Is Eco-Phenomenology?" in *Eco-Phenomenology: Back to the Earth Itself*, ed. Charles S. Brown and Ted Toadvine (Albany: State University of New York Press, 2003).

2. Val Plumwood concurs that contemporary environmental philosophy should pursue the joint tasks of (1) revaluing nature in its materiality (rather than attributing to nature any additional conceptual or spiritual dimension, we should reconceive matter as itself having agency and mind-like characteristics), and (2) reconceiving human beings as ecologically situated, not positioned in a transcendent realm of culture or reason. See Plumwood, *Environmental Culture*, esp. pp. 45–56.

WORKS CITED

Allison, Henry. *Kant's Transcendental Idealism*. New Haven: Yale University Press, 1983.

———. *Kant's Theory of Freedom*. Cambridge: Cambridge University Press, 1990.

Ameriks, Karl. "Recent Work on Hegel: The Rehabilitation of an Epistemologist." *Philosophy and Phenomenological Research* 52, no. 1 (1992): 177–202.

Barnes, Rachel, ed. *Monet by Monet: Artists by Themselves*. Devon: Webb and Bower, 1990.

Beaumont, Bertrand. "Hegel and the Seven Planets." In *The Hegel Myths and Legends*. Edited by Jon Stewart. Evanston, IL: Northwestern University Press, 1996.

Beiser, Frederick C. *The Fate of Reason: German Philosophy from Kant to Fichte*. Cambridge, MA: Harvard University Press, 1987.

———. "Introduction: Hegel and the Problem of Metaphysics." In *The Cambridge Companion to Hegel*. Edited by Frederick C. Beiser. Cambridge: Cambridge University Press, 1993.

———. *German Idealism: The Struggle against Subjectivism, 1781–1801*. Cambridge, MA: Harvard University Press, 2002.

———, ed. *The Early Political Writings of the German Romantics*. Cambridge: Cambridge University Press, 1996.

Belshaw, Christopher. *Environmental Philosophy: Reason, Nature, and Human Concern*. Chesham, Buckinghamshire: Acumen, 2001.

Bonsiepen, Wolfgang. "Hegels Raum-Zeit Lehre." *Hegel-Studien* 20 (1985): 9–38.

————. "Hegels kritische Auseinandersetzung mit der zeitgenössischen Evolutionstheorie." In *Hegels Philosophie der Natur*. Edited by Rolf-Peter Horstmann and Michael J. Petry. Stuttgart: Klett-Cotta, 1986.

————. "Hegels Vorlesungen über Naturphilosophie." *Hegel-Studien* 26 (1991): 40–54.

Boothby, Richard. *Freud as Philosopher*. New York: Routledge, 2001.

Bowie, Andrew. *Schelling and Modern European Philosophy: An Introduction*. London: Routledge, 1993.

————. *From Romanticism to Critical Theory*. London: Routledge, 1997.

Breidbach, Otto. *Das Organische in Hegels Denken: Studie zur Naturphilosophie und Biologie um 1800*. Würzburg: Königshausen und Neumann, 1982.

————. "Hegels Evolutionskritik." *Hegel-Studien* 22 (1987): 165–72.

Brinkmann, Klaus. "Schellings Hegel-Kritik." In *Die Ontologische Option*. Edited by Klaus Hartmann. Berlin: De Gruyter, 1976.

Buchdahl, Gerd. "Conceptual Analysis and Scientific Theory in Hegel's Philosophy of Nature (with Special Reference to Hegel's Optics)." In *Hegel and the Sciences*. Edited by Robert S. Cohen and Marx W. Wartofsky. Dordrecht: Reidel, 1984.

————. "Hegel's Philosophy of Nature and the Structure of Science." In *Hegel*. Edited by Michael Inwood. Oxford: Oxford University Press, 1985.

————. "Hegel on the Interaction between Science and Philosophy." In *Hegel and Newtonianism*. Edited by Michael J. Petry. Dordrecht: Kluwer, 1993.

Burbidge, John W. "Concept and Time in Hegel." *Dialogue: Canadian Philosophical Review* 12, no. 3 (1973): 403–22.

————. "The Necessity of Contingency." In *Art and Logic in Hegel's Philosophy*. Edited by Warren E. Steinkraus and Kenneth I. Schmitz. Atlantic Highlands, NJ: Humanities Press, 1980.

————. *On Hegel's Logic: Fragments of a Commentary*. Atlantic Highlands, NJ: Humanities Press, 1981.

————. "Challenge to Hegel: Contraries and Contradictories in Schelling's Late Philosophy." In *Hegel on Logic and Religion*. Albany: State University of New York Press, 1992.

————. "Hegel's Conception of Logic." In *The Cambridge Companion to Hegel*. Edited by Frederick C. Beiser. Cambridge: Cambridge University Press, 1993.

————. *Real Process: How Logic and Chemistry Combine in Hegel's Philosophy of Nature*. Toronto: University of Toronto Press, 1996.

Butler, Judith. *Subjects of Desire: Hegelian Reflections in Twentieth-Century France*. New York: Columbia University Press, 1987.

Caneva, Kenneth L. "Physics and *Naturphilosophie*: A Reconnaissance." *History of Science* 35 (1997): 35–107.

Capek, Milic. "Hegel and the Organic View of Nature." In *Hegel and the Sciences*. Edited by Robert S. Cohen and Marx W. Wartofsky. Dordrecht: Reidel, 1984.

Clark, Wendy L., and J. M. Fritzman. "Reducing Spirit to Substance: Dove on Hegel's Method." *Idealistic Studies* 32, no. 2 (2002): 73–100.

Collingwood, R. G. *The Idea of History*. Edited by T. M. Knox. Oxford: Clarendon Press, 1946.

Collins, Ardis B. "Hegel on Language, Citizenship, and the Educational Function of the Workplace: The Marxist Challenge." *Owl of Minerva* 32, no. 1 (2000): 21–43.

Compton, John J. "A Comment on Buchdahl's 'Conceptual Analysis and Scientific Theory in Hegel's Philosophy of Nature.' " In *Hegel and the Sciences*. Edited by Robert S. Cohen and Marx W. Wartofsky. Dordrecht: Reidel, 1984.

———. "Phenomenology and the Philosophy of Nature." *Man and World* 21 (1988): 65–89.

Cunningham, Andrew, and Nicholas Jardine, ed. *Romanticism and the Sciences*. Cambridge: Cambridge University Press, 1990.

Dahlstrom, Daniel O. "Hegel's Appropriation of Kant's Account of Teleology in Nature." In *Hegel and the Philosophy of Nature*. Edited by Stephen Houlgate. Albany: State University of New York Press, 1998.

De Nys, Martin J. " 'Sense-certainty' and Universality: Hegel's Entrance into the *Phenomenology*." In vol. 3 of *G. W. F. Hegel: Critical Assessments*. Edited by Robert Stern. London: Routledge, 1993.

Drees, Martin. "The Logic of Hegel's Philosophy of Nature." In *Hegel and Newtonianism*. Edited by Michael J. Petry. Dordrecht: Kluwer, 1993.

———. "Evolution and Emanation of Spirit in Hegel's *Philosophy of Nature*." *Bulletin of the Hegel Society of Great Britain* 26 (1992): 52–61.

Engelhardt, Dietrich von. *Hegel und die Chemie: Studie zur Philosophie und Wissenschaft der Natur um 1800*. Wiesbaden: Pressler, 1976.

Esposito, Joseph L. *Schelling's Idealism and Philosophy of Nature*. Lewisburg, PA: Bucknell University Press, 1977.

Falkenburg, Brigitte. *Die Form der Materie*. Frankfurt: Athenäum, 1987.

———. "How to Save the Phenomena: Meaning and Reference in Hegel's Philosophy of Nature." In *Hegel and the Philosophy of Nature*. Edited by Stephen Houlgate. Albany: State University of New York Press, 1998.

Fay, Brian. *Contemporary Philosophy of Social Science*. Oxford: Blackwell, 1996.

Ferrarin, Alfredo. *Hegel and Aristotle*. Cambridge: Cambridge University Press, 2001.

Ferrini, Cinzia. "Features of Irony and Alleged Errors in Hegel's *De Orbitis Planetarum*." *Hegel-Jahrbuch* (1991): 459–77.

Feuerbach, Ludwig. "Provisional Theses for the Reformation of Philosophy." 1843. In *The Young Hegelians: An Anthology*. Edited by Lawrence S. Stepelevich. Atlantic Highlands, NJ: Humanities Press, 1983.

Fichte, J. G. "Some Lectures Concerning the Vocation of the Scholar." 1794. In *Early Philosophical Writings*. Edited and translated by Daniel Breazeale. Ithaca: Cornell University Press, 1988.

———. *The Vocation of Man*. 1800. Translated by Peter Prauss. Indianapolis: Hackett, 1987.

Findlay, John N. *Hegel: A Re-Examination*. London: Allen and Unwin, 1958.

———. Foreword to *Philosophy of Nature*, by G. W. F. Hegel. Translated by A. V. Miller. Oxford: Clarendon Press, 1970.

Foltz, Bruce V. *Inhabiting the Earth: Heidegger, Environmental Ethics, and the Metaphysics of Nature*. Atlantic Highlands, NJ: Humanities Press, 1995.

Forster, Michael. *Hegel and Skepticism*. Cambridge, MA: Harvard University Press, 1989.

———. *Hegel's Idea of a Phenomenology of Spirit*. Chicago: University of Chicago Press, 1998.

Gadamer, Hans-Georg. *Truth and Method*. 1960. Second ed., revised. Edited by Joel Weinsheimer and Donald G. Marshall. London: Sheed and Ward, 1989.

Gardner, Sebastian. "German Idealism." *Proceedings of the Aristotelian Society* Supplement 76 (2002): 211–28.

George, Michael, and Andrew Vincent. Introduction to *The Philosophical Propaedeutic*, by G. W. F. Hegel. Translated by A. V. Miller. Oxford: Blackwell, 1986.

Gies, Manfred. "Naturphilosophie und Naturwissenschaft bei Hegel." In *Hegel und die Naturwissenschaften*. Edited by Michael J. Petry. Stuttgart: Frommann-Holzboog, 1987.

Giovanni, George di, and H. S. Harris, ed. and trans. *Between Kant and Hegel: Texts in the Development of Post-Kantian Idealism*. Revised edition. Indianapolis: Hackett, 2000.

Gloy, Karen, and Paul Burger, ed. *Die Naturphilosophie im Deutschen Idealismus*. Stuttgart-Bad Cannstatt: Frommann-Holzboog, 1993.

Goethe, Johann Wolfgang von. *Scientific Studies*. Edited and translated by Douglas Miller. Princeton: Princeton University Press, 1988.

Goodpaster, Kenneth. "On Being Morally Considerable." *Journal of Philosophy* 75 (1978): 308–25.

———. "From Egoism to Environmentalism." In *Ethics and Problems of the Twenty-first Century*. Edited by Kenneth Goodpaster and Kenneth M. Sayre. Notre Dame, IN: University of Notre Dame Press, 1979.

Gower, Barry. "Speculation in Physics: The History and Practice of *Naturphilosophie*." *Studies in History and Philosophy of Science* 3, no. 4 (1973): 301–56.

Greene, Murray. *Hegel on the Soul: A Speculative Anthropology*. The Hague: Nijhoff, 1972.

Grier, Philip T. "Abstract and Concrete in Hegel's Logic." In *Essays on Hegel's Logic*. Edited by George di Giovanni. Albany: State University of New York Press, 1990.

Habermas, Jürgen. *Knowledge and Human Interests*. Translated by Jeremy J. Shapiro. London: Heinemann, 1978.

Halper, Edward. "The Logic of Hegel's *Philosophy of Nature*: Nature, Space, and Time." In *Hegel and the Philosophy of Nature*. Edited by Stephen Houlgate. Albany: State University of New York Press, 1998.

Hardimon, Michael. *Hegel's Social Philosophy: The Project of Reconciliation*. Cambridge: Cambridge University Press, 1994.

Harris, Errol E. "The Philosophy of Nature in Hegel's System." *Review of Metaphysics* 3 (1949–1950): 213–28.

———. "The *Naturphilosophie* Updated." *Owl of Minerva* 10, no. 2 (1978): 2–7.

———. "Hegel and the Natural Sciences." In *The Spirit of Hegel*. Atlantic Highlands, NJ: Humanities Press, 1993.

Harris, H. S. *Hegel's Ladder*. 2 vols. Indianapolis: Hackett, 1997.

Hartmann, Klaus. *Studies in Foundational Philosophy*. Amsterdam: Rodopi, 1988.

Hegel, G. W. F. *Miscellaneous Writings*. Edited by Jon Stewart. Evanston, IL: Northwestern University Press, 2002.

———. *Naturphilosophie Band I: Die Vorlesung von 1819/20*. Edited by Manfred Gies. Napoli: Bibliopolis, 1982.

———. *Vorlesung über Naturphilosophie Berlin 1821/22, Nachschrift von Boris von Uexküll*. Edited by Gilles Marmasse and Thomas Posch. Frankfurt: Peter Lang, 2002.

———. *Vorlesung über Naturphilosophie Berlin 1823/24, Nachschrift von K. G. J. v. Griesheim*. Edited by Gilles Marmasse. Frankfurt: Peter Lang, 2000.

Heidegger, Martin. "Modern Science, Metaphysics, and Mathematics" 1962. In *Basic Writings*. Second ed., revised. Edited by David Farrell Krell. London: Routledge, 1993.

Henrich, Dieter. "Hegels Theorie über den Zufall." *Kant-Studien* 50 (1958–1959): 131–48.

Hollis, Martin. *The Philosophy of Social Science: An Introduction*. Cambridge: Cambridge University Press, 1994.

Horkheimer, Max. *Eclipse of Reason*. 1947. New York: Continuum, 1974.

Horstmann, Rolf-Peter. "Logifizierte Natur oder naturalisierte Logik?" In *Hegels Philosophie der Natur: Beziehungen zwischen empirischer und spekulativer Naturerkenntnis*. Edited by Rolf-Peter Horstmann and Michael J. Petry. Stuttgart: Klett-Cotta, 1986.

Hösle, Vittorio. "Raum, Zeit, Bewegung." In *Hegel und die Naturwissenschaften*. Edited by Michael J. Petry. Stuttgart: Frommann-Holzboog, 1987.

Houlgate, Stephen. "Necessity and Contingency in Hegel's *Science of Logic*." *Owl of Minerva* 27, no. 1 (1995): 37–49.

———. "Schelling's Critique of Hegel's *Science of Logic*." *Review of Metaphysics* 53 (1999): 99–128.

———. "Logic and Nature in Hegel's Philosophy: A Response to John W. Burbidge." *Owl of Minerva* 34, 1 (2002–2003): 107–25.

Husserl, Edmund. *The Crisis of the European Sciences and Transcendental Phenomenology*. 1954. Translated by David Carr. Evanston, IL: Northwestern University Press, 1970.

Ihmig, Karl-Norbert. *Hegels Deutung der Gravitation. Eine Studie zu Hegel und Newton*. Frankfurt: Athenäum, 1989.

Ilting, Karl-Heinz. "Hegels Philosophie des Organischen." In *Hegel und die Naturwissenschaften*. Edited by Michael J. Petry. Stuttgart: Frommann-Holzboog, 1987.

Inwood, Michael. "Solomon, Hegel, and Truth." *Review of Metaphysics* 31, no. 2 (1977): 272–82.

———. *Hegel.* London: Routledge, 1983.

———. *A Hegel Dictionary.* Oxford: Blackwell, 1992.

Janaway, Christopher. "Will and Nature." In *The Cambridge Companion to Schopenhauer.* Edited by Christopher Janaway. Cambridge: Cambridge University Press, 1999.

Johnson, Lawrence. *A Morally Deep World.* Cambridge: Cambridge University Press, 1991.

Kalenberg, Thomas. *Die Befreiung der Natur: Natur und Selbstbewußtsein in der Philosophie Hegels.* Hamburg: Meiner, 1997.

Kant, Immanuel. *Critique of Pure Reason.* 1781. Translated by Norman Kemp Smith. London: MacMillan, 1929.

———. "Metaphysical Foundations of Natural Science." 1786. In *Philosophy of Material Nature.* Translated by James W. Ellington. Indianapolis: Hackett, 1985.

———. *The Metaphysics of Morals.* 1797. Translated and edited by Mary Gregor. Cambridge: Cambridge University Press, 1996.

Kierkegaard, Søren. *Concluding Unscientific Postscript.* 1846. Edited and translated by Howard V. Hong and Edna H. Hong. Princeton: Princeton University Press, 1992.

Kojève, Alexandre. *Introduction to the Reading of Hegel.* 1947. Edited by Allan Bloom. Translated by James H. Nichols, Jr. New York: Basic Books, 1969.

Kolb, David. *The Critique of Pure Modernity: Hegel, Heidegger, and After.* Chicago: University of Chicago Press, 1986.

Korsgaard, Christine. "Two Distinctions in Goodness." In *Creating the Kingdom of Ends.* Cambridge: Cambridge University Press, 1996.

Krell, David Farrell. *Son of Spirit.* Albany: State University of New York Press, 1997.

———. *Contagion: Sexuality, Disease, and Death in German Idealism and Romanticism.* Bloomington: Indiana University Press, 1998.

Kuhn, Thomas. "Energy Conservation as an Example of Simultaneous Discovery." In *Critical Problems in the History of Science.* Edited by M. Clagett. Madison: University of Wisconsin Press, 1959.

Lacoue-Labarthe, Philippe, and Jean-Luc Nancy. *The Literary Absolute: The Theory of Literature in German Romanticism.* Translated by Philip Barnard and Cheryl Lester. Albany: State University of New York Press, 1988.

Lamb, David. *Hegel: From Foundation to System.* The Hague: Nijhoff, 1980.

Larmore, Charles. *The Romantic Legacy.* New York: Columbia University Press, 1996.

Leiss, William. *The Domination of Nature.* New York: Braziller, 1972.

Leopold, Aldo. *A Sand County Almanac.* New York: Oxford University Press, 1949.

Lloyd, Genevieve. "Feminism in History of Philosophy." In *The Cambridge Companion to Feminism in Philosophy.* Edited by Miranda Fricker and Jennifer Hornsby. Cambridge: Cambridge University Press, 2000.

Lucas, George R. "A Re-Interpretation of Hegel's Philosophy of Nature." *Journal of the History of Philosophy* 22 (1984): 103–13.

Mackenzie, Millicent. *Hegel's Educational Theory and Practice.* London: Swan Sonnenschein, 1909.

Maker, William. "The Very Idea of the Idea of Nature." In *Hegel and the Philosophy of Nature.* Edited by Stephen Houlgate. Albany: State University of New York Press, 1998.

Marcuse, Herbert. *One-Dimensional Man.* Boston: Beacon Press, 1964.

Marmasse, Gilles. Foreword to *Vorlesung über Naturphilosophie Berlin 1823/24, Nachschrift von K. G. J. v. Griesheim,* by G. W. F. Hegel. Frankfurt: Peter Lang, 2000.

Marx, Karl. "Economic and Philosophical Manuscripts." 1844. In *Marx: Early Writings.* Translated by Rodney Livingstone and Gregor Benton. Harmondsworth: Penguin, 1975.

McCarney, Joseph. *Hegel on History.* London: Routledge, 2002.

McDowell, John. *Mind and World.* Cambridge, MA: Harvard University Press, 1994.

McMullin, Ernan. "Philosophies of Nature." *The New Scholasticism* 43 (1969): 29–74.

Mendelssohn, Moses. "On the Question: What Is Enlightenment?" In *What Is Enlightenment? Eighteenth-Century Questions and Twentieth-Century Answers.* Edited by James Schmidt. Berkeley: University of California Press, 1996.

Mill, John Stuart. "Nature." [1874]. In *Nature and Utility of Religion.* Edited by George Nakhnikian. New York: Bobbs-Merrill, 1958.

Miller, Elaine P. "The Figure of Self-Sacrifice in Hegel's *Naturphilosophie*." *Philosophy Today* 41 Supplement (1997): 41–8.

Miller, Jr., Mitchell H. "The Attainment of the Absolute Standpoint in Hegel's *Phenomenology of Spirit*." In *The Phenomenology of Spirit Reader: Critical and Interpretive Essays*. Edited by Jon Stewart. Albany: State University of New York Press, 1998.

Moore, G. E. "The Conception of Intrinsic Value." In *Philosophical Studies*. Second edition. London: Routledge and Kegan Paul, 1960.

Nagel, Thomas. "Panpsychism." In *Mortal Questions*. Cambridge: Cambridge University Press, 1979.

Nietzsche, Friedrich. *On the Genealogy of Morality*. Translated by Carol Diethe. Cambridge: Cambridge University Press, 1994.

O'Neill, John. "The Varieties of Intrinsic Value." *Monist* 75, no. 2 (1992): 119–37.

———. "Humanism and Nature." *Radical Philosophy* 66 (1994): 21–9.

Palmer, Clare. *Environmental Ethics and Process Thinking*. Oxford: Clarendon Press, 1998.

Passmore, John. "Attitudes to Nature." In *Environmental Ethics*. Edited by Robert Elliott. Oxford: Oxford University Press, 1995.

Patten, Alan. *Hegel's Idea of Freedom*. Oxford: Oxford University Press, 1999.

Petersen, Mark C. E. "Animals Eating Empiricists: Assimilation and Subjectivity in Hegel's Philosophy of Nature." *Owl of Minerva* 23, no. 1 (1991): 49–62.

———. "The Role of Practical and Theoretical Approaches in Hegel's *Philosophy of Nature*." *Owl of Minerva* 27, no. 2 (1996): 155–65.

Petry, Michael J. Introduction to *Philosophy of Nature*, by G. W. F. Hegel. Edited and translated by Michael J. Petry. 3 vols. London: Allen and Unwin, 1970.

———. "Hegel's Dialectic and the Natural Sciences." *Hegel-Jahrbuch* 19 (1975): 452–56.

———. Introduction to *The Berlin Phenomenology*, by G. W. F. Hegel. Edited and translated by Michael J. Petry. 3 vols. Dordrecht: Reidel, 1981.

———. "Hegel, Francoeur, and Pohl." In *Hegels Philosophie der Natur: Beziehungen zwischen empirischer und spekulativer Naturerkenntnis*. Edited by Rolf-Peter Horstmann and Michael J. Petry. Stuttgart: Klett-Cotta, 1986.

———, ed. *Hegel und die Naturwissenschaften*. Stuttgart: Frommann-Holzboog, 1987.

————, ed. *Hegel and Newtonianism*. Dordrecht: Kluwer, 1993.

Pillow, Kirk. *Sublime Understanding: Aesthetic Reflection in Kant and Hegel*. Cambridge, MA: MIT Press, 2000.

Pinkard, Terry. *Hegel's Dialectic: The Explanation of Possibility*. Philadelphia: Temple University Press, 1988.

————. *Hegel: A Biography*. Cambridge: Cambridge University Press, 2000.

Pippin, Robert B. *Hegel's Idealism: The Satisfactions of Self-Consciousness*. Cambridge: Cambridge University Press, 1989.

Plumwood, Val. "The Ecopolitics Debate and the Politics of Nature." In *Ecological Feminism*. Edited by Karen J. Warren. New York: Routledge, 1993.

————. *Environmental Culture: The Ecological Crisis of Reason*. London: Routledge, 2002.

Poggi, Stefano, and Maurizio Bossi, eds. *Romanticism in Science: Science in Europe, 1790–1840*. Dordrecht: Kluwer, 1994.

Priest, Graham. *Beyond the Limits of Thought*. Cambridge: Cambridge University Press, 1995.

Ramet, Pedro. "Kantian and Hegelian Perspectives on Duty." *Southern Journal of Philosophy* 21, no. 2 (1983): 281–99.

Regan, Tom. "The Nature and Possibility of an Environmental Ethic." *Environmental Ethics* 3 (1981): 19–34.

————. *The Case for Animal Rights*. New York: Routledge, 1983.

Reid, Jeffrey. "Hegel and the State University: The University of Berlin and its Founding Contradictions." *Owl of Minerva* 32, no. 1 (2000): 5–19.

Reusswig, Fritz. *Natur und Geist: Grundlinien einer ökologischen Sittlichkeit nach Hegel*. Frankfurt: Campus, 1993.

Richards, Robert J. *The Romantic Conception of Life: Science and Philosophy in the Age of Goethe*. Chicago: University of Chicago Press, 2002.

Ritter, Joachim. *Hegel and the French Revolution: Essays on the Philosophy of Right*. Translated by Richard Dien Winfield. Cambridge, MA: MIT Press, 1982.

Rorty, Richard. "The Historiography of Philosophy: Four Genres." In *Philosophy in History*. Edited by Richard Rorty, J. B. Schneewind, and Quentin Skinner. Cambridge: Cambridge University Press, 1984.

Rosen, Michael. "From *Vorstellung* to Thought: Is a 'Non-Metaphysical' View of Hegel Possible?" In vol. 3 of *G. W. F. Hegel: Critical Assessments*. Edited by Robert Stern. London: Routledge, 1993.

Rosenfeld, Michel. "Hegel and the Dialectics of Contract." In *Hegel and Legal Theory*. Edited by Drucilla Cornell, Michel Rosenfeld, and David Gray Carlson. New York: Routledge, 1991.

Sallis, John. *Force of Imagination: The Sense of the Elemental*. Bloomington: Indiana University Press, 2000.

Santoro-Brienza, Liberato. "Aristotle and Hegel on Nature: Some Similarities." *Bulletin of the Hegel Society of Great Britain* 26 (1992): 13–29.

Schelling, F. W. J. *Ideas for a Philosophy of Nature*. 1797. Translated by Errol E. Harris and Peter Heath. Cambridge: Cambridge University Press, 1988.

———. *On the History of Modern Philosophy*. Translated by Andrew Bowie. Cambridge: Cambridge University Press, 1994.

Schmidt, James. "A *Paideia* for the 'Bürger als Bourgeois': The Conception of 'Civil Society' in Hegel's Political Thought." *History of Political Thought* 2, no. 3 (1981): 469–93.

Sepper, Dennis L. *Goethe Contra Newton: Polemics and the Project for a New Science of Color*. Cambridge: Cambridge University Press, 1988.

Sextus Empiricus. *Outlines of Scepticism*. Translated and edited by Julia Annas and Jonathan Barnes. Cambridge: Cambridge University Press, 2000.

Skinner, Quentin. "Meaning and Understanding in the History of Ideas." *History and Theory* 8 (1969): 3–53.

Snelders, H. A. M. "Romanticism and Naturphilosophie and the Inorganic Natural Sciences 1797–1840: An Introductory Survey." *Studies in Romanticism* 9 (1970): 193–215.

Soll, Ivan. *An Introduction to Hegel's Metaphysics*. Chicago: Chicago University Press, 1969.

Solomon, Robert. "Hegel's Epistemology." In *Hegel*. Edited by Michael Inwood. Oxford: Oxford University Press, 1985.

Stern, Robert. *Hegel, Kant and the Structure of the Object*. London: Routledge, 1990.

———. "Going Beyond the Kantian Philosophy: On McDowell's Hegelian Critique of Kant." *European Journal of Philosophy* 7, no. 2 (1999): 247–69.

———. *Hegel and the Phenomenology of Spirit*. London: Routledge, 2002.

Stewart, Jon. "Hegel and the Myth of Reason." In *The Hegel Myths and Legends*. Edited by Jon Stewart. Evanston, IL: Northwestern University Press, 1996.

Stillman, Peter G. "Property, Freedom and Individuality in Hegel's and Marx's Political Thought." In *Nomos* 22: *Property*. Edited by J. Roland Pennock and John W. Chapman. New York: New York University Press, 1980.

Surber, Jere Paul. Introduction to *The Difference between The Fichtean and Schellingian Systems of Philosophy*, by G. W. F. Hegel. Arascadero, CA: Ridgeview, 1978.

Taylor, Charles. "The Opening Arguments of the *Phenomenology*." In *Hegel: A Collection of Critical Essays*. Edited by Alasdair MacIntyre. New York: Doubleday, 1972.

———. *Hegel*. Cambridge: Cambridge University Press, 1975.

———. *Sources of the Self*. Cambridge: Cambridge University Press, 1989.

Taylor, Paul W. "Are Humans Superior to Animals and Plants?" *Environmental Ethics* 6 (1984): 149–60.

———. *Respect for Nature: A Theory of Environmental Ethics*. Princeton: Princeton University Press, 1986.

Vasseleu, Cathryn. *Textures of Light: Vision and Touch in Irigaray, Levinas, and Merleau-Ponty*. London: Routledge, 1998.

Waldron, Jeremy. *The Right to Private Property*. Oxford: Clarendon Press, 1988.

Wandschneider, Dieter. *Raum, Zeit, Relativität: Grundbestimmungen der Physik in der Perspektive der Hegelschen Naturphilosophie*. Frankfurt: Klostermann, 1982.

———. "Nature and the Dialectic of Nature in Hegel's Objective Idealism." *Bulletin of the Hegel Society of Great Britain* 26 (1992): 30–51.

———, and Vittorio Hösle. "Die Entäusserung der Idee zur Natur und ihre zeitliche Entfaltung als Geist bei Hegel." *Hegel-Studien* 18 (1983): 173–99.

Warren, Mary Anne. *Moral Status: Obligations to Persons and Other Living Things*. Oxford: Oxford University Press, 1997.

Wartenberg, Thomas. "Hegel's Idealism: The Logic of Conceptuality." In *The Cambridge Companion to Hegel*. Edited by Frederick C. Beiser. Cambridge: Cambridge University Press, 1993.

Webb, Thomas R. "The Problem of Empirical Knowledge in Hegel's Philosophy of Nature." *Hegel-Studien* 15 (1980): 171–86.

Weber, Max. "Science as a Vocation." 1919. In *From Max Weber: Essays in Sociology*. Translated and edited by H. H. Gerth and C. Wright Mills. London: Routledge, 1948.

Westphal, Kenneth R. "Hegel's Solution to the Dilemma of the Criterion." In *The Phenomenology of Spirit Reader: Critical and Interpretive Essays.* Edited by Jon Stewart. Albany: State University of New York Press, 1998.

———. *Hegel's Epistemological Realism.* Dordrecht: Kluwer, 1989.

White, Alan. *Absolute Knowledge: Hegel and the Problem of Metaphysics.* Athens, OH: Ohio University Press, 1983.

Wicks, Robert. "Hegel's Aesthetics: An Overview." In *The Cambridge Companion to Hegel.* Edited by Frederick C. Beiser. Cambridge: Cambridge University Press, 1993.

Williams, Robert R. "Reason, Authority, and Recognition in Hegel's Theory of Education." *Owl of Minerva* 32, no. 1 (2000): 45–63.

Winfield, Richard Dean. "Space, Time, and Matter: Conceiving Nature without Foundations." In *Hegel and the Philosophy of Nature.* Edited by Stephen Houlgate. Albany: State University of New York Press, 1998.

Wood, Allen. *Hegel's Ethical Thought.* Cambridge: Cambridge University Press, 1990.

Wood, David. "What is Eco-Phenomenology?" In *Eco-Phenomenology: Back to the Earth Itself.* Edited by Charles S. Brown and Ted Toadvine. Albany: State University of New York Press, 2003.

Wyss, Beat. *Hegel's Art History and the Critique of Modernity.* Translated by Caroline Dobson Saltzwedel. Cambridge: Cambridge University Press, 1999.

INDEX